# Freedom

## versus

# Suppression and Censorship

---

With a Study of the
Attitudes of Midwestern Public Librarians
and a
Bibliography of Censorship

---

## Charles H. Busha

Preface by
Allan Pratt

Introduction by
Peter Hiatt

1972

---

LIBRARIES UNLIMITED, INC.,   LITTLETON, COLO.

Library of Congress Card Number 72-91672
International Standard Book Number 0-87287-057-X

LIBRARIES UNLIMITED, INC.
P.O. Box 263
Littleton, Colorado 80120

Research Studies in Library Science, No. 8

## RESEARCH STUDIES IN LIBRARY SCIENCE
Bohdan S. Wynar, Editor

No. 1. *Middle Class Attitudes and Public Library Use.* By Charles Evans, with an Introduction by Lawrence Allen.

No. 2. *Critical Guide to Catholic Reference Books.* By James Patrick McCabe, with an Introduction by Russell E. Bidlack.

No. 3. *An Analysis of Vocabulary Control in Library of Congress Classification and Subject Headings.* By John Phillip Immroth, with an Introduction by Jay E. Daily.

No. 4. *Research Methods in Library Science. A Bibliographic Guide.* By Bohdan S. Wynar.

No. 5. *Library Management: Behavior-Based Personnel Systems. A Framework for Analysis.* By Robert E. Kemper.

No. 6. *Computerizing the Card Catalog in the University Library: A Survey of User Requirements.* By Richard P. Palmer, with an Introduction by Kenneth R. Shaffer.

No. 7. *Toward a Philosophy of Educational Librarianship.* By John M. Christ.

No. 8. *Freedom versus Suppression and Censorship.* By Charles H. Busha, with an Introduction by Peter Hiatt, and a Preface by Allan Pratt.

No. 9. *The Role of the State Library in Adult Education: A Critical Analysis of Nine Southeastern State Library Agencies.* By Donald D. Foos, with an Introduction by Harold Goldstein.

# ACKNOWLEDGMENTS

Chapters 5 through 8 of this book consist of a revised version of a dissertation written in 1971 for the Ph.D. degree at the Graduate Library School of Indiana University. Consequently, I am most grateful for the guidance and encouragement given to me in the completion of that study by members of my research committee: Professors Peter Hiatt, Haynes McMullen, Allan D. Pratt, and G. Cleveland Wilhoit, Jr.

Without the financial support which I received through the U. S. Office of Education fellowship program, the study would not have been possible. I am also most appreciative of Professor Margaret I. Rusvold's contributions toward establishing that program at Indiana University.

Chapters 1 through 4 and the bibliography of censorship in Part III were written and compiled after the dissertation was completed; while the author is solely responsible for the contents of these parts of the present book, without the help of Dorothy Marie Kibler, my former graduate assistant, the additional work necessary in preparing the manuscript would otherwise have delayed the book's publication indefinitely. Miss Kibler, who is now a member of the University of Iowa library's reference staff, conducted numerous bibliographic searches and also assisted in proofreading. The meticulous attention which she gave to the preparation of the manuscript is deeply appreciated.

My gratitude is also extended to the 624 public librarians in Illinois, Indiana, Michigan, Ohio, and Wisconsin who participated in the opinion research upon which the dissertation was based. Part II of this book was made possible by the cooperation of those respondents.

Graduate Library School
Indiana University
Bloomington, Indiana                                                    Charles Busha

5

# TABLE OF CONTENTS

Acknowledgments  . . . . . . . . . . . . . . . . . . . . . . . . . . . . . . . . . . . . . .   5
Preface
    by Allan Pratt . . . . . . . . . . . . . . . . . . . . . . . . . . . . . . . . . . . . . .  11
Introduction
    by Peter Hiatt . . . . . . . . . . . . . . . . . . . . . . . . . . . . . . . . . . . . . .  19

## PART I
## REPRESSIONS AND FREEDOMS

### CHAPTER 1 – THE NATURE OF CENSORSHIP
The Suppression of Information  . . . . . . . . . . . . . . . . . . . . . .  23
Restrictions on Expression  . . . . . . . . . . . . . . . . . . . . . . . . . .  28
Religion and Conservatism  . . . . . . . . . . . . . . . . . . . . . . . . . .  34

### CHAPTER 2 – CENSORSHIP IN ACTION
The Ginzburg Case  . . . . . . . . . . . . . . . . . . . . . . . . . . . . . . .  40
Incidences of Censorship  . . . . . . . . . . . . . . . . . . . . . . . . . . .  50
Organized Censors and Their Friends . . . . . . . . . . . . . . . . . . .  54

### CHAPTER 3 – PROTECTION OF INDIVIDUAL RIGHTS
Conventionality vs. Creativity  . . . . . . . . . . . . . . . . . . . . . . . .  62
Freedom of Choice . . . . . . . . . . . . . . . . . . . . . . . . . . . . . . . .  64
The Bill of Rights . . . . . . . . . . . . . . . . . . . . . . . . . . . . . . . . .  66
The Library Bill of Rights . . . . . . . . . . . . . . . . . . . . . . . . . . .  69
Defending Intellectual Freedom . . . . . . . . . . . . . . . . . . . . . . .  69

### CHAPTER 4 – BOOK SELECTION IN PUBLIC LIBRARIES
The Library as a Social Institution  . . . . . . . . . . . . . . . . . . . .  75
What Should the Librarian Purchase? . . . . . . . . . . . . . . . . . . .  76
Controversial Works . . . . . . . . . . . . . . . . . . . . . . . . . . . . . . .  80

### CHAPTER 5 – FACING THE CHALLENGE
The Public Librarian and Censorship  . . . . . . . . . . . . . . . . . . .  83
The Public Librarian and the Freedom to Read . . . . . . . . . . . .  86
Intramural or Self-Imposed Censorship . . . . . . . . . . . . . . . . . .  87
The Fiske Censorship Study . . . . . . . . . . . . . . . . . . . . . . . . . .  88

# PART II
## ATTITUDES OF MIDWESTERN PUBLIC LIBRARIANS
## TOWARD INTELLECTUAL FREEDOM AND CENSORSHIP:
## A STUDY

CHAPTER 6 – INTRODUCTION TO THE STUDY AND
METHODOLOGY
Purpose of the Study . . . . . . . . . . . . . . . . . . . . . . . . . . . . .   93
Selection of the Sample and Development of the Questionnaire . .   95
The Population . . . . . . . . . . . . . . . . . . . . . . . . . . . . . . . . .   95
Determination of the Type of Sample . . . . . . . . . . . . . . . . . .   98
Choosing the Sample . . . . . . . . . . . . . . . . . . . . . . . . . . . . .   100
The Variables . . . . . . . . . . . . . . . . . . . . . . . . . . . . . . . . . .   100
The Questionnaire . . . . . . . . . . . . . . . . . . . . . . . . . . . . . . .   101
Pre-Testing the Questionnaire . . . . . . . . . . . . . . . . . . . . . . .   104
Organization of the Measuring Instrument . . . . . . . . . . . . . . .   105
Mailing and Return of the Questionnaires . . . . . . . . . . . . . . .   107


CHAPTER 7 – ANALYSIS OF THE DATA
Some Characteristics of the Sample . . . . . . . . . . . . . . . . . . . .   109
Scoring and Coding of Item Responses . . . . . . . . . . . . . . . . .   110
Measures for Central Tendency and Variability . . . . . . . . . . . .   114
Censorship Item Analysis . . . . . . . . . . . . . . . . . . . . . . . . . . .   114
Intellectual Freedom Item Analysis . . . . . . . . . . . . . . . . . . . .   117
F Scale Item Analysis . . . . . . . . . . . . . . . . . . . . . . . . . . . . .   119
Item Analysis of Section II . . . . . . . . . . . . . . . . . . . . . . . . .   120
Testing the Null Hypotheses . . . . . . . . . . . . . . . . . . . . . . . .   120
Relationship of Variables to Attitude Scores . . . . . . . . . . . . . .   123
    Educational-Attainment Level . . . . . . . . . . . . . . . . . . . .   124
    Population-Size Categories . . . . . . . . . . . . . . . . . . . . . . .   127
    Age Groups . . . . . . . . . . . . . . . . . . . . . . . . . . . . . . . .   130
    Sex of Respondents . . . . . . . . . . . . . . . . . . . . . . . . . . .   132
    State Where Employed . . . . . . . . . . . . . . . . . . . . . . . . .   132
    Job Classification . . . . . . . . . . . . . . . . . . . . . . . . . . . . .   135


CHAPTER 8 – SUMMARY AND CONCLUSIONS
Purposes and Procedures of the Study . . . . . . . . . . . . . . . . . .   139
Reliability of the Censorship Scale . . . . . . . . . . . . . . . . . . . .   140
Pro- and Anti-Censorship Librarians . . . . . . . . . . . . . . . . . . .   141
Relationship of Attitudes to Variables . . . . . . . . . . . . . . . . . .   143
Conclusions and Recommendations . . . . . . . . . . . . . . . . . . . .   147
Implications of the Study . . . . . . . . . . . . . . . . . . . . . . . . . .   147
Recommendations for Additional Research . . . . . . . . . . . . . . .   149
In Conclusion . . . . . . . . . . . . . . . . . . . . . . . . . . . . . . . . . .   150

# PART III
## BIBLIOGRAPHY OF CENSORSHIP
### 1950–1971

Introduction . . . . . . . . . . . . . . . . . . . . . . . . . . . . . . . . . . 153
Section A: Books, Dissertations, Studies, Reports and Pamphlets;
    An Annotated List . . . . . . . . . . . . . . . . . . . . . . . . . . . . 155
Section B: Theses . . . . . . . . . . . . . . . . . . . . . . . . . . . . . . . 186
Section C: Articles and Parts of Larger Works . . . . . . . . . . . . . . . . 188

# APPENDIX I
## LETTERS AND THE SURVEY INSTRUMENT

A.  Cover Letter to Respondents and Follow-up Letters . . . . . . . . . . 199
B.  The Questionnaire with Percentages of Responses to
    All Items . . . . . . . . . . . . . . . . . . . . . . . . . . . . . . . . . . . 202

# APPENDIX II
## INTELLECTUAL FREEDOM STATEMENTS ADOPTED BY
## THE AMERICAN LIBRARY ASSOCIATION

A.  What to Do Before the Censor Comes—and After . . . . . . . . . . . . 213
B.  Library Bill of Rights . . . . . . . . . . . . . . . . . . . . . . . . . . . . 215
C.  School Library Bill of Rights . . . . . . . . . . . . . . . . . . . . . . . 216
D.  Statement on Labeling . . . . . . . . . . . . . . . . . . . . . . . . . . . 217
E.  Resolution on Challenged Materials . . . . . . . . . . . . . . . . . . . 218
F.  What the American Library Association Can Do for You
    to Help Combat Censorship . . . . . . . . . . . . . . . . . . . . . . . 219
G.  The Freedom to Read Statement . . . . . . . . . . . . . . . . . . . . . 228

Index . . . . . . . . . . . . . . . . . . . . . . . . . . . . . . . . . . . . . . . . 233

# PREFACE

It is always comforting to have suspicions confirmed. In a world in which one is forever discovering that what was thought to be true turns out not to be so, the appearance of a soundly documented and meticulous piece of research which corroborates one's opinions is an occasion to be savored, if not celebrated. Charles Busha's research as described in Part II of this book is such an occurrence.

He deserves congratulations on at least two counts. First, he has firmly established the correlation between attitudes toward censorship and the authoritarian attitudes measured by Adorno's F-scale. Second, and of perhaps more immediate relevance to librarians, he has established that Midwestern librarians profess a more liberal attitude with respect to intellectual freedom than they apparently practice. Though it is hazardous to extrapolate from a selected sample to the entire public library population, one would not be very surprised to discover that Dr. Busha's Midwestern librarians are fairly representative of the profession's beliefs over the entire country. Certainly one would expect regional differences, but on the whole the Midwesterners are probably "typical" of public librarians throughout the United States.

The bibliography of censorship, which he has provided in Part III, is worthy of special attention. It brings together the most significant works on the issue published in English in the last decade, as well as some earlier items of historical interest. His careful annotations of the major works are of particular value in describing their salient points.

The contrast Dr. Busha found between theory and practice or between preachment and performance is not, of course, unique to librarians. It is all-too-commonly characteristic of most of us. In the librarians' case, however, the contrast between these two concepts has a special uniqueness, because the very *raison d'être* of the profession is founded on a paradox. One of the fundamental assumptions underlying the library profession is so basic that it is rarely stated. This assumption is that reading does in fact make a difference; that a person can be changed in some way by reading a book. Carter and Bonk describe this as ". . . the faith accepted by our society that the reading of books is a good thing, that it leads to desirable ends, and that books have the power to alter people for the better."[1]

This same belief is implied in the *Minimum Standards for Public Library Systems, 1966*. The library's materials are provided:

> To facilitate informal self education of all people in the community
> To enrich and further develop the subjects on which individuals are
> undertaking formal education

To meet the informational needs of all

To support the educational, civic, and cultural activities of groups and organizations

To encourage wholesome recreation and constructive use of leisure time.[2]

ALA could hardly assert that the library could facilitate, enrich, meet, support, and encourage anything unless the underlying assumption was that the reading of books can in fact cause changes in readers.

Along with this assumption, librarians hold another belief. They are opposed to censorship in nearly every form. Though Dr. Busha's work shows that librarians may seem to be more opposed to censorship than their actual practices would indicate, it is by and large true that the profession as a whole does oppose censorship.

It has apparently been little noted, or scarcely reported, that there is a contradiction in these two views which cannot easily be explained away. Indeed, reading can change people. But there is no assurance that all changes are necessarily for the good. Since it is absurd to assert that only good changes are possible, never bad ones, there is at least a *prima facie* case for restricting the nature of what is made available for reading. Asheim makes a significant point in a 1953 article:

> What other reason is there for censorship than the assumption that the condemned book will have a harmful effect upon its readers—or at least on some of them? . . . If we have no evidence that books are harmful we have less that they are not, and it is quite understandable that those who favor censorship should advocate wariness against materials which may be harmful.[3]

His remarks may be turned around. What other reason is there for selection of books than the assumption that the selected books will have a beneficial effect upon readers—or at least upon some of them?

A few years ago the U. S. Food and Drug Administration changed its policy with respect to permitting new drugs to appear on the market. The prior policy had permitted the marketing of any drugs for which no ill effects were demonstrated in tests. The new policy requires that the manufacturer provide evidence of positive benefit of the drug in question. This change was, by and large, heartily approved by the liberal members of society. Any such similar attempt by the government to require at least some evidence of the benefits of a particular book would be bitterly opposed by the same group. Their opposition to the production, sale, and marketing of inferior products in one part of the market does not extend to similar actions in another part.

American society is full of similar examples of government regulation, permissible quality standards and the like, directed at insuring certain minimum quality goods. The recent consumerism movement is aimed at similar goals. Books, and communications media in general, are exempt from this regulatory effort—mainly, of course, due to the provisions of the First Amendment: "Congress shall make no law . . . abridging the freedom of speech, or of the press." This amendment has been the rock upon which has foundered a multitude of both state and federal statutes aimed at regulating what is communicated.

With respect to the position of librarians in this matter, there are two basic questions. The first and broader one is the opposition to censorship in general. Whether or not any library would in fact purchase *The Housewife's Handbook on Selective Promiscuity* (Documentary Books, 1962)—one of the items at issue in the Ginzburg case[4]—is irrelevant to Ginzburg's right, or lack thereof, to publish and sell it. Operating on the basic premise that one has the right to publish and sell whatever one pleases, the library profession should recognize Ginzburg's right to publish his materials, even though some librarians considered it of no value to their collections.

The more difficult and practical question for librarians is what they will in fact buy for their collections. The act of buying certain titles instead of others implies that those bought are preferable to—in some sense "better" than—those not purchased. Hence, the librarian must be prepared to defend his choices. This is a particularly sensitive issue, since public funds are frequently involved.

Librarians typically defend their selection on two grounds: 1) librarians are better qualified than others to select appropriate materials for their communities; and 2) particular segments of the community which object to a given title fail to take into account the broad view of the needs of all library users. Librarians repeatedly defend their obligation to represent all viewpoints on controversial matters, but these arguments are unconvincing in many cases. They do not convince the pro-censorship groups because these groups already have a predilection for censorship. These groups view the matter as a struggle between their value judgments and the librarian's. These arguments sometimes also fail to convince more serious students of the matter as well, primarily because the librarian's avowed principles are in notable contrast to his actual performance.

A certain hypocrisy becomes evident when librarians' statements are compared with their actions. Where, for example, does one find a library which has a "balanced" collection on the topic of racial segregation? Despite the fact that many pro-segregation titles are badly written, the principle that one should select a badly written book if it is the only thing available would require that such titles be obtained in the interests of balance. Similarly, legal and medical titles are ordinarily not provided in public libraries, on the grounds that such works are too susceptible to misinterpretation by the laymen. On the other hand, *Everything You Always Wanted to Know About Sex; But Were Afraid to Ask, Explained* (McKay, 1969) is widely available through the libraries of even relatively conservative communities despite the distinct possibility that the unwary reader is at least as liable to cause problems for himself (and others) if he uses this book's advice uncritically, as he would be if he used the unselected medical or legal titles unwisely. Such examples of "unbalanced" collections are widespread. Books on hunting and automotive care are commonly available, while those on casting of horoscopes are scarce. Yet it is clear that many more people are injured by careless use of guns and autos than by careless use of horoscopes.

Librarians violate their principles not only by omission, as above, but by commission as well. How does *Memoirs of a Woman of Pleasure* (Putnam, 1963) make any positive contribution to the ALA-supported objectives quoted earlier?

Or any of a number of other titles? The only possible purpose such titles could support is the "catch-all" final objective, and it is difficult to see how one can make a case for them under any generally accepted definition of "wholesome recreation" or "constructive use of leisure time."

A good part of this divergence between professed principles and actual practice may be attributed to the lack of a consistent and defensible underlying philosophy. The librarian's liberalism is, by and large, based on eighteenth-century views of the equality of man—the same views which contributed so heavily to the development of the U. S. Constitution. However, these views have been strongly attacked. Darwinism, the decline of once widely held religious beliefs, Freudian psychology, and world events at large have led many to the conclusion that mankind is an unnecessary, if not deleterious, addition to life-forms on the planet.

Psychological research in particular has contributed to this rather dismal view of man. The Freudian view—man struggling with his id and/or superego— and the belief that man's basic innate urges are destructive and evil, have been most influential. It is fair to say that the entire *Weltanschauung* of contemporary society has been irrevocably altered by Freudian psychology. This pessimistic view of mankind has been reinforced by the behavioristic school of psychology as well. The principal exponent of this basically negative view of man, B. F. Skinner, is quite blunt:

> The hypothesis that man is not free is essential to the application of scientific method to the study of human behavior. The free inner man who is held responsible for the behavior of the external biological organism is only a pre-scientific substitute for the kinds of causes which are discovered in the course of a scientific investigation. All these alternative causes lie outside the individual.[5]

Skinner has made his views even more explicit in his recent work, *Beyond Freedom and Dignity*, in which he puts forth the view that man can be held "accountable" for neither his successes nor his failures.[6] This statement directly challenges the humanistic belief in free will and the ability to choose for oneself. It is a belief, however, which is held either explicitly, as in the case of Skinner, or implicitly, as in the case of many other social scientists. Librarians have traditionally found themselves in the camp of the humanists, rather than the scientists. Being thus aligned, they have found it difficult to counter the "scientific" arguments of their opponents and hard to justify their efforts toward such non-quantifiable goals as "facilitating informal self-education . . ." Since librarians have relied basically on humanistic justifications, it has been difficult for them to deal with those who favor a pragmatic, scientific, objective, efficient, results-oriented, manipulative society (those who have "science" on their side). While it is true that people will give lip service to those standard platitudes regarding the worth of a liberal education, pragmatism and "scientific" logic will win in most cases.

The inability to deal effectively with the "what-good-is-it?" argument has been compounded by the librarian's professed neutrality. This neutrality makes it likely that he will be taken for a person with no particularly strong views at all, and hence ineffectual. Librarians are not, on the whole, taken very seriously by those who have economic or political power. Currently, programs are most successful when their proponents can justify them in terms of pragmatic and demonstrable "usefulness," i.e., when the "what-good-is-it?" question is answered in contemporary terms. Librarians can seldom justify their programs on this "scientific" basis.

There is in fact a philosophical/psychological basis which can justify the librarians' position. While Freudian and behavioristic views of man have been opposed by some almost from their beginnings, it has been only recently that a reasonable, well-formulated alternative to both has come into being. It has become known as humanistic psychology. (It is sometimes called third force psychology—Freudianism and behaviorism being the first two.) It makes two major assertions which challenge the basic assumptions of earlier psychologies: 1) the basic inner drives of man are not evil, and 2) it is possible to establish an objective and scientific set of ethics. Abraham H. Maslow was probably the foremost exponent of humanistic psychology. As a result of his research, Maslow concluded:

1.  We have, each of us, an essentially biologically based inner nature, which is to some degree 'natural,' intrinsic, given, and in a certain limited sense, unchangeable, or, at least, unchanging.
2.  Each person's inner nature is in part unique to himself and in part species-wide.
3.  It is possible to study this inner nature scientifically and to discover what it is like—(not *invent—discover*).
4.  This inner nature, as much as we know of it so far, seems not to be intrinsically or primarily or necessarily evil. The basic needs (for life, for safety and security, for belongingness and affection, for respect and self-respect, and for self-actualization), the basic human emotions and the basic human capacities are on their face either neutral, pre-moral or positively 'good.' Destructiveness, sadism, cruelty, seem so far to be not intrinsic, but rather they seem to be violent reactions *against* frustration of our intrinsic needs, emotions and capacities. Anger is *in itself* not evil, nor is fear, laziness or even ignorance. Of course, these can and do lead to evil behavior, but they needn't. This result is not intrinsically necessary. Human nature is not nearly as bad as it has been thought to be. In fact it can be said that the possibilities of human nature have customarily been sold short. [emphasis in original]
5.  Since this inner nature is good or neutral rather than bad, it is best to bring it out and to encourage it rather than to suppress it. If it is permitted to guide our life, we grow healthy, fruitful, and happy.
6.  If this essential core of the person is denied or suppressed he gets sick sometimes in obvious ways, sometimes in subtle ways, sometimes immediately, sometimes later.[7]

The contrast between Maslow's view of the nature of man and the view of "conventional" psychologies is evident. It is, however, the only psychology which is consistent with extra-psychological experience and writings. Shadowings and similarities, extensions and extrapolations of the implications of humanistic psychology can be found in many other writers, who are outside the field of psychology. There are obvious similarities between Maslow's concept of man and theological writings. There is little difference except in the nature of the explanations between "B-cognition" described by Maslow[8] and the classical descriptions of mystical or transcendental experiences. Similarly there is little difference between Maslow's assertion that healthy people can trust their impulses and St. Thomas' dictum: "Love God, and do what you will."

The recognition of the advantages of being a self-actualizing person, and the description of such a person as a hero, a personality type to be striven for, is evident in much other literature. Riesman's "autonomous man"[9] is similar. Reich's Consciousness III man shares many of the same characteristics.[10] Ayn Rand, despite the heavy rationalist elements of her objectivist philosophy, is describing the same kind of ideal person. Certainly the protagonists of her novels are autonomous men. She states quite clearly that she set out to create heroic models of man, not "well-adjusted" ones.[11]

There is insufficient space here to trace the concept of "hero" in literature or history, but enough has been suggested to indicate that heroes have similar self-concepts and that they bear a great resemblance to "autonomous man." The same theme is sounded in Hayek's *Road to Serfdom*.[12] This polemic against planning is not so much anti-planning as it is pro-individual. Hayek attacks centralized planning sharply on the grounds that it inevitably leads to totalitarianism. His almost mystic faith in competition is unwarranted, but his real point is that it is preferable, even at the cost of some apparent injustice, to leave alone rather than regulate men's lives.

Clearly, the viewpoints expressed by all these authors—which might be lumped together under the term "individualism"—represent value judgments. There is a strong resemblance between them and the ideals of Jeffersonian democracy. The library profession has consistently maintained in principle, if not in practice, that these same ideals of individuality—freedom from censorship, the right to read, and so forth—constitute the basis of the profession's value structure. However neglected it may be in practice, the notion of individual freedom is inherent in the philosophical statements of librarians.

One of the difficult questions facing the library profession in contemporary society is the problem of justification of this set of beliefs. There is an increasing tendency on the part of society to regulate matters. In the name of rationality and logic, more and more things are planned, controlled, and administered. Maximizing predictability and minimizing risk are goals of many organizations, public and private. When faced with arguments that certain things are bad to read, or are inimical to society in some way, librarians find that they must fall back on eighteenth-century humanistic arguments about the nature of free men. They appeal to the Founding Fathers, to the writings of the Age of Enlightenment. Though these arguments have some value, like wrapping oneself in the flag, they are of decreasing effectiveness in contemporary society. They lack the scientific basis; they are not substantiated by hard evidence. Similar arguments based on Hayek, Rand, or other writers suffer from the same defect.

Humanistic psychology offers a scientific basis for defending the library profession's value system. For the first time it becomes possible for librarians to argue: our policies are the way they are because they reflect our best judgment on how we can meet the basic human psychological needs for growth. In justification for our view of what these needs are, we offer the following: 1) humanistic arguments from Plato to the present day, which emphasize the importance of spontaneity, liberty, and the uniqueness of each individual; and 2) the results of psychological investigations which demonstrate that given the opportunity to choose freely, people will choose wisely, becoming better persons—and furthermore that when denied these choices, people become neurotic and unwell. It is entirely true that some people may make poor choices, but the ability to choose, rightly or wrongly, is essential for human growth. To limit this is to warp the natural course of that growth.

Humanistic psychology offers a rich, meaningful and even inspiring view of man in society which is of particular relevance to the library profession. It is a psychology/philosophy which is optimistic about man, convinced of his worth, congruent with history, and which encompasses all facets of man's experience. In addition, it presents verifiable data, proceeds from logical hypotheses, and forms a framework upon which a consistent set of theories and principles of operation can be based.

It is certainly true that humanistic psychology presents a view of only the potentialities of man, not necessarily his actualities. There is some evidence that its perspective is "truer" than the Freudian or behavioristic alternatives, but there is also evidence that there are many elements of truth in these less optimistic alternatives. These alternatives are, however, based on a set of values no less than is humanistic psychology. But because these alternatives present such a dim view of man, they are accepted as objective facts, rather than value judgments.

It is impossible for an individual *not* to have values. Just as there must be *some* kind of weather, a person must have *some* set of values, whether they are fundamentalist or relativist. Within limits, one can choose the set of values he or she prefers to live by. Rationally, the set which promotes "happiness" or ability to function should be chosen. The same is true of a profession. Each profession has a set of values which influences the way in which duties of members are performed and the way in which practitioners are educated. If these values are difficult to justify in the face of cultural pressure, they will be defended less and less strongly, then finally abandoned for another set. Humanistic psychology presents a new defense for the librarian's values—a set of values which is worth defending, and which, if abandoned, will contribute to a decline in the quality of life and society.

Indiana University
August 1, 1972                                                        Allan Pratt

# FOOTNOTES

[1] Mary D. Carter and Wallace J. Bonk, *Building Library Collections* (Metuchen, N. J.: Scarecrow Press, 1969), p. 2.

[2] *Minimum Standards for Public Library Systems, 1966* (Chicago: American Library Association, 1967), p. 9.

[3] Lester Asheim, "Censorship or Selection," *Wilson Library Bulletin*, September 1953, p. 65.

[4] Ginzburg v. United States, 383 U. S. Reports 463 (1966).

[5] B. F. Skinner, *Science and Human Behavior* (New York: Macmillan, 1953), p. 447.

[6] B. F. Skinner, *Beyond Freedom and Dignity* (New York: Knopf, 1971).

[7] Abraham Maslow, *Toward a Psychology of Being*, 2d ed. (New York: Van Nostrand Reinhold Co., 1968), pp. 3-4.

[8] Abraham Maslow, *Religion, Values, and Peak-Experiences* (New York: Viking Press, 1970), pp. 19ff.

[9] David Reisman, *The Lonely Crowd* (New Haven, Conn.: Yale University Press, 1950), pp. 285ff.

[10] Charles Reich, *The Greening of America* (New York: Bantam Books, 1971), pp. 233ff.

[11] Ayn Rand, *The Romantic Manifesto* (New York: New American Library, 1971), p. 127.

[12] Friedrich A. von Hayek, *The Road to Serfdom* (Chicago, Ill.: University of Chicago Press, 1944).

# INTRODUCTION

Charles Busha's censorship investigation, which forms Part II of *Freedom versus Suppression and Censorship*, has a number of implications for the library profession, including the following: 1) librarians can no longer afford the intellectual luxury of assuming that only elsewhere—say, in California—do we practice the restriction of access of ideas and 2) the suggestion that education, particularly continuing education, would most probably have a very positive effect on the degree to which librarians are committed to freedom of access to recorded ideas.

Marjorie Fiske's report of repressive practices of librarians, *Book Selection and Censorship*, was a milestone; it has already become a classic of library literature. The Fiske study revealed that much of the responsibility for "censorship" of public and school library materials in certain California libraries could be placed on librarians, not on someone "out there." Yet for a number of years the question has been: Can the Fiske conclusions be extrapolated to librarians in other states and regions? Many librarians chose to hide behind the possibility that Fiske's findings were not indicative of libraries at large, only of institutions in California. As a result of Dr. Busha's research reported in this book, that possibility no longer exists—especially in the Midwest, where, as a matter of fact, there was considerable resistance to the implications of the Fiske report.

The studies by Fiske and Busha, which used different methodologies and which examined dissimilar geographic and cultural areas, support strikingly similar conclusions: An uncomfortable number of librarians do practice censorship and do support certain types of suppression in libraries. Only the most irrational among us will continue to hide behind the refrain "But we're different here."

Fiske found that some librarians (nearly one-fifth of the book selectors in her sample) avoided purchasing books they believed to be of a controversial nature and that some others restricted circulation of such works if purchased. Dr. Busha's study finds a "marked disparity between attitudes of many public librarians toward intellectual freedom as a concept and toward censorship as an activity" in the Midwest of the United States. We can no longer escape the evidence that some librarians practice censorship.

The various "explosions"—information, research, publications, media—are constantly increasing society's need for instant access to a broad range of information and ideas in all forms and shades. Yet Busha tells us that apparently all too often librarians have opinions and attitudes which are creating barriers between man's recorded ideas and his access to them. Can anything be done about it? About us? Dr. Busha has stated:

The association found between the amount of formal education completed by respondents and their attitudes toward censorship may have implications for the education of librarians. This study revealed that with each amount of increase in the degree of formal education completed by respondents, there was, almost without exception, a corresponding decrease in the approval of repressive measures on the right to read and the freedom of inquiry. In view of this finding, continuing education in the form of courses taken for credit may be an important, perhaps even essential, method for promoting among librarians an active commitment to the preservation of the freedom to read for everyone. Less formal methods of education, such as on-the-job or in-service training, workshops, and institutes, might have similar effects on librarians' attitudes toward censorship; however, this study did not identify or isolate these as variables. Such informal education could have been an intervening variable and could account for the fact that a few of the librarians with limited formal education expressed quite liberal views.

I am in accord with those statements and would like to elaborate further by examining the potential role of continuing education as it relates to library-practiced or intramural censorship.

Most educators agree that trying to change attitudes is difficult, often impossible. This is true of formal and of informal education. I was first forcibly made aware of this in my own teaching experience. After presenting what I felt was a particularly effective series of lectures on intellectual freedom, I capped what I believed to be incisive and penetrating verbal essays with an examination which required students to take one of the ALA "Library Bill of Rights" statements and argue *against* it. I had hoped that the exercise would clinch my argument that those whom librarians oppose in their efforts to display the full range of man's recorded ideas are not all bigots or unintelligent. Very sound arguments can be raised against intellectual freedom, and I felt these future professionals needed to be prepared to deal with them.

The first exam paper that I read was all too revealing of one teacher's failure to change attitudes. "I cannot argue against intellectual freedom as you ask. I so believe in what you have taught us that I would put into jail anyone who would argue against intellectual freedom." The student was a former Nazi SS officer.

Educational experts, especially those with experience in adult education methods, claim that we *can* change behavior. Indeed, one of the potential strengths of continuing education, informal education, or adult education is the factor that it permits more emphasis on immediate needs than does formal education. Certainly, continuing education in librarianship is apt to be aimed at helping librarians do their jobs more effectively. And, often the methodology is far more flexible, working with real-life situations and building on the practitioner's own experience and background. The reinforcement of learning with others who share similar needs is one of the most effective avenues to behavioral change.

In censorship clinics, selection policy seminars, and even in the "reaching the unreached" institutes I have led, participants have always wanted to come to grips with their immediate on-the-job problems. Reports of post-workshop changes in behavior are typical.

If we are to heed the warnings implicit in Dr. Busha's study of censorship attitudes among librarians, I would suggest that the area of continuing education is the most important as well as the most effective place to start. But with *whom* should we start? Trustees? Busha comments:

> Boards of trustees of public libraries are responsible for the selection and appointment of head librarians and are, as well, responsible for setting policies under which public librarians operate. To what extent do these boards support the application of intellectual freedom policies to book-selection practices and to library services? Are trustees willing to defend actions of librarians who actively support the principles of the freedom to read in public libraries?

Community leaders? Busha has questioned:

> What are the attitudes of community leaders toward the freedom to read and access to information? Librarians with restrictive attitudes frequently justify a need for censorship by referring to the general climate of opinion within their communities.

Librarians? A profile constructed by Dr. Busha of the censorship-prone public librarian shows a middle-aged librarian heading a library in a community of less than 35,000. She probably has had some college work. If she is older, she is even more apt to agree with authoritarian beliefs.

Perhaps we should start with the librarian. My experience has empirically demonstrated that this group is often highly sensitive to community interests. That sensitivity can be a two-way street—it can lead to real, in-depth community service, or it can lead to an increasingly restrictive library program. But we certainly need to be concerned with all levels of library personnel, and we need to be concerned with all types of libraries. The public library is hardly alone in facing the problems of censorship or in finding solutions.

Librarians can ill afford to reject their responsibility to see that all citizens have access to the full range of man's recorded thoughts—good and bad, old and new, acceptable and repulsive. Charles Busha reminds us in his book that we need once more to look objectively at our own professional commitments to intellectual freedom. I find myself once again impressed with the objectivity and directness of his censorship study in Part II of this book. *Freedom versus Suppression and Censorship* is a provoking and exciting book. Its charge to the library profession is clear.

Boulder, Colorado
August 10, 1972

Peter Hiatt, Director
Continuing Education Program for Library Personnel
Western Interstate Commission for Higher
Education

# PART I

# REPRESSIONS AND FREEDOMS

# CHAPTER 1
# THE NATURE OF CENSORSHIP

*While democracy must have its organization
and controls, its vital breath is individual
liberty.*
—Charles Evans Hughes

*Tyranny, like hell, is not easily conquered;
yet we have this consolation with us, that
the harder the conflict the more glorious
the triumph.*
—Thomas Paine

## The Suppression of Information

Liberation may very well become the byword of the 1970s; to liberate is a very fashionable activity, and to be liberated is a very fashionable state of mind. A number of interest groups have established liberation "fronts," and, in keeping with the temper of the times, even librarians could be expected at any moment to create a boisterous and spirited movement to set books and other materials free and to promote the right to read. Although such an event is not likely to occur, this book is appropriately concerned with one concept of liberation—the setting free of ideas and information. It is an attempt to explain why librarians should practice two of our treasured, constitutionally guaranteed freedoms, the freedom to read and the freedom of speech, and to investigate the attitudes of public librarians toward the concept of intellectual freedom. And, in no small amount, it is hoped that the treatise on intellectual freedom and censorship in Part I of this book, as well as the study of librarians' attitudes about freedoms and suppressions in Part II, will also proivde an answer to the question of how the exercise of these freedoms can be efficaciously accomplished by librarians in our media-oriented society.

The era of the 1950s, 1960s, and 1970s has been fittingly described as a time of information overdose: a period in which knowledge could be and still is disseminated instantaneously via a superfluity of televisions, radios, telephones, fascimile transmission devices, films, books, newspapers, magazines, and many other media of communication. But ironically our age is also a phase in time in which there is a need for even more facts and figures. Despite our sophisticated communication networks and our profusion of electronic devices for the transmission and reception of messages, there appears to be an acute and even greater need today than anytime in the past for the liberation of information. Although the government of the United States has usually been regarded among all nations as one of the most liberal disseminators of information to its citizens, the demands for knowledge have become so relentless in recent years that the federal bureaucracy has been severely criticized for its security classification system for certain types of data and for the cloaks of secrecy with which it has shrouded many government decisions and activities, particularly those pertaining to the war in Vietnam.

So extraordinary has the need for more information become on the part of American citizens that in recent years citizens have exerted strong pressures on government authorities to pass on to the people, via the communication media, all matters of special, public interest. Governments, including those at local and county levels, have been accused of press control; such developments as the Pentagon Papers, disguised threats against news networks, and the infrequency of presidential press conferences have been viewed by some observers as obvious examples of a pattern of governmental information control. While many Americans have seemed uninterested in the freedom *versus* secrecy-of-information issue and have been relatively content with the federal government's performance in letting the people know what is going on, members of the mass media and others engaged in occupations or activities closely related to the dissemination of information have been quite outspoken in their criticism of the administration's performance in this area.

In summarizing suppression and intellectual freedom activities of the 1950s and 1960s, Dan Lacy, a former managing director of the American Book Publishers Council who was appointed by the President to his National Advisory Commission on Libraries, outlined five examples of the methods by which two presidential administrations have attempted to repress the flow of information from the federal government to American citizens: 1) Vice-president Agnew's attack on the mass media, particularly the television networks, for their criticism of President Nixon's policies; 2) the use of Federal investigative power in attemps to pressure or intimidate news correspondents whose comments on the administration's performance had been less than favorable; 3) the use of charges of conspiracy in an apparent attempt to associate critics of the government with acts of criminality; 4) the use of court or Congressional subpoena to force newsmen to reveal their sources of information or to turn over to the Federal government materials such as notes and film sequences; and 5) the prevention of the publication of classified documents by injunction or by criminal prosecution.[1]

In an obvious response to vociferous anti-secrecy critics, President Nixon issued an executive order, effective as of June 1, 1972, in an attempt to liberalize and to curtail the federal government's control of information. In signing the order, the President made the following statement:

> The many abuses of the security system can no longer be tolerated. Fundamental to our way of life is the belief that when information which properly belongs to the public is systematically withheld by those in power, the people soon become ignorant of their own affairs, distrustful of those who manage them, and—eventually—incapable of determining their own destinies.

Despite the concern the President expressed for the free dissemination of information, there have been incidents during Nixon's administration which would lead one to believe that our present chief executive is not always sensitive to the dangers of censorship and threats against freedom of the press. In the summer of 1972, for example, an organization called the National Committee for Impeachment of President Nixon placed an advertisement in *The New York Times*. The notice urged the impeachment of the chief executive because of his Vietnam war policies, and press workers of *The Times* refused to print it. Simply because they did not agree with its contents, some pressmen demanded deletion of the advertisement from the newspaper. Newspaper officials refused to give in to the demands, and, after a considerable delay in the publication schedule, the workers were persuaded to print the paper. If management of *The Times* had permitted censorship by its mechanical workers, a precedent could have been set for the exercise of restrictions by press employees on anything in newspapers to which they might object. Despite the lip service given by the present administration to freedom of the press and freedom of expression, Donald F. Rogers, special consultant to the President for labor affairs, told the New York Printing Pressman's Union No. 2 that their protest against the impeachment advertisement made Mr. Nixon feel "good," and he extended the President's personal gratitude to them. Such action on the part of an administration official represents approval of forms of suppressive acts against freedom of the press. No attempts, blatant or subtle, by press employees to censor newspapers should be allowed or encouraged in a democratic country, even though a president of the United States expresses his approval of such action. In a recent press interview, Kingman Brewster, Jr., President of Yale University, stated that the Nixon administration has been "excessively impatient" with constitutional safeguards. The pressmen's episode appears to be one such example. Indeed, respect for law and order has been heavily emphasized in recent years, often to the detriment of respect for individual rights.

While the vice-president, Spiro T. Agnew, has demonstrated an adroitness for condemning members of the press for attitudes and comments critical of the federal administration, that is as far as such attacks should be allowed to go in the United States. Elected officials and their administrations are subject to constant scrutiny; criticism of federal and state policies, programs, and activities helps insure a healthier democracy. The press in the United States ought to be a sounding board and a voice of the people, not of the government. Newspapers, as well as such organs of the press as magazines and journals, are frequently manipulated as tools of totalitarian régimes; however, the U. S. Constitution explicitly forbids Congress to pass laws which abridge freedom of the press. Through an interpretation of the Fourteenth Amendment in 1868, the Supreme Court made freedom of the press also binding on the states. That freedom should not only protect the press from state and federal bureaucracies but should also extend to newspapers the right to reject private and commercial advertisements which conflict with established editorial policies. In consideration of editorial policies and of the press's responsibility to its publics, newspapers should also be able to reject political advertisements from extreme left- and right-wing groups. In recent years there has been more and more concern, in relation to a free and responsible press, over published attacks and criticisms aimed at persons or institutions. In a democracy, such victims should also be given newspaper space to answer charges, regardless of whether they are valid or invalid.

In the spring of 1972 the Food and Drug Administration (FDA) of the federal government announced that beginning in the summer of 1972 90 per cent of its records would be opened to the public. Most of the material had been classified and unavailable for examination by private citizens, and one wonders why such things as laboratory tests on food and drug products and letters to the FDA from businessmen and politicians were not heretofore available. The public can only speculate that numerous other government agencies also maintain secret files containing information to which citizens should have access. Apparently, some federal officials prefer to operate in privacy and secrecy as much as possible, but the American taxpayer has a right to know, for example, whether a drug product is effective, ineffective, or dangerous and whether a canned food industry meets federal standards.

In a democratic society it is intolerable for the burden of proof to be placed on private citizens to show why they ought to be able to read a public document. Confidentiality of government records is sometimes justified to protect the privacy of individuals; however, candor should be the rule rather than the exception. In the past two decades the federal government has obviously carried the security issue to excess, and much of the overclassification of documents as secret or top secret has been, without a doubt, a measure to prevent public knowledge of various activities of government agencies.

The civil liberties movement which apparently reached its peak in the fifties has been somewhat of a counterpart of the demands of citizens for fewer restrictions on information. The American Civil Liberties Union has been quite active in recent years in providing legal and financial aid to persons who feel their constitutional rights have been violated. Promoters of civil liberties have spoken out strongly in support of the rights, privileges, and immunities of citizens; they have attempted to stimulate and to promote the legal protection of citizens from undue government interference. The issue of the invasion of citizens' privacy has become almost as strong among the defenders of civil liberties as the question of the control of information has been among those who seek a freer exchange of information and ideas. There is, after all, a very close relationship between these two endeavors. The 1971 U. S. Congress hearing of the Subcommittee on Constitutional Rights disclosed the extent to which citizens' rights and privacies have been infringed upon by such government agencies as the Justice Department, particularly the Federal Bureau of Investigation; various branches of the military under the auspices of the Defense Department; the Internal Revenue Service; the Passport Division of the State Department; and the Social Security Administration, not to mention state and local agencies such as welfare and police departments.

Grave concern has also been expressed in recent years over the development of data banks of information about citizens by government agencies, such as those maintained by the F.B.I., and the collection of information to be placed in various departmental dossiers. Many critics of these activities have claimed that such government action has moved us one step closer to the Orwellian style Big Brother predicted in *1984*. Dossiers maintained by the Federal Bureau of Investigation, with their welter of confirmed and unconfirmed gossip, scandal, and hearsay, stand as a monument to the bureaucratic powers of J. Edgar

Hoover, the late director of that agency who was often described by his admirers and supporters as "a fearless fighter and implacable foe of the godless tyranny of cancerous communism." Indeed, Hoover was a professional politician of the old school, and his blanket methods and authoritarian actions seemed terribly out of place in a democratic society and in the subtle world of intelligence. Hoover managed to use his ruthless talents to compile and store away vast amounts of information concerning the personal lives of millions of American citizens.

Violations of library users' privacies by agents of the federal government have also become a matter of concern among librarians, particularly those who have a healthy suspicion of imperious bureaucracies. In July 1970, agents of the Internal Revenue Service (IRS) requested access to public library circulation records in Milwaukee, Atlanta, and DeKalb County, Georgia. The IRS was attempting to identify readers of materials dealing with the manufacturing of explosives. Many practicing librarians and the Office of Intellectual Freedom of the American Library Association protested the IRS action, maintaining that circulation records of libraries are strictly confidential for the protection of users' rights to privacy. Librarians cannot allow the confidentiality of library users' reading habits to be eroded in favor of the objectives of government agents engaged in crime control. The right to read, to borrow materials, and to obtain information confidentially from libraries should not be infringed upon by local, state, or federal snoopers; for since when has reading become a crime?

From time to time, the U. S. Congress has either intentionally or inadvertently made overt jurisdictional attempts to repress the flow of information. One of the unfortunate weaknesses of the American system of government is the belief among many citizens, as well as government officials, that if a problem arises all we have to do is pass a law which will take care of it. Such has been the case with the "control" of obscenity and pornography. Congressional action aimed at eliminating the availability of pornography and similar sexually-oriented materials was taken in such legislation as the Comstock Act of 1873, which was an upshot of the efforts of Anthony Comstock, a puritanical crusader and one of the organizers of the New York Society for the Suppression of Vice. The Smoot-Hawley Tariff Bill of 1929, as well as certain actions of Congressmen such as Senators Joseph McCarthy, Barry Goldwater, and Strom Thurmond were designed in part to control objectionable materials.

Congress has also enacted several laws tantamount to repression, the first of which were the Alien and Sedition Acts of 1798. At that time, war with France appeared eminent, and the need was felt to oust "dangerous" aliens and to impeach those individuals who might write or speak "with intent to defame" the government, the Congress, or the President. The Alien and Sedition Acts of 1798 delineate the first legislation which seriously threatened freedom of speech and freedom of the press in the United States. The Espionage Act of 1917 was the antecedent of widespread enforcement for the first time of censorship by the United States government, and it represents legislation which far exceeded the needs of national safety during wartime. The Smith Act of 1940 was the first legislation to curb freedom of speech and freedom of the press during peacetime. Until the Smith Act was put into effect, no federal legislation had been enacted since 1798 which was aimed at subduing offenses, other than treason, against the authority of the government. The Smith Act was designed to prevent the advocacy of or the conspiracy to advocate forcible overthrow of the government. The act was employed numerous times after 1948 to combat communist activities within the nation.

A cursory examination of legislative acts of an inhibiting nature will demonstrate that a number of repressive laws passed during periods of crises have served as instruments of restraint upon the freedom of speech and the freedom of the press. Professor Norman Dorsen points out in *Frontiers of Civil Liberties*, however, that the degree to which a nation will protect individual liberty during a period of turmoil such as wartime or internal social strife may well be the ultimate test of the country's political morality.[2]

Even in the absence of any new legislation designed to control or to restrain individual freedoms, Congressional hearings have often focused attention on special problems such as crime and juvenile delinquency, which various legislators have sometimes attempted to link with "undesirable" materials such as comic books, films, television programs, and pornography. These hearings have often caused repercussions deleterious to intellectual freedom, particularly in reference to the animation of renewed interest in the control of materials deemed to be objectionable by some person or group. Congressional hearings have often set into motion reenforcement of almost forgotten and antiquated repressive laws, many of which were founded, contrary to the Bill of Rights of the United States Constitution, on the idea that individual rights must by capitulated when they come in conflict with matters relating to national safety or to the "best interest" of the nation. A "clear and present danger" criterion was devised by the U. S. Supreme Court after World War I, for example, to determine whether acts related to the scope of freedom of speech and press helped to bring about those conditions which Congress had a right to prevent. In yet another repressive move, an Office of Censorship was established by executive order on December 19, 1941, and that agency was quite active during World War II.

### Restrictions on Expression

The causes of censorship are extremely complicated; however, they have been classified into four major categories; psychological, political, paternal, and social. Psychological causes stem from a compulsive need of some people to restrain others from uttering disturbing or distasteful thoughts or images. Political causes are related to the interests of governments and governing bodies in maintaining stability and in preventing communications or utterances which threaten existing policies. Paternal causes of censorship are those which originate from the desire of parents to have their children confronted only with those influences which might allow them to develop along lines deemed acceptable or attractive. Social causes are related to the desires of administrators and citizens to preserve a wholesome society and to reduce crime and abnormal behavior.[3]

While official and unofficial censorship is a restriction placed on some form of public expression, it can be of two basic types: 1) preventative censorship, the restriction of material prior to publication or issue, and 2) punitive censorship, the restriction after materials have been distributed. Censorship in the 1950s was politically oriented, for the most part; however, in the decade of the 1960s most official and unofficial suppression of intellectual freedom in the United States took the form of restrictions on publications, performances, or films which were sexually oriented. Grounds for suppression in most censorship controversies in recent years have concentrated on charges of obscenity against offending agents or materials.

Censorship controversies are usually inextricably embroiled in confrontations between two schools of thought; each is convinced that its philosophy reflects the best interest of the community. The censor aims to protect persons from "evils" or "dangerous" ideas, and the anti-censor endeavors to bolster the freedom of choice whereby people can expose themselves to any ideas, or even "evils," which interest them. Two experts in the legal aspects of pornography and obscenity, Professors Lockhart and McClure of the University of Minnesota, have characterized the censor as:

> ... seldom a person who appreciates esthetic values or understands the nature and function of imaginative literature. His interests lie elsewhere. Often an emotionally disturbed person, he sets out to look for smut and consequently finds it almost everywhere ... He is rarely an educated person ... He is often ... an intemperate person with a paranoid personality.[4]

The chance of reconciling positions held by the two sides in any particular censorship controversy, therefore, is normally quite slim; both schools of thought are usually steadfastly held. On the one hand, those who oppose censorship are convinced that freedom of expression and freedom of information are the cornerstones of American democracy; on the other hand, those who want more controls on publications and other media would like to insure that decency will prevail or that a particular opinion toward an issue will be predominant.

Censors frequently claim that a high correlation exists between rising crime rates and the unrestricted dissemination of certain types of books and materials containing ideas in conflict with their own. A frequent charge of censors and their allies, consequently, is that increased crime rates are the result of the permissiveness of our times and the availability of pernicious materials. However, the issue that more vice and crime actually exists today per capita than in the past is open for debate; no doubt we are made more aware of the extent of crime by our more sophisticated mass media of communication and by our improved, systematic methods of collecting, analyzing, and reporting crime statistics. In addition, the word "crime" has been increasingly used in recent years as a synonym for cultural, political, and social deviance as well as a description of such acts as murder, rape, and extortion.

Those people who theorize a casual relationship between the reading of pernicious literature and criminalism have apparently failed to recognize that individuals predisposed to crime and other anti-social activities are usually not interested in literary pursuits. People tend to choose selectively the books and periodicals, as well as the television programs and motion pictures, which support their existing predispositions and value systems. Consequently, would-be criminals, if they read at all, would most likely ferret out and read materials which already interest them or which support their concern with violence and acts of criminality. Pernicious materials cannot be blamed, therefore, for originating criminal tendencies. The casual relationship which some people attempt to establish between pornography, obscenity, and other "harmful" materials with grave offenses perpetrated against society has not been verified.

Insofar as television, radio, newspapers, and magazines are concerned, these mass communication media have been shown repeatedly to be ineffectual as tools for profoundly affecting the thoughts and actions of people. Presently, we can only hypothesize from available evidence that depictions of violence, as well as sexually-explicit materials, *might* at the most aggravate the latent criminal tendency; however, here again, the mutual relationship is indeed nebulous and in need of verification by rigorous research. Amitai Etzioni, professor of sociology at Columbia University and director of the Center for Policy Research, has underscored the fact that ". . . persons are more likely to heed spouses, relatives, friends, and 'opinion leaders' than broadcasted or printed records" when it comes to matters of opinion change and behavioral influences.[5]

In contrast to those who would suppress books and other materials in the name of "law and order," the promoters of intellectual freedom are quick to point out the close connection between freedom and creativity and to proclaim that secrecy and controls are millstones around the necks of a society struggling to maintain, if not to achieve, democracy. They are also quick to question whether the censorship of books and materials containing accounts or depictions of sexual acts and violence actually protects society from depravity and brutality. The philosophic concept of intellectual freedom is associated with that of metaphysical doubt, humility, and the tolerance—even encouragement—of experiment and change, and progress in all areas of human endeavor. Intellectual freedom can be realized in any society only through the exercise of understanding and tolerance. Charles Rembar, a principal defense attorney in a number of major censorship cases and a former editor of the *Columbia Law Review*, dissents from the generally-accepted idea that more unrestricted expression in our society is a sign of moral decay among the people. He does not believe, contrary to the claims of many of those who are pro-censorship, that styles of expression and customs of behavior are all one, or that a firm connection exists between changes in sexual morality and the changes in different kinds of morality. Mr. Rembar has stated:

> I would assert the wisdom of the law's separation of expression and conduct, and suggest that the removal of artificial restrictions on expression may help to establish a sounder morality.[6]

Anti-censors contend that the individual should be allowed to exercise his or her right to the freedom to read; they urge those who pass public judgments on publications and other communication media to use evaluative criteria such as content and the contribution to knowledge of the work under consideration. Considerations about the author's or producer's political leanings, religious affiliations, or personal life should not form the basis of a work's value, according to the anti-censor. Those who oppose censorship also encourage publishers to distribute controversial books, but, at the same time, to exercise a reasonable degree of self-policing of their products. The anti-censor feels very strongly that the publisher, not an agent of the government, ought to decide what is or is not to be published.

In a theoretical context, librarians tend to accept the principles of academic and intellectual freedom, but in view of findings of research conducted in this area, implementation of concepts of tolerance has apparently often been lacking, most probably because of the many variables and complexities which surround censorship struggles. Public librarians, who are servants of the public and in direct contact with the taxpaying users of libraries, are frequently in the firing line of censorship controversies, particularly when they involve highly controversial subject matter such as sex and questions of morality. They are constantly faced with the problem of whether limitations should be placed in their communities on library users' freedom of access to certain materials, and, if so, the proper restrictions that librarians should impose. Consequently, there is little wonder that in some instances those public librarians lacking a firm commitment to intellectual freedom have at times practiced censorship of both a subtle and an overt nature as they build their library collections and as they make resources available to library users.

Without a doubt, the extreme sexual frankness—sometimes called the "new morality"—in so many aspects of our contemporary society (particularly the arts and literature) will force those librarians inclined toward restrictive practices to liberalize their services and collections. Standards of morality have changed dramatically in the past two decades; many books found objectionable only a few years ago now seem innocuous. Librarians have often pondered unnecessarily over the wisdom of adding a controversial book to library collections, only to discover later, after having decided to place the work on the shelves, that the work appears quite mild, tame, and harmless in view of subsequent, more recently-published works.

The time has certainly come for librarians to flex their muscles and to stand firm in their profession's commitment to the protection of readers' rights. Librarians must recognize that they are living in an age in which the values of the present decade are considerably less affected by and less sympathetic to the prudishness of the past—even of the previous decade. The trend of present-day writers to "tell it like it is" is a facet of the realistic movement in literature, which attempts to describe life without idealization. Librarians must awaken to the reality that some readers want to read works incorporating the sordid and the trivial as well as the noble and dramatic aspects of the human condition and that the library user ought to be able to find representative works of all of these in their local public library.

Tolerance of unpopular ideas, faith in the ultimate ability of the American citizen to reject preposterous ideas and to adopt more practicable ones, and freedom of expression and inquiry all entail perpetual struggles. In view of past events and present trends, the goal of achieving intellectual freedom will most probably continue to require increasing efforts. It is much easier, for example, to merely quash unpopular ideas; after all, suppression is society's first inclination. Who has not seen, for example, the overt and subtle persecution in recent years of persons who have violated middle-class beliefs—the freaks, radicals, homosexuals, vagabonds, etc. It is more convenient to stifle and to suppress critics than to counteract their ideas with logically formulated and well-presented conflicting ideas. Consequently, repression is often the method adopted by the herd and the throng. In order to counter-balance this seemingly natural, herd-like instinct of man, we must learn to subdue the very society which, if left alone, would stagnate and eventually destroy itself intellectually. A society's best insurance policy against censorship and repression appears to be an educated and intellectually demanding citizenry.

Unfortunately, there has been a long history of anti-intellectualism in the United States; perhaps the educated and thinking people of our nation have been a bit too active in dissecting the myths of the masses and in questioning the prevailing popular values and beliefs, By their very nature, intellectuals are inclined to encourage thought and discussion. Our total educational system, from elementary to higher education levels, is a reflection of the general faith of concerned Americans in thought and discussion as a means of accomplishing peaceful change and progress. The right of scholars to teach, to conduct research, and to publish without restrictions or restraints from the institutions with which they are affiliated is generally recognized and respected in academic communities.

We have at least been providential in that our college and university professors have been guaranteed a fair degree of academic freedom in their open investigations and research, as well as in their promotion of knowledge. However, the freedom granted to professors has not always been of an absolute or complete nature. In some cases the pursuit of scholarly activities and research has been jeopardized, and censorship pressures have been exerted. The late Alfred Kinsey, the founder and first director of the Institute of Sex Research at Indiana University, was the object of considerable extralegal pressures designed to prohibit or to restrain the study of human sexual behavior. Commenting on the right to conduct research in the area of sexual behavior, Dr. Kinsey said:

> It is incomprehensible that we should know so little about such an important subject as sex, unless you realize the multiplicity of forces which have operated to dissuate the scientist, to intimidate the scientist, and to force him to cease research in these areas.[7]

Academic freedom, the freedom of speech, and the freedom of the press are all very important to those who attempt to make our world a better informed, more sexually enlightened world. But the censor is an anxious man who is always ready to rally around the banner of other anxious men campaigning to eliminate what they deem to be a tide of heresy, permissiveness, and promiscuity.

Although science and the forces of authoritarianism have been traditional enemies, the scientific community is not always completely adverse to practicing a bit of repression and censorship itself. The case of Immanual Velikovsky, physician and psychologist, is an excellent example. In the 1950s Dr. Velikovsky wrote two books, *Worlds in Collision*[8] and *Earth in Upheaval*[9], both of which became popular best-sellers and very controversial among scholars and scientists. Theories of "cosmic catastrophism" and "terrestrial cataclysms," which, according to the author, cause drastic changes in orbits and structures of planets, were explained in the two volumes. Dr. Velikovsky claimed that the earth has suffered devastating natural catastrophies, even in the period since the appearance of man in the not-so-distant historical past. In *Worlds in Collision* an attempt was made to explain how upheavals sculpted our planet's surface approximately 3,500 years ago, when a comet passed close by Earth and the Earth ceased temporarily to rotate on its axis. Velikovsky also maintained that the catastrophe altered the course of the Earth's history by bringing about an end to Egypt's Middle Kingdom, wiping out existing established civilizations, and contributing to the Exodus of Jews from the Holy Land.

Some American scientists attempted to suppress *Worlds in Collision*; others were satisfied to criticize severely the interdisciplinary synthesis Velikovsky attempted to explain in the book. The work was censured by a number of prominent scientists, including Cecilia Payne-Gasposchkin, the Phillips astronomer at Harvard College; Harlow Shapley, of the Harvard University Observatory; and John Q. Stewart, astronomical physicist at Princeton University. Dr. Shapley, who claimed to be speaking for his fellow astronomers, called Velikovsky's theories "rubbish and nonsense."[10] Dr. Stewart also outlined detailed and biting criticism of the author's theories in *Harper's Magazine.*[11] The executive director of the American Geological Institute, Dr. David Delo, said of Valikovsky: "He appears to be bypassing all the scientific observations of a multitude of geologists made during the past 100 years."[12] Dr. Payne-Gaposchkin, writing in the *Reporter*, claimed: "A heavy body that merely passed by [the Earth] could not have more than a very small effect on the Earth's rotation."[13] Historian Carl Kraeling, director of the Oriental Institute of the University of Chicago, concluded: "There is nothing we as historians can do about Dr. Velikovsky's work other than smile and go about our business."[14] In addition to criticism and censure, scientists even threatened Macmillan's scientific textbook department, the publisher of *Worlds in Collision*, with a boycott, and the work was withdrawn and handed over to another firm, Doubleday & Company, which did not publish textbooks.

Recent discoveries resulting from man's space explorations and studies of the surface of the moon have caused scientists to reexamine some of Velikovsky's theories with a realization that there appears to be much more than a grain of truth there than was originally recognized. Some have even maintained that Velikovsky has already been vindicated by recent findings; as a matter of fact, during the same year in which *Worlds in Collision* was published, a number of sound scientific works dealing with collisions within the solar system also appeared in journals and other publications. Since that time, they have been appearing with increasing frequency. Only in 1972, *Pensée* magazine published, through the Student Academic Freedom Forum, a special issue entitled *Immanuel Velikovsky Reconsidered*,[15] which attempts to survey the evidence relevant to Velikovsky's theories and to determine how much of yesterday's heresy is today's science.

The persecution and censure of Dr. Velikovsky by American scientists for his unique theories stands as an example of a suppressive act by some scholars in an apparent attempt to keep discoveries and new scientific claims well within the prevailing currents and existing theories of the established scientific community. Such action is not at all dissimilar to the activities of more professional censors who operate in non-scientific fields such as human behavior, in which restraining yokes are placed around the necks of anyone who happens to stray from the well-trodden path. An editorial in the *Saturday Evening Post* at the height of the controversy over Velikovsky's *Worlds in Collision* is still particularly germane today (22 years later). The editorial stated in part:

> Dr. Velikovsky's offense seems to be that he writes better than most scientists and in his book expounds a theory of astronomical activity which differs widely from orthodox theories.[16]

That statement touches the heart of an important matter: should we stifle those who disagree with what has been firmly established and comfortably codified as unalterable law, or should those who challenge our sacred cows be given a fair hearing in the marketplace of ideas?

## Religion and Conservatism

Puritanism has had a stultifying effect on American society, even though the sturdy character and strong moral principles of early Puritans contributed heavily to the development of self-government in the United States. The early Puritans banned drama, prohibited religious music, inhibited the reading of certain types of books and poetry, and excluded the observance of Christmas, which they associated with paganism. The Puritans of seventeenth-century America lost a great deal of their influence and power when some clergymen and laymen forsook reason, fell into emotionalism, and let the Salem witch hunts get out of control. But this is not to say that the effects of the Puritan movement were terminated with the downfall of its powerful and influential leaders; the inhabiting Puritan ethic has persisted for several centuries.

In contrast to the commonly held belief that the first settlers in America were freedom-loving and tolerant people who escaped from various religious and political tyrannies of Europe to establish a free society, John P. Roche states in *Aspects of Liberty*:

> Colonial America was an open society dotted with closed enclaves, and one could generally settle with his co-believers in safety and comfort and exercise the right of oppression.[17]

The same view is also held by Leonard W. Levy, who stated in *Legacy of Suppression*:

> The persistent image of colonial America as a society in which freedom of expression was cherished is an hallucination of sentiment that ignores history ... The American people simply did not understand that freedom of thought and expression means equal freedom for the other fellow, especially the one with hated ideas.[18]

Notwithstanding historical developments which occurred during and after Puritanism's heyday—not to mention the current contemporary spirit of freedom—the net effect of organized religion today is still a restraining one on the public lives (but not necessarily the private lives) of many Americans. Virtue, which was highly valued among the Puritans and their imitators, as well as a distinguishing characteristic of many non-sectarian aspects of our culture, has

34

been overemphasized and has often endangered the individual's intellectual and emotional well-being. The Puritan ethic contributed, no doubt, to a climate of repression and morbidity, prerequisites for the anti-intellectual atmosphere which has frequently discouraged inquiry in the United States and which has often equated the acquisition of knowledge with unnecessary, if not eccentric, foolishness.

The concept of sin and the idea that celebration, mirth, and many forms of recreation are closely related to wickedness is part of our Christian heritage. The Christian churches, both Roman Catholic and Protestant, have served as powerful conservative influences for many years. Even in the fifteenth century, soon after the advent of printing in about 1450, pervasive censorship was practiced by the church in Europe. Within the Roman Catholic hierarchy and institutions, as well as among some Protestant groups, a disregard for the civil liberties of political and social non-conformists and dissenters has frequently been evident. Modern-day Puritans, our present religious bigots and fundamentalists, still believe and promote the idea that the path to righteousness is one of solemnity and seriousness. They adhere rather strongly to the philosophy of salvation through suffering and labor; they look favorably at religious and economic colonialization; and they prize capitalistic free-enterprise ideas rather highly.

One need not examine our present society very carefully to realize that the prevailing concepts of morality are deep-rooted in a spirit of religious repression. Religious puritanism has always associated sex with sin, and there is every reason to believe that it has contributed heavily to the development of a guilt-ridden and hypocritical society. The often-encountered idea, for example, that morality involves restraint, self-sacrifice, and solemnity is a carry-over and a by-product of the Protestant ethic, which has tended to influence, if not to encourage, followers of religions to accept doctrines as absolutes. The permissiveness or unrestrained morality of our present age has come under the critical, watchful eye of many organized religions. While some persons believe that the "new morality" and "situation ethics" amount to immorality, others believe that they are indeed moral; still others contend that sexual behavior has no direct bearing upon the philosophical aspects of morality.

Democracy is based upon individual choice and majority consent, but religions are usually based on revealed "truths." Consequently, religions tend to submerge individual will to that of the dogma and teaching of various church doctrines, but when learning and intellectuality are highly valued concurrently with an appreciation of life and its full enjoyment, a freer and more liberal prospect for living results, not only in relation to social, economic, and political aspects of our culture, but in spiritual and religious realms as well.

The church and religious-sponsored bodies have at times practiced or attempted the censorship of reading materials. In 1938 the National Office for Decent Literature (NODL) was established by the Roman Catholic bishops of the United States "to set in motion the moral forces of the entire community . . . against the lascivious type of literature which threatens moral, social, and national life." A reviewing committee evaluates magazines and pocket-size books on the basis of a NODL code consisting of nine points; when at least six reviewers decide that a book being considered violates the code, the publication is placed on the list of objectionable works. Evaluations of publications are then distributed to individuals and to organizations interested in the promotion of "decent literature." Among the main purposes of the National Office for Decent Literature is the removal of objectionable materials from distribution places which are accessible by young people and the promotion of worthwhile reading habits during the formative years of young people.[19]

In a critical examination of the activities of the National Office for Decent Literature, John Fisher claimed in *Harper's Magazine*: "A little band of Catholics is now conducting a shocking attack on the rights of their fellow citizens." The article, appropriately entitled "The Harm Good People Do," declared that the activities of the NODL were so un-American that they equated or exceeded communist tactics at repression and that the organization was harming the nation, the Catholic Church, and the cause of freedom. According to Fisher, members of the National Office for Decent Literature are well-meaning people with sincere intentions; however, he expresses concern that the organization's "misguided" attempts to cope with a serious national problem are doing grave harm to democracy. In describing the activities of the NODL, Mr. Fisher complained:

> Its chief method is to put pressure on news dealers, drug stores, and booksellers, to force them to remove from their stacks every item on the NODL blacklist. Included on this list are reprint editions of books by Ernest Hemingway, William Faulkner, John Dos Passos, George Orwell, John O'Hara, Paul Hyde Bonner, Emile Zola, Arthur Koestler, and Joyce Cary. In some places—notably Detroit, Peoria, and the suburbs of Boston—the organization has enlisted the local police to threaten booksellers who are slow to 'cooperate.'[20]

The question of the relationship and influence of organized religion on non-sectarian aspects of our culture has often been posed. There is considerable evidence that many religious followers and persons who attend church frequently attempt to transmit, by means of the non-sectarian institutions with which they are employed or affiliated, religions' tendencies to repress a free spirit. Without a doubt, the cumulative effect of organized religions upon many of our social institutions, including libraries, has been of a leveling nature. Much of the social strife our nation has witnessed in recent years has resulted at least partially because of the rejection by many Americans of the Puritan ethic, which was systematically woven into so many of our nation's mores, manners, and laws. We cannot deny that the miasma of thought control which some of our institutions, including schools and libraries, have attempted is related to our religious heritage, particularly the Puritan ethic. By contributing to and supporting the prevailing values of our society, religious organizations and their supporters have usually upheld the status quo. Conformity, rather than freedom of thought and action, appears to be the mainstay of most organized religions.

As our nation has changed from an agrarian to an urban society, we have witnessed the rise of many different and often competing life-styles and world outlooks. Our society has become pluralistic and heterogeneous, replete with groups which not only completely reject the Puritan ethic but which also do not respect or hanker after the past. The rallying cry of the youth movement has been a need for knowledge, kindness, and courage, and there has also been a significant rejection by many persons, particularly our youth, of the traditions of the past. The social revolution taking place today among the young people is undoubtedly related to the repressive and artificial climate in which children of the Western world have been forced for centuries. But young people appear to be reaching sexual maturity earlier than previous generations; they begin dating earlier than did their parents, and some girls in their early teens now take birth control pills. Many of the nation's youth have expressed increasing hope for and faith in a bold new future guided by fearless intelligence rather than the dead past. Those who now advocate a new freedom cry out for the elimination of all social, economic, and political influences which cause discontent and disaffection among all the people of the world. They rebel against the loyalty demanded of the establishment and label it conformity and ethnocentric nationalism; they disagree with the uncritical idea that the United States of America is a finished product, without fault and complete in every respect.

Many of the critics of our present society are quick to point out that some of our institutions have fostered morality in the form of narrowly defined rules of conduct, which are not perceived as instruments of human happiness. Critics of our present society also frequently question any established morals which do not have human fulfillment and happiness as their purpose. By rejecting organized religion on a rather extensive scale, our young people tend to be less ethnocentric. The rejection of hypocrisy; the emphasis on cooperation, rather than competition; the obtainment of truth by direct involvement and participation; the rejection of artificial forms of authority; and the rejection of laws, rules, and mores which interfere with natural expression and function are characteristic traits of many of those young people who are involved in the student revolt. While "the movement" among the young people has frequently been called a political revolution, it is actually a cultural revolution which views politics merely as an instrument to achieve intellectual, artistic, and social reforms.

An important consideration in relation to religion and libraries deals with book-selection policies, and, within this context, the influence of the Puritan ethic on the development of public library collections should be examined. According to the principles of book selection fostered by the American Library Association, public librarians should develop collections following the principle that the library provides for greater popular choice of ideas and opinions. The extent to which collections have satisfied the needs of taxpaying supporters of libraries has usually been the operational index of the success or failure of most public libraries. Librarians have generally made a practice of conducting community surveys to determine, insofar as possible, the information needs of their publics; within the limits of budgets and propriety, they have then attempted to obtain the needed materials and to make them available in their collections.

Librarians hardly need to be reminded that the first public libraries were established in the United States as institutions of social and moral reform and of public education. Public libraries have often been called "The People's University." With such humanitarian goals, it is quite natural that librarians and boards of trustees of libraries have encouraged the reading of only "good books" and that some books characterized thus so by librarians were not always those which the public clamored to read and to obtain from libraries. Consequently, one can see that librarians have been caught between two somewhat opposing principles of selection: 1) the idea that librarians should collect and disseminate only books which will improve or uplift their patrons (books whose worth and literary merit have been well established and whose contents reflect the prevailing political, religious, economic, and aesthetic values of the community) and 2) the school of thought that each reader should be the final judge of what is appropriate for him to read and should be able to choose freely from a collection containing not only the "good" and the "bad" but the mediocre as well. In following the first principle, librarians would neglect demands for books which they consider unworthy or "bad"; consequently, they would not necessarily provide what library users want to see and read. They would ignore the idea that the terms *good books* and *bad books* are relative, and that what is deemed desirable by patron *A* might be thought to be undesirable by patron *B*.

Therefore, a public library's book-selection policy should be flexible and should allow for the inclusion of works and materials which the librarians believe will be of value as contributions to library users' emotional, intellectual, and moral competencies. Also to be included, however, are those somewhat questionable books and materials needed or requested by the public which contain various unorthodox opinions, discussions of controversial questions, and extreme political views of either a left- or right-wing nature. Librarians, then, should not set themselves up as judges of what readers should or should not read. When a controversial or likely-to-be controversial work is being considered for purchase, librarians should remind themselves that if the book is not expressly forbidden by law (that is, if it is not a case of unquestionable treason, libel, or obscenity), the publication *could be* added to the collection legally. How many librarians have ignored these important considerations when attempting to decide on questionable books and have relied singly on their personal values? Such action is understandably a rejection of the concepts of intellectual freedom expressed in the *Library Bill of Rights*,[2][1] which has been widely promoted within the library profession. The complete text of the *Library Bill of Rights* is provided in the appendix for those who are not familiar with the document or for those who might wish to refresh their memories with its contents.

## FOOTNOTES

[1] Dan Lacy, "Suppression and Intellectual Freedom," *American Libraries* 3(1972):810.

[2] Norman Dorsen, *Frontiers of Civil Liberties* (New York: Pantheon Books, Random House, 1968), p. 109.

[3] Neville March Hunnings, *Film Censors and the Law* (London: George

Allen & Unwin Ltd., 1967), p. 383.

[4] William B. Lockhart and Robert C. McClure, "Literature, the Law of Obscenity, and the Constitution," *Minnesota Law Review* 38(1954):295-372.

[5] Amitai Etzioni, "Human Beings Are Not Very Easy to Change After All," *Saturday Review* 55(1972):45.

[6] Charles Rembar, *The End of Obscenity; the Trials of Lady Chatterley, Tropic of Cancer, and Fanny Hill* (New York: Random House, 1968), pp. 492-93.

[7] Cornelia V. Christenson, *Kinsey: A Biography* (Bloomington: Indiana University Press, 1971), p. 217.

[8] Immanuel Velikovsky, *Worlds in Collision* (New York: Macmillan, 1950).

[9] Immanuel Velikovsky, *Earth in Upheaval* (Garden City, N. Y.: Doubleday, 1955).

[10] *Science News Letter* 57(1950):119.

[11] John Q. Stewart, "Disciplines in Collision," *Harper's Magazine* 202(1951):57-63.

[12] *Science News Letter* 57(1950):119.

[13] Cecilia Payne-Gasposchkin, "Nonsense, Dr. Velikovsky," *The Reporter* 2(1950):37-40.

[14] *Science News Letter* 57(1950):119.

[15] Stephen L. Talbott, ed., *Immanuel Velikovsky Reconsidered* (Portland, Ore.: Pensée Magazine, 1972).

[16] "The 1950 Silly Season Looks Unusually Silly" [Editorial], *Saturday Evening Post* 223(1950):12.

[17] John P. Roche, "American Liberty: An Examination of the 'Tradition' of Freedom," in *Aspects of Liberty*, eds. Milton R. Konvitz and Clinton Rossiter (Ithaca: Cornell University Press, 1958), p. 137.

[18] Leonard W. Levy, *Legacy of Suppression; Freedom of Speech and Press in Early American History* (Cambridge: The Belknap Press of Harvard University Press, 1960), p. 18.

[19] *Encyclopedia of Associations*, National Organizations of the United States (Detroit: Gale Research Co., 1970), 1:767.

[20] John Fisher, "The Harm Good People Do," *Harper's Magazine* 213(1956):14.

[21] The *Library Bill of Rights* was adopted June 18, 1948, by the Council of the American Library Association and was amended February 1, 1961, and June 27, 1967.

# CHAPTER 2
# CENSORSHIP IN ACTION

*Liberty, to be secure for any, must be secure for all—even the most miserable merchants of hatred and unpopular ideas.*
—Hugo Black

*Any country that has sexual censorship will eventually have political censorship.*
—Kenneth Tynan

## The Ginzburg Case

On Valentine's Day of 1962, Ralph Ginzburg published the first issue of *Eros*, a magazine devoted to the subjects of love and sex. The publication was designed by Herb Lubalin, winner of the 1962 Art Director of the Year Award, given by the National Society of Art Directors. On December 19, 1962, while the fifth issue of *Eros* was still on the printing press, Ginzburg was served with an indictment charging him with a violation of the Comstock Act of 1873—more specifically, with criminal use of the United States mails in connection with *Eros*, *Liaison*, and *The Housewife's Handbook on Selective Promiscuity*. Ginzburg was tried and convicted in a Philadelphia federal court, presided over by Judge Ralph C. Boyd of the United States District Court for the Eastern District of Pennsylvania. He was sentenced to a five-year prison term and was fined $42,000.

An appeal by Ginzburg to the United States Court of Appeals, Third District, was denied, and on March 21, 1966, the United States Supreme Court also ruled against the publisher of *Eros*. On February 17, 1972, prior to turning himself in to a federal marshal for imprisonment, Ginzburg declared, as he held a parchment copy of the Bill of Rights of the U. S. Constitution in his hand: "Every day I remain in prison this Bill of Rights is a meaningless piece of paper." The publisher then began a reduced sentence of three years at the Allentown Farm Camp in Pennsylvania.

While the U. S. Supreme Court did not declare that *Eros* and Ginzburg's other publications were obscene, it upheld the lower court's conviction on grounds of what the Court called "pandering," namely, the techniques used by the publisher to advertise and promote his materials. The Ginzburg case was the first in which such a standard had been applied, and it has not been used since. The irony of the Ginzburg decision is that in the period between the publisher's trial and his confinement in prison—a period of almost ten years—the nation has witnessed what appears to be a liberalization of moral and sexual standards and expression as well as a proliferation of sexually explicit publications. Many of these recent publications far exceed the tastelessness of *The Housewife's Handbook on Selective Promiscuity*, and they are being promoted and distributed through the mails as well as in thousands of "adult book stores" over the nation. On his way to prison it is highly possible, indeed most probable, that Ginzburg passed by a number of such shops which were selling explicit sexual publications and related pornographic materials. The President's Commission on Obscenity and Pornography, which was appointed by President Johnson late in 1967, investigated the traffic and distribution of sexually oriented materials in the United States up to August 1970. On the basis of a 15-month study, a number of conclusions were made and reported in the *Technical Report of the Commission on Obscenity and Pornography*[1]; these conclusions are reprinted here as a clear indication of the current market for sexually explicit materials.

The first basic conclusion is that at the present time sexual stimuli in the media discussed (books, magazines, motion pictures and mail order) are extremely commonplace. The degree of explicitness varies considerably within and between these media, depending upon the audience sought by the producer. However, in all media and for all audiences, the degree of sexual explicitness has greatly increased since 1960. This trend rapidly accelerated during 1969 and 1970. The 1960s saw a shift of such major proportions that the degree of explicitness at the frontier in 1960 is now found in mass media widely distributed to the general buying public. During this same period, the most explicit materials available on the open market became more and more graphic. By August 1970, the most explicit materials available "above the counter" were approximately equivalent to the most explicit materials ever produced for covert sale.

In conjunction with these changes, the sub-industries producing the most explicit "adults only" publications and motion pictures openly available have solidified and expanded. In proper perspective, production of "adults only" materials remains a relatively minor business in the total U. S. economy. Nonetheless, some producers of explicit materials can and do find the business very lucrative, especially when judged on an individual basis.

The second major conclusion to be drawn from the data is that there is a significant market for sexually oriented materials of varying degrees of explicitness in all media. To the producers of such materials, whether aimed at mass distribution or at the limited "adults only" market, the opinion of the general public exerts a very limited influence. For example, the views of the general public about the sexual content of general release motion pictures or widely distributed books and magazines cannot be determinative of a producer's business judgment. The view of the actual purchaser of a particular media is all important. This is not more than simple good business sense. It is clear that a significant proportion of the customers of the various media discussed will purchase a variety of sexually oriented materials.

The final conclusion based on the study of the 1970 market is that the most explicit materials available are approximately equal to the self-labeled "pornography" openly sold in Denmark and Sweden. The 16mm motion pictures exhibited in many cities in the United States in public theaters (sometimes with a "private club" facade) do not differ one iota from the "pornographic sex films" exhibited in Denmark. While it is true that the self-labeled "pornographic" magazines sold in Denmark are not ordinarily sold openly in this country, the American version of such publications is virtually as explicit. The only difference between Danish "pornographic magazines" and the current crop of American "adults only" illustrated paperback books and magazines is that the latter contain a significant amount of textual material. The degree of sexual explicitness in the photographs contained in both are identical. Thus, with only this minor reservation, it can be stated that the so-called "Danish experiment" is currently underway in the United States.

Predictions for the future are hazardous, at best. However, the author is willing to venture that, in the absence of new and sweeping rulings by the Supreme Court, distribution of the most explicit possible sexual materials will increase both in volume and in nationwide coverage (at least in metropolitan areas) in the near future. That is, "16mm stag films" shown in theaters open to the public and illustrated publications containing photographs of graphic coitus, fellatio, cunnilingus, etc. will capture much, if not all, of the "adults only" market.

The degree of explicitness in more widely distributed materials, *i.e.*, mass market books and magazines and general release motion pictures, will probably not change markedly in the near future.

Long range predictions about the future of sexually oriented materials are beyond the competence of the author. Only time will tell whether today's American version of the Danish experiment will continue unabated and become an ingrained part of society, or whether the buying public will grow tired of such materials. In addition, the market does not operate in a vacuum. It is possible that new court decisions will reverse the apparent trend of the marketplace.

On January 30, 1972, several weeks before he began his prison sentence, Ralph Ginzburg placed a full-page advertisement in *The New York Times* under the caption "Don't Send Me to Prison!" The letter, written without the knowledge of Ginzburg's legal counsel, accused the courts of suppression and of creating a special crime in order to obtain a conviction. Because of the importance of Ginzburg's statement in the contemporary censorship struggle, the entire text of the letter is reprinted here by permission of the author as it appeared in the January 30, 1972, issue of *The New York Times*:

DON'T
SEND ME
TO PRISON!
An Open Letter
To the United States
Supreme Court:

I am a publisher who tried to give America its first beautiful, intellectual, emotionally mature magazine devoted to the subjects of love and sex. Its name was EROS. For nearly ten years I have been harassed and persecuted for this and now, for the second time, I have been condemned to prison by your honorable court.

You have made a terrible mistake. You have misjudged me, you have misunderstood my publications, you have mocked the Constitution.

The First Amendment declares that "Congress shall make no law . . . abridging the freedom of speech, or of the press." Upon that Amendment, and its implied guarantee, I have based my career as a publisher. I have not hesitated to challenge Goliaths with my sling. I have done all this in the expectation that, should the need arise, the U. S. Supreme Court would defend me in my rights. Instead, you have betrayed me.

You have suppressed my publications, you have concocted a special crime ("pandering") in order to convict me, and you have condemned me to prison.

This is a critical hour for America. Never in our history have the youth of this nation been as completely disillusioned with their elders as they are at the present time. At every turn, they see their hopes and aspirations thwarted, their ideals crushed by the dead hand of the past. Nowhere will America's decadence be more evident than in my imprisonment. The youth of this nation know my publications. They know that they stand for Beauty, Truth, and Love. They know that they are anything but immoral. They know that I am anything but criminal. And, though this may surprise you, they consider me something of a public benefactor, not an enemy of the people. The only question in their minds is whether the Supreme Court will have the courage to admit that it has made a mistake, and whether, by some miracle, something will be done to end this travesty of justice.

The machinery for you to correct this grievous error exists. Any one of the Court's nine Justices has the power to stay the execution of my sentence. Any four Justices have the power (under RULES OF THE SUPREME COURT OF THE UNITED STATES, Part VII, 30, entitled "Jurisdiction to Issue Extraordinary Writs") to issue a writ of mandamus ordering my case returned to the Supreme Court for reconsideration.

The big question is: Will you act? Will you have the mettle to confess error, to reconsider my case, to reverse my conviction? Will you use the EROS case—which involved publications of supreme quality and testimony by some of America's most distingushed literary, artistic, scientific, and religious figures—as the basis for a landmark decision? Will you nullify the unenforceable, demoralizing, costly, hypocritical, confusing, outdated, and obscene "obscenity" laws once and for all? Will you demonstrate to the world that the United States, though nearing its bicentennial, is still capable of change? Or will you ignore my plea and earn for yourself—and, thereby, for our society under law—the contempt of free men everywhere?

Ralph Ginzburg
110 West 40th Street, New York, N.Y. 10018

This letter has been written without the knowledge of my legal counsel.

For those who had assumed that the nation was moving toward a state of literary frankness and permissiveness in which problems of censorship appeared to be rapidly diminishing insofar as legal questions were concerned, the Court's decision in the Ginzburg case was surprising. While a temper of liberalism permeated many of the Court's decisions of the 1960s, the Court was often attacked for its liberality. Many promoters of intellectual freedom felt that the liberal legal decisions of that period represented an inexorable move toward increased freedoms; however, some Americans viewed the rulings as blueprints for a licentious society. In view of the Court's concern for the protection of individual freedoms in many of the cases of the 1950s and 1960s, particularly those involving civil rights, the decisions should have been widely acclaimed; however, criticism by certain elements in our nation has frequently demonstrated a general disinterest for the defense of liberties guaranteed by the Bill of Rights. Much of the apathy toward preserving individual liberties has probably been due to ignorance, which has characterized a great deal of the popular reaction to the Court's decisions. But Americans must become more concerned; the U. S. Constitution is much too important to be left to the courts alone.

In an examination of approximately 70 legal decisions, William Hachten concluded in 1968 that court rulings of the decade of the sixties could be characterized by change and that the direction of that change was unmistakably toward increased freedoms. He pointed out that there is, at the level of constitutional law, greater freedom of the press today than at any time in the history of the Republic.[2] The Ginzburg decision shattered the assumption, however, that the courts were well on their way toward establishing a rather lenient national policy toward pornography and obscenity in relation to individual rights. Apparently, the decision was but another manifestation that local, state, and federal courts have always been unable to effectively cope with problems of obscenity and pornography.

Richard Kuh, former assistant district attorney of New York, has pointed out that some judges, especially the Justices of the U. S. Supreme Court, have been fearlessly attempting to salvage something of the anti-pornography laws but that "in the process they have burdened themselves with interminable censorship chores, have been beset with abuse for their opinions, and have ended up giving little guidance to anybody."[3] Olga and Edwin Hoyt pointed out in *Censorship in America* that the courts took rather lenient positions in obscenity cases of the 1960s and that decisions handed down demonstrated the very subjective nature of the obscenity question. The Hoyts also noted that despite many conflicting judicial views, the same statutes and precedents tended to be employed but that when judges concurred in decisions, it was often for very different reasons, including diversified interpretations of existing laws. These writers also noted that community standards during the period were in a transitional state of flux; strong feelings toward purity were counteracted by laxity and tolerance.[4]

The composition of the U. S. Supreme Court in itself also has a great bearing on the kinds of decisions reached in cases which are brought before our nation's highest tribunal. The Court's decisions are dependent to a very great extent on whether judges are predominantly liberal or predominantly conservative. Past performance of the justices has shown that when the majority of the judges are strong and devoted to liberty, the Court will emphasize individual liberties; when most of them are irresolute, faltering, or complacent about the basics of freedom, the Court's decisions do not tend to support individual liberties.

The move to impeach liberal Associate Supreme Court Justice William O. Douglas, a champion of civil rights and individual liberties, was an apparent attempt by House minority leader Gerald C. Ford to rid the Court of a liberal voice out-of-step with the "law and order" conservatism of the Nixon administration. A number of Court-watchers viewed the attempt to purge the tribunal of Douglas' liberality as a reprisal against Senate forces which had rejected the appointment of conservatives Clement F. Haynesworth, Jr., and G. Harrold Carswell. It was also a conservative reaction to increased concern among the judges for liberal causes such as the constitutional rights of the individual, the desegregation of public schools, the proportional representation in state legislatures, and antitrust cases. Indeed, stacking the highest court of the nation to achieve either liberal or conservative rulings has been practiced by a number of presidents; Franklin D. Roosevelt's struggle with the U. S. Supreme Court in the 1930s and the liberalization of the Court after 1938 stand as an excellent example of that activity.

In an apparent effort to keep his promise to curb riots, disorders, and lawlessness, President Nixon has appointed four rather conservative justices to the U. S. Supreme Court during his administration. Each appointment was obviously made in an effort to shift the balance away from the protection of individual rights to the protection of "law and order." However, in the recent wiretap ruling handed down and written by Justice Lewis F. Powell, Jr., a conservative legal scholar and a Nixon appointee, the U. S. Supreme Court upheld a Michigan lower court, which found the use of wiretap evidence unlawful in a conspiracy trial. The Supreme Court declared that wiretaps cannot be used against suspected domestic radicals without a court order. The decision clearly indicates that even though the Court might have drifted to the right toward conservatism, it has not strayed too far from the protection of constitutional guarantees of freedom.

The five-to-four death sentence decision handed down by the Supreme Court in June 1972, which declared capital punishment a violation of the U. S. Constitution, clearly demonstrates the liberal versus conservative dichotomy of the present Court. All nine justices filed statements in the death penalty decision, and Justices William O. Douglas, William J. Brennan, Jr., Thurgood Marshall, and, with some reservations, Potter Stewart and Byron R. White, were in the majority. The first three justices listed are frequently referred to as "Warren Court liberals." The four Nixon appointees, Chief Justice Warren E. Burger and Justices Harry A. Blackmun, Lewis F. Powell, Jr., and William H. Rehnquist, were in favor of maintaining the death sentence. During the 1972 Court term, a distinct division between liberal and conservative justices was definitely discernible. Justices Douglas, Brennan, and Marshall were rather consistently on the same side of issues, and the four Nixon appointees banded together with rather uniform regularity. With the death penalty decision as one of the exceptions, five-to-four decisions have allowed the Court to drift slowly to the right and have produced recent rulings such as the declaration that a member of Congress can be called before a grand jury to explain how classified government documents were obtained and put into the hands of private publishers, the decision that newsmen do not have the right to protect their sources of information when called before a grand jury, and the ruling that urban shopping center malls may be declared off-limits to peaceful pamphleteers such as antiwar protesters.

In the Ginzburg case four members of the U. S. Supreme Court dissented: Justices Black, Douglas, Harlan, and Stewart. The opinion of the Court, however, was written by Justice Brennan, whose statement included these remarks:

> The circulars sent for EROS and Liaison stressed the sexual candor of the respective publications, and openly boasted that publishers would take full advantage of what they regarded as an unrestricted license allowed by law in the expression of sex and sexual matters ... The evidence, in our view, was relevant in determining the ultimate question of obscenity and, in the context of this record, serves to resolve all ambiguity and doubt ... Where the purveyor's sole emphasis is on the sexually provocative aspects of his publications, that fact may be decisive in the determination of obscenity. Certainly in a prosecution which, as here, does not necessarily imply suppression of the materials involved, the fact that they originate or are used as subject of pandering is relevant to the application of the *Roth* test ... We perceive no threat to the First Amendment guarantees in thus holding that in close cases evidence of pandering may be probative with respect to the nature of the material in question and thus satisfy the *Roth* test. No weight is ascribed to the fact that petitioners have profited from the sale of publications which we have assumed but do not hold cannot themselves be adjudged obscene in the abstract; to sanction consideration of this fact might indeed include self-censorship, and offend the frequently

stated principle that commercial activity, in itself, is no justification for narrowing the protection of expression secured by the First Amendment. Rather the fact that each of these publications was created or exploited entirely on the basis of its appeal to prurient interests strengthens the conclusion that the transactions here were sales of illicit merchandise, not sales of constitutionally protected matter.[5]

In contrast to the Court's decision, Justice Black, one of the four dissenters in the Ginzburg case, included the following comments in his statement:

It is obvious that the effect of the Court's decision in the three cases handed down today is to make it exceedingly dangerous for people to discuss either orally or in writing anything about sex. Sex is a fact of life. Its pervasive influence is felt throughout the world and it cannot be ignored. Like all other facts of life it can lead to difficulty and trouble and sorrow and pain. But while it may lead to abuses, and has in many instances, no words need be spoken in order for people to know that the subject is one pleasantly interwoven in all human activities and involves the very substance of the creation of life itself . . . I find it difficult to see how talk about sex can be placed under the kind of censorship the Court here approves without subjecting our society to more dangers than we can anticipate at the moment. It was to avoid exactly such dangers that the First Amendment was written and adopted. For myself I would follow the course which I believe is required by the First Amendment, that is, recognize that sex at least as much as any other aspect of life is so much a part of our society that its discussion should not be made a crime.[6]

The opinion of Justice Douglas was clearly the most passionate condemnation of what he believed to be repression. In dissenting from the Court's majority decision, Justice Douglas said in part:

Today's condemnation of the use of sex symbols to sell literature engrafts another exception on First Amendment rights that is as unwarranted as the judge-made exception concerning obscenity . . . A book should stand on its own, irrespective of the reasons why it was written or the wiles used in selling it. I cannot imagine any promotional effort that would make chapters 7 and 8 of the Song of Solomon any the less or any more worthy of First Amendment protection than does their unostentatious inclusion in the average edition of the Bible . . . I find it difficult to say that a publication has no "social importance" because it caters to the taste of the most unorthodox among us. We members of this Court should be among the last to say what should be orthodox in literature. An omniscience would be required which few in our whole society possess . . . It is shocking to me for us to send to prison anyone for publishing anything, especially tracts so distant from any incitement to action as the ones before us.[7]

Another dissenting opinion of Justice Stewart was also noteworthy for its defense of freedoms outlined in the Bill of Rights; the justice wrote in his decision:

Censorship reflects a society's lack of confidence in itself. It is a hallmark of an authoritarian regime. Long ago those who wrote our First Amendment charted a different course. They believe a society can be truly strong only when it is truly free. In the realm of expression they put their faith, for better or worse, in enlightened choice of the people, free from the interferences of a policeman's intrusive thumb or a judge's heavy hand. So it is that the Constitution protects coarse expression as well as refined, and vulgarity no less than elegance. A book worthless to me may convey something of value to my neighbor. In the free society to which our Constitution has committed us, it is for each to choose for himself . . . Today the Court assumes the power to deny Ralph Ginzburg the protection of the First Amendment because it disapproves of his "sordid business." That is a power the Court does not possess. For the First Amendment protects us all with an equal hand. It applies to Ralph Ginzburg with no less completeness and force than to G. P. Putnam's Sons. In upholding and enforcing the Bill of Rights, this Court has no power to pick or to choose. When we lose sight of that fixed star of constitutional adjudication, we lose our way. For then we forsake a government of law and are left with government by Big Brother.[8]

Despite these rather liberal dissenting opinions, the majority of the justices disagreed, and the Court ruled against Ginzburg. In a *Library Journal* editorial which expressed deep concern about the decision in the *Eros* case, Karl Nyren stated that Ginzburg's publication was no great shocker when it was being issued and that in light of what has come after it from other publishing houses, the magazine now appears stodgy. In defending Ginzburg's rights, as well as those of others who offend merely by action or gesture, the editor of *Library Journal* also declared:

Those individuals who move society to change through persistent minor transgressions against the current taboos—moral, political, religious, artistic, etc.—make the rest of us uncomfortable, and we understandably go along with giving them an occasional backhand to express our discomfort. But that's as far as it ought to go. When a government agency commits an atrocity like the Ginzburg crucifixion, we must protest in the sternest possible way. The alternative is acquiescence to an action which, by extension, could legitimize the abrogation of the democratic process itself.[9]

Indeed, every American citizen must be concerned with defending the Constitution which expresses our value system. They should also be concerned with the increasing tendency of the federal government to become more and more distant from citizens.

Looking at the case from a legal standpoint, Ginzburg's conviction by the lower court and the upholding of that conviction by the U. S. Supreme Court are representative of the present paradox in which our nation finds itself in respect to liberties and the issue of sexual freedom. In recent years, a sexual explosion has occurred; voices have cried out in condemnation of the repressiveness of laws relating to sexual expression and action. Many citizens now feel that the available pornographic materials are often prepared for use by a special and limited audience, particularly adults who request and desire sexually explicit materials. Critics of our present anti-pornography and obscenity laws maintain that the rights to freedom of speech and press entitle persons to satisfy their personal, intellectual, and emotional needs by reading and viewing sexually-oriented publications if they so desire. The popularity of motion pictures, plays, and publications which treat the subject of sex directly and frankly is a clear indication that large segments of the American population are not offended by a wide range of sexual expression in many of our media of communication. However, counteracting the demands for freedom of sexual expression, other segments of our society have cried out for more laws and legislation to protect the nation from what they believe to be sexual excesses and permissiveness.

According to Donald Sharp, editor of *Commentaries on Obscenity*, the ruling in *U. S. v. Ginzburg* confused the legal issues over obscenity by opposing the liberal trend in which the U. S. Supreme Court had earlier set a pace.[10] Without a doubt, the Ginzburg case stands as a legal example of the very confusing state of affairs in which we now find ourselves in a period of transition in respect to social expression and action. It is becoming more and more evident today that numerous sections of our penal code deal with acts that are classified as criminal only because they are on our society's checklist of "crimes." Some of them are crimes without victims and are spelled out in laws designed to protect customs which have been elevated almost into divine sanction. Who is injured, for example, when a prostitute engages in the affairs of her trade, when two consenting adults participate in homosexual activities, or when someone holds in his or her possession pornographic or obscene publications? Clearly, our penal code is in need of a complete revision to eliminate those acts that are not evil in themselves but are prohibited only because certain segments of our population have labeled them morally offensive and believe that they should be punishable by our criminal justice system. We need, in other words, to resist the temptation to elevate custom into legal sanction and to recognize it for what it actually is: the accumulated habit of centuries, nothing more.

The present necessity for librarians to be on guard constantly to protect readers' rights is another facet of the social complexity of our present society. As we approach the last quarter of the twentieth century, it is somewhat paradoxical that librarians must still concern themselves in our so-called "permissive" era with the protection of the freedom to read and with the maintenance of intellectual freedom in American libraries. Such concern might appear unwarranted—unless one realizes that our contemporary era is replete with inconsistencies; many of our current social problems are the exact opposite of what we might logically expect to find in view of the collective know-how and advanced technology our nation has achieved. We had, for example, in the 1972 presidential election year an aspirant for the highest elected position in our federal government who hailed from the Deep South and who had consistently supported repressive causes, yet who had a very substantial following among the people—even in the North. And despite our ability to travel to the moon and back, we have not learned to grapple effectively with the ecological problems of the planet Earth. There is apparently more than a grain of truth in the frequently-echoed charge from many of our young people that technology has not liberated man from drudgery and disease but has been used by some of the elders of our nation as an instrument to impose conformity and order.

Of more immediate concern to librarians, however, is another paradox which contradicts the "tempo of the times." It is becoming increasing apparent that, along with our rather sophisticated bibliographical and information systems, our proliferation of electronic communication devices (publishing agencies, abstracting services, and clearing houses for information), and our social and cultural innovations, our times have apparently also ushered in forces which attempt to control or to restrict the flow of information. The nation seems to be entering a period in which a certain segment of the populace (the American establishment) is struggling to preserve whatever remains of the status quo, and the maintenance of the established order appears to be intrinsically associated with the control of information. Indeed, there is considerable evidence from legislative bodies; courts; academic institutions; local, state, and federal government agencies; and local communities themselves that our nation faces in the decade of the seventies a period of renewed censorship and other repressive activity.

### Incidences of Censorship

During the past five-year period (1967 to 1972), censors and their friends have been quite busy. A cursory examination of issues of the American Library Association's *Newsletter on Intellectual Freedom*,[11] which attempts to report incidents of repression and censorship in libraries, will demonstrate the degree to which public and school libraries have been targets for numerous attacks by would-be censors. The examples reported here represent only a few of the incidents reported in selected recent issues of the *Newsletter*; perhaps the following briefly related episodes will serve to indicate that, far from being an activity of the past, censorship of library materials is taking place in all regions of the nation at an intensity and a frequency that somewhat belies the present trend of so-called "permissiveness."

(1) The police chief of Warwick, Rhode Island conducted a search of the public library for "smut," and he was happy to report negative results. The *Providence* (R. I.) *Journal* commented that the police had verified the cleanliness of the library. The editors wondered (apparently with tongue in cheek) how many other public libraries in the nation could claim a police department's seal of approval, and they commented on the pleasure of knowing that the city of Warwick was so free of crime that the police chief could find time to prowl among the shelves of the local public library.

(2) In Coldwater, Michigan, the board of trustees fired the director of the public library without giving a reason; however, the librarian claimed

that he was released because of books which he had added to the library collection, including such works as *Woodstock Nation* (Vintage Books, 1969) and *Revolution for the Hell of It* (Dial Press, 1968). The mayor of the city reacted to the situation by stating: "We've got a pretty nice little town here, and we'd like to keep it that way."

(3) In North Miami, Florida, the city manager requested the public library to remove from its shelves *The Sensuous Woman* (Lyle Stuart, 1969); however, the librarian ignored the request as there was a three-month waiting list for the book.

(4) A patron of the Welsh Road Branch, Free Library of Philadelphia objected to Jerry Rubin's *Do It!* (Simon and Schuster, 1970); the Northeast Philadelphia Chamber of Commerce demanded that the library director explain who had approved the book for purchase and on what basis it was selected for the library's collection. Faced with continuing controversy, the library's board of trustees decided to intercede; a vote was taken among board members which resulted in a ten-to-three decision against removing the work from the collection.

(5) In Tulsa, Oklahoma, a resident asked the Tulsa Public Library to remove two periodicals, *Evergreen Review* and *Ramparts*, from its collection on grounds that they were seditious, pornographic, and inappropriate for the expenditure of tax-payers' money.

(6) In Memphis, Tennessee, a "well-known" citizen complained to the mayor about the book *Portnoy's Complaint* (Random House, 1969), which was in the Memphis Public Library's collection. The mayor announced that the book was one of the filthiest that he had ever seen; he then asked the public library to set up some standard of decency for the purchase of library books.

(7) In Reseda, California, a city councilman made a request to the West Valley Regional Library for the removal of *Evergreen Review* from its collection. The councilman claimed that he was not practicing censorship but was concerned only with the expenditure of taxpayers' money for "filth" to be placed in libraries.

(8) Three people suggested in Denver, Colorado, that the inclusion of "revolutionary" books in the Denver Public Library's collection should be investigated by the city council. The protestors objected to what they called "anti-American" works promoting riot and revolution; however, the city council took no action.

A number of incidents of censorship by librarians themselves were also reported in recent years in the *Newsletter on Intellectual Freedom.* Only a selected number of events will be listed as representative examples.

(1) In Clifton, New Jersey, the public library board banned the book *Sensuous Woman* because the mayor of the city had attempted to prohibit the purchase of the work for the library's collection.

(2) The Montgomery, Alabama *Journal* reported that the public librarian of that city had sold a collection of "pornographic books" found hidden in the library. Apparently the books had been stored in an out-of-the-way place by a previous library administrator. Included in the collection were scholarly works on sex, marriage, birth control, and biology.

The librarian was reported as saying that the collection would not be replaced because there was no demand for that type of material in Montgomery.

(3) In Freeport, Illinois, the head librarian of the public library ordered the removal of a controversial page from the 1970 Caldecott award picture book, *Sylvester and the Magic Pebble* (Windmill Books, 1969), when a library patron complained that policemen were depicted as pigs in the publication.

(4) In North Little Rock, Arkansas, the head of the public library told a newspaperman that she had worked 13 years for the library and that censorship had always been in effect there. She reported that any book was removed from the library at the request of an adult patron and that a "censorship shelf" was used to restrict circulation of such works as *The Sensuous Woman*, *Human Sexual Inadequacy* (Little, Brown, 1970), and *Homosexuality in America* (Castle Books, 1960).

(5) The *Seattle Times* reported that in Spokane, Washington, the head librarian at the Spokane Public Library was storing certain books away from the public in view of the conservative nature of the community. The librarian, according to the newspaper, claimed that all books were listed in the card catalog and that requested books which had been stored in the basement of the library could be brought up when needed by patrons.

(6) In a study to determine whether censorship was being practiced in the Cuyahoga County (Ohio) Public Library, one librarian openly advocated intramural censorship, and many others indicated their approval of some form of library restrictive measures for certain books and materials in practice, if not in theory.

School libraries have also been targets for censorship pressures. The *Newsletter on Intellectual Freedom* has reported numerous incidents in these institutions; however, only a few will be included here.

(1) The sheriff of Camden, South Carolina, objected to Salinger's *The Catcher in the Rye* (Little, Brown, 1951) on grounds that parts of the book were obscene; the Kershaw County superintendent of education announced that the book was being withdrawn from school reading lists and from public school library shelves of the county.

(2) In Williamsville, New York, school administrators were publicly censured by a group of citizens for having *Soul on Ice* by Eldridge Cleaver (McGraw-Hill, 1967) in the high school library.

(3) A Schurz High School teacher in Chicago filed suit in Cook County Circuit Court seeking a mandatory injunction to ban certain books from the school's library on grounds that the works defamed Italian-Americans. Objectionable books included the following: *The Vallachi Papers* (G. P. Putnam's Sons, 1968), *The Mafia and Politics* (Chatto & Windus, 1966), *The Secret Rulers* (Duell, Sloan and Pearce, 1966), and *The Honored Society* (Putnam, 1964).

(4) Petitions were circulated in Manistique, Michigan to have two books removed from school library shelves. The objectionable works were physically removed by a woman who spearheaded the petition drive in

an apparent attempt to insure that they would not be placed back on library shelves.

(5) *Sylvester and the Magic Pebble*, in which a policeman is portrayed as a pig, was removed from public school libraries in Toledo, Ohio, in view of a protest from the president of the Toledo Police Patrolmen's Association.

(6) In Shawnee Mission, Kansas, a high school advisory board voted unanimously to recommend to the board of trustees the removal of *The Catcher in the Rye* from a reading list for a literature class. Someone had claimed that the book contained 860 obscenities.

(7) In Conway, New Hampshire, a school superintendent apologized to parents of a high school student who had complained about an "obscene" book entitled *The New Underground Theater* (Bantam Books, 1968), which was a collection of contemporary plays. Parents who made the complaint were informed that the work had been withdrawn and destroyed and, furthermore, that the student who made the complaint was being placed in a class other than the one in which an assignment had been made to read the objectionable book.

While most librarians will emphatically deny that they practice any form of intramural censorship, a subtle kind of restriction is sometimes undertaken in libraries. That technique is the placing of controversial or likely-to-be-controversial books and materials on restricted shelves in out-of-the-way, inaccessible places, sometimes marking such works with a symbol or letter which designates them for special handling or for restricted circulation. The practice of marking controversial books is known as "labeling," and it has been strongly discouraged by the American Library Association as a form of intramural censorship which forces readers to accept the librarian's prejudgment that a work is dangerous or subversive.

An example of the labeling practice was recently reported in the Fort Wayne, Indiana, *Journal-Gazette* on July 9, 1972. In an article entitled "'Q' Represents Questionable: Sex, Butterflies, Motorcycles," the newspaper reported that the Fort Wayne-Allen County Public Library had developed a system for handling books with "high sex interest" or with "a certain attitude or presentation of sex." A large letter "Q" is marked on the spine of "questionable" books that are deemed to be unfit for the public shelves by the library's staff reviewer. According to the newspaper article, such books are stored in the library's basement or sub-basement and are made available only if a borrower can give the exact title of the wanted book. Included in the collection are books by Vladimir Nabokov, James Baldwin, John O'Hara, William Inge, Gore Vidal, and William Styron. The *Journal-Gazette* article also reported that other libraries in the Fort Wayne area were labeling books; a Decatur, Indiana librarian was quoted as saying:

I'm one of the cowards. I put a red band on the books with questionable material. They say you shouldn't do it, but I'm not brave enough. I don't want mothers complaining to me about their children reading improper material. Some of these are really good novels . . . there are just one or two pages of terrible material. Some were recommended highly by *Library Journal* or other selection aids, but they seem to be getting more liberal with their reviews, lately. We are a small library and don't have much of a budget. I don't order many books in that classification. I order very carefully.

A letter written to the author by a Midwestern public librarian provides a firsthand account of a librarian's encounter in 1970 with a would-be censor; part of the letter is reprinted here:

> Intellectual freedom, of course, is a delicate issue, more so now than at perhaps any other time in our history. The truly frightening aspect of the contemporary issue, I think, is that the militant censors . . . are prosecuting their work in the name of 'patriotism.' There is nothing new in this but the public approbation which the censors are garnering is. Any librarian who thinks it can't happen here is deluding himself. Not three weeks ago I was the object of a thirty-minute telephone tirade from a gentleman who was up tight about the library's subscription to *Ramparts*, a magazine which, although he admitted he had never read, he was convinced was part of a communist plot to overthrow the government. To his mind, it followed that the library was thus part of this plot and that I, as librarian, was a member of some group which, I suppose, he would identify, along with Gov. Wallace, as 'pointy-headed intellectuals.' I discovered that it was impossible to reason with such a person or even to interrupt his passionate monologue.

### Organized Censors and Their Friends

The growth of extremist groups in the sixties has had a noticeable impact on the free flow of information from certain American public libraries. Many of the politically oriented groups which have sprung up have made sizable inroads on political and social institutions, including schools and public libraries. Ultra-right and far-left groups have established a foothold in almost every state of the nation in an apparent attempt to undermine the confidence of citizens in their elected officials, their social institutions, and their democratic form of government. An episode that occurred in Cincinnati will illustrate what groups such as the John Birch Society, the Constitutional Heritage Club, the American Legion, and other organizations which employ vigilante-type tactics can do to disturb or inhibit intellectual freedom in libraries. The Public Library of Cincinnati and Hamilton County was pressured by those groups in 1971 to remove "pornographic and revolution-inciting literature" from its branch libraries. Members of right-wing groups objected to works by Leroi Jones, which they labeled "obscene racist garbage," and to such books as *Red Star Over China* (New York: Grove Press, 1968), *The Bolshevik Revolution* (New York: International Publishers, 1967), and *Ramparts* magazine.

At the time of the writing of this book, the Public Library of Cincinnati and Hamilton County was still the object of an intense effort on the part of a group of citizens who called themselves "Real Friends of the Public Library" to force librarians to place more works expressing anti-United Nations sentiments on library book shelves and to rid the collection of publications that depict acts of murder, robbery, incest, the use of narcotics, or other "acts provocative of corrupt morals, crime or juvenile delinquency." An attorney employed by the Real Friends group which opposed the library's existing selection policies notified the library's board of trustees in June 1972 that litigation would be instigated if the policies of the library were not brought into conformity with a section of the Ohio Revised Code pertaining to dissemination of material to persons under 18 years of age. A letter written to the library board by another lawyer who opposed the pro-censorship group's actions was printed in a July 1972 issue of the *Cincinnati Enquirer*, and part of it is reprinted below:

> In some countries of the world, libraries can carry out the publications approved by the government in power. In others, private institutions or pressure groups dictate or influence decisions on what the public will be allowed to read. I am here to urge this board to resist as strongly as possible the demands of any individuals or groups to participate in making final decisions as to what will or will not be shelved in the public libraries. Criticism, exposure and argument, not suppression, are the proper weapons of a democratic society.

A strong counterattack has also been launched against critics of the library's selection policies in Cincinnati including the Woman's City Club, the Jewish Community Relations Council, and the American Civil Liberties Union. Cincinnati's censorship attempts represent a concerted effort to oppose local library policies on the part of pressure groups which are apparently well-organized. Extremist groups with such action programs are quite aware that the most fertile soil for planting their ideas is the sensitive local governing unit, where officials might be inclined to submit to their unrealistic demands rather than to openly resist such pressures. After all, controversies require time and effort, not to mention the emotional strain they place on both librarian and board member. Some local officials might be inclined, therefore, to concede a few constitutionally-guaranteed freedoms rather than to take the risk of losing their positions and of facing the persistent emotional harangues of irrational super-patriots. But librarians and trustees must keep in mind that repressive forces promoting distrust and hatred can be tolerated only at a very great cost to democracy. The old proverb which states "Give them an inch, and they'll take a mile" ought to be kept in mind when dealing with extremist groups.

A popular misconception among extremist groups is that they alone have the truth and can save the nation, states, and communities from internal and external "enemies." The Radical Left tends to discredit and to tear down existing institutions regarded as instruments of capitalistic oppression and control; it accuses the United States of being a racist, war-bent society. Leftists also regard the American economy as a junkie in need of constant "fixes" and always on the verge of self-destruction. The Far Right is opposed to anti-war demonstrations and student riots, which are regarded as manifestations of a "freaking fag revolution"; ultra-conservatives stand ever ready to shear the heads of "dirty commie hippies." The Radical Right aspires to save the nation from what it believes is an almost imminent takeover by the communists. Members of the John Birch Society attribute most of the nation's vice, discontent, crime, lust, free love, and immorality to "infidel, commie liberals," whom they regard almost as devils disguised as humans. Birchers and other far-right groups would be classified among those pro-censorship groups which Saul Maloff has characterized as regarding repressive laws against "'smut peddlers' as self-evidently good in themselves."[12]

Perhaps the most efficiently-organized, best-financed, and largest ultra-conservative group in the United States is the John Birch Society. Members of that organization have adopted tactics outlined by Robert Welch in *The Blue Book of the John Birch Society* (Belmont, Mass.: John Birch Society, 1961), and for over a decade they have conducted assaults on private and public institutions, including libraries. In order to understand why and how Birchers have waged censorship campaigns, an examination of the organization's purposes and aims is in order. Founded in December 1958 by Robert Welch and 11 other "concerned" citizens in an Indianapolis hotel, the John Birch Society takes its name from a Baptist missionary who was killed in 1945 by Communist Chinese just after V-J Day. The Society has as its primary purpose the elimination of communist influences in the United States, and to that could be added "less government, more responsibility, and a better world." With a selected membership, the Society is now comprised of approximately 90,000 members in some 4,000 semi-secret chapters in the 50 states and the District of Columbia. Like most other ultra-right organizations, the John Birch Society is strongly opposed to the United Nations, foreign aid, sex education in public schools, international entanglements, and cultural exchanges with communist nations. Among its special projects, the Society has fought to repeal the federal income tax, to impeach former U. S. Supreme Court Chief Justice Earl Warren, and to rid churches of any interest in applying Christian teachings to contemporary social and political problems. The John Birch Society maintains approximately 350 American Opinion Bookstores in which are available hundreds of books, periodicals, record albums, and tapes, all devoted to ultra-right causes and issues. A speakers bureau is also sponsored by the Society.[13]

At the local grass-roots level, the John Birch Society has apparently attached importance to community groups and civic organizations as instruments for obtaining its objectives. Members have made what appears to be a concerted effort to infiltrate these groups and to accomplish the Society's aims by planting Birchers in positions of authority and responsibility. Public library boards of trustees have apparently been viewed as prime targets, and Birchers have even turned up as public library employees. One such librarian lost her job in Boxford, Massachusetts, after she promoted and distributed Birch ideas and literature to patrons in the library.[14] A conspiracy theory of history has been expounded by the John Birch Society. John Stormer's book, *None Dare Call It Treason* (Florissant, Missouri: Liberty Bell Press, 1964), is devoted to that topic, and over 7,000,000 copies have been sold. It has also been strongly promoted and distributed by the Society.

One fact is preeminent in characterizing members of the John Birch Society: they are not interested in attempting to reason and to understand opposing viewpoints, being quick to brand those who disagree with them as "communists." Birchers are also inclined to expound unrelentlessly upon ultra-conservative viewpoints *ad nauseam* and to disregard logic and reason. As has frequently been noted ". . . every new member added to the Birch Society becomes one more American spreading dissention, division, suspicion, fear, and discord in his own heart and among his fellow citizens."[15] Gerald Schomp, a former paid professional coordinator of the John Birch Society, became disenchanted with the Society's program and policies and wrote a book about his experiences entitled *Birchism Was My Business*. Schomp accused Birchers of exploiting anxieties and fears among the people and noted that the John Birch Society is a permanently-organized group designed to systematically and effectively coordinate all right-wing forces in the United States. The former Bircher noted that the Society has a solid recruiting program employing modern techniques of communication and that, with its strong financial backing, the organization has always been able to do a thorough and efficient job with its projects.[16]

As a super-patriotic but extremely anti-democratic organization, the John Birch Society is opposed to the enlargement of civil rights; it has promoted the notion that the civil rights movement in the United States originated with, is implemented by, and is under the direct control of communists who work undercover to subvert our government, culture, and institutions. Because Birch Society members believe that many of our existing civil rights laws are unconstitutional, the U. S. Supreme Court has been an institution against which they have directed considerable criticism, especially in reference to the Court's interpretation of individual rights as outlined in the Constitution.[17] Birchers have also repeatedly labeled the Supreme Court as a part of a grandiose plot to destroy the United States.

When members of the Society first began their campaigns against public library materials, librarians found themselves unprepared, thus particularly vulnerable; however, many of them soon learned to be more dexterous at putting up a firm stand for intellectual freedom. Librarians quickly identified Birch causes and tactics, and they found means of coping with the organized censors. As Milton A. Waldor has pointed out in "Attacking the Right to Read," Chapter Six of his book *Peddlers of Fear*,[18] the methods outlined by Robert Welch in his program of action lend themselves very readily to assaults on public libraries, and because public libraries contain books devoted to numerous subjects and areas of knowledge, Birchers have always been able to locate something in any library which they might consider "pornographic" or "pro-communist." Consequently, it is not surprising that in communities and cities over the nation, members of the John Birch Society and its sympathizers have taken librarians to task for disseminating books or other materials which the ultra-rightists deplore.

Indeed, many of the librarian's actual confrontations with systematized would-be censors have been instigated and carefully orchestrated by groups that have attempted to rid library collections of what is believed to be subversive, obscene, or merely hostile to conservative causes. If an idea in a book, film, periodical, or some other medium does not conform to the Bircher's view of the world, for example, he does not hesitate to condemn it, along with the librarian who makes it available to users of libraries. Some of the techniques employed by these groups have been outlined by Milton Waldor, and they are paraphrased here: 1) condemnation of books and materials which right-wing groups believe to be inappropriate for libraries, 2) recommendation (often insistence) that ultra-conservative literature be placed in libraries along with ready charges of unfairness or discrimination if the works are declined, 3) demand that committees comprised of non-librarians be called upon to accomplish library book selection as opposed to professionally-recommended methods, 4) infiltration or take-over of boards of trustees in what is an obvious effort to submerge existing library policies to those of the rightists, and 5) to attempt to force the resignation of librarians who do not submit to repressive, right-wing demands.[19]

As stated earlier, librarians have learned in more than a decade of isolated as well as coordinated incidents to cope more effectively with censorship pressures from organized groups; yet, witch hunters are still on the prowl. In April 1972 the LJ/SLA *Hotline* reported that Birchers were at their old tactics and were looking into public libraries to insure that copies of *The Blue Book* were not only purchased but kept available on library shelves. *Hotline* warned librarians: "If you say no to them they will make a lightning draw of a copy of the Library Bill of Rights and read to you the appropriate passages. The book costs $3, and few librarians can justify not stocking it. The question is, if this campaign really works, what's the next title they'll pick for you?" Therefore, it appears that, while librarians have become more adept at warding off Birchers, these right-wingers have also refined their techniques.

In 1963, members of the Birch Society demanded the removal of *The Dictionary of American Slang* (New York: Crowell, 1960) from the Tulare County Library in California after the *Bulletin of the John Birch Society* urged opposition to the work in local communities. The censorship attempt came after California's Superintendent of Public Instruction, Max Rafferty, who was well known for his ultra-conservative views, claimed that the dictionary was "a practicing handbook of sexual perversion." An open hearing was held by the county board of supervisors to determine whether the volume should be allowed to remain in the library, and a petition for the removal of the dictionary from the library was presented which had been signed by 2,000 citizens objecting to "obscene" words in the reference book. The county librarian, Mrs. Hilda Collins, prepared a statement to be read before the board at its hearing. She said:

> Like all the books bought in the library, this [*Dictionary of American Slang*] was ordered after reading the reviews in book review publications, which were favorable. This book is a standard reliable reference work of 609 pages containing over 20,000 definitions of over 8,000 words. It deals with the origin, history, and usage of slang words and phrases; entries come from every period of American history. Its treatment of taboo words relating to sex is factual and historical; such words form only a small part of the whole, and taboo and derogatory terms are clearly indicated as such. The book is intended for the use of scholars in the fields of literature, history, language, and psychology.[20]

Despite the emotional verbal blasts directed by the assembled Birchers and their followers against the schools, the library, and the dictionary itself, the board of

58

supervisors voted unanimously against the censors and in favor of the county librarian. Although the dictionary was kept in the library, those who had objected to it immediately began an attack on board members, who were quickly branded as communists.

Only this year (1972) Piri Thomas' book *Down These Main Streets* (New York: Knopf, 1967) was the object of another Bircher attack. In Salinas, California, the book had been assigned in a public high school elective course devoted to literature of "forgotten Americans." An autobiography of a New York City Puerto Rican who became a junkie, thief, and convict, the book has been described as "by no means genteel" and a work "written without apology." When the father of a student objected to the reading of the book by his son, the local Birch Society got into the act and distributed a leaflet quoting selected risqué passages out of context from the objectionable work. A local conservative newspaper, *The Californian* assisted the Birch cause by stirring up local emotions over the issue to the point that the Salinas Union High School District trustees decided to ban the work from schools. One trustee found it difficult to believe that the autobiography could have been assigned without someone having realized along the line that it was "controversial." Despite the ban in Salinas on *Down These Main Streets*, favorable reviews had been published on the book in *The New York Times*, *Life*, and *The Nation*.[21]

The censor was not so successful in another attempt at repression in Minneapolis. In 1970, the mayor of that city, who had once been a policeman, threatened to withhold operating funds from the Minneapolis Public Library if such underground publications as *Rolling Stone*, *Black Panther*, and *New Left Notes* were not removed from the shelves. The mayor's attempt at coercion was not successful, having been met with strong resistance from the library director, Erwin Gaines; the state librarian, Hannis Smith; and the chairman of ALA's Intellectual Freedom Committee, David K. Berninghausen. Minneapolis citizens also came to the defense of the library: A *Star* newspaper poll showed that in a sample of 600 adults, 64 percent were opposed to restrictions on adult reading. Before a hearing conducted by the Board of Estimate, library director Gaines stated: ". . . a library worthy of the name must be a repository of information about the major controversies of society and if passions run high at this moment it is because there are sharp divisions about the course this nation should follow . . . The great strength of the underground press is that it reports events and opinions not easily obtained other places. The library would be poorer without them."[22]

Despite the inconceivable amount of knowledge that we now have at our disposal about almost any problem or issue of interest to man, extremist groups appear to suffer from a common ailment—a myopic inability to assimilate information in a logical fashion so that they can establish alternatives and realistic priorities for their own daily actions and problems as well as for those of their communities, state, and nation. Extremists look for a scapegoat, and for the right-wingers it is usually communists or socialists. Behind every progressive move made by society, the Far Right perceives a communist lurking in the backgournd, and it endows him with super-human power and influence. Ultra-conservatives view a world shrouded in a cloud of doom and destruction. They seek naive, simplistic solutions to many of our complex social and economic problems. Without a doubt, the Far Right is opposed to almost all forms of progress, and its adherents prefer to look at the world through a rear-view mirror. Despite the fact that extremists of the Right have often been dismissed as ineffective eccentrics and malcontents, there appears to be a new confidence in its voice. It appears to have reached a segment of "Middle America." Those in our nation who feel neglected and forgotten by the government—and by almost every other group—listen to these radicals, who do not sound so crazy any more. Everett Moore claims that "Despite the liberalizing influences of the past decade and tremendous anti-censorship progress in the courts, there are currently even more threats to intellectual freedom." Moore believes that we might be entering another period similar to the McCarthy era, and he suggests that Spiro Agnew is its new spiritual leader.[23]

Senator Jacob K. Javits of New York, who has been a frequent target of Birchers as well as other ultra-right organizations, had this to say about ultra-conservative groups at a symposium held at Princeton University:

> I am confident ultra-conservatism will be exposed as an ineffective approach to the complex challenges of modern life . . . Ultra-conservatism cannot effectively meet the critical problems of equal opportunity, productivity, hard core unemployment or modern social welfare. It cannot cope with our pressing needs in education, housing or medical care—in whatever way they are supplied: public means, private means, or a mixture of both . . . the ultra-conservative approach can lead to movements that feed on our national frustrations and can undermine our national heritage of freedom. The John Birch Society has now come along to remind us again that the principles of a free society can be eroded from the extreme right as well as the extreme left.[24]

The Citizens for Decent Literature, Inc. (CDL) is another nationally organized group that has promoted censorship. It was founded in 1957 and has national headquarters in Los Angeles. The CDL is comprised of 300 local groups over the nation which have as their goals the support of existing laws against pornographic literature and its distribution, the creation of an awareness among the American people of the pornographic material being distributed through the nation's newsstands and bookstores, and the assistance in the arrest and prosecution of publishers and distributors of pornographic materials. The group, which maintains a speakers bureau, also circulates films, pamphlets, and other materials designed to curtail or to control pornography and obscenity in current literature.[25]

## FOOTNOTES

[1] U. S. Commission on Obscenity and Pornography, *Technical Report of the Commission on Obscenity and Pornography*, vol. 3, The Marketplace: The Industry (Washington: U. S. Government Printing Office, 1971), pp. 207-208.

[2] William A. Hachten, *The Supreme Court on Freedom of the Press* (Ames: The Iowa State University Press, 1968), p. 306.

[3] Richard H. Kuh, *Foolish Figleaves? Pornography in—and out of—Court* (New York: The Macmillan Company, 1967), p. 323.

[4] Olga C. and Edwin P. Hoyt, *Censorship in America* (New York: Seabury Press, 1970), pp. 51-55.

[5] Ginzburg v. United States, 383 U. S. Reports 463 (1966)

[6] *Ibid.*

[7] *Ibid.*

[8] *Ibid.*

[9] "On the Crucifixion of Punks," (Editorial) *Library Journal* 97(1972): 1221.

[10] Donald B. Sharp, ed., *Commentaries on Obscenity* (Metuchen, N. J.: The Scarecrow Press, Inc., 1970), p. 10.

[11] The *Newsletter on Intellectual Freedom* began publication with the November 1952 issue and is a publication of the Intellectual Freedom Committee of the American Library Association.

[12] Saul Maloff, "Comstock's Complaint," *Commonweal* 91(1969):362.

[13] *Encyclopedia of Associations*, National Organizations of the United States (Detroit: Gale Research Co., 1970), 1:756.

[14] Benjamin R. Epstein and Arnold Forster, *The Radical Right: Report on the John Birch Society* (New York: Random House, 1967), pp. 164-65.

[15] Lester DeKoster, *The Citizen and the John Birch Society* (Grand Rapids: William B. Eerdmans Publishing Co., 1967), p. 9.

[16] Gerald Schomp, *Birchism Was My Business* (New York: The Macmillan Company, 1970), pp. 22-23.

[17] Benjamin R. Epstein and Arnold Forster, *Report on the John Birch Society* (New York: Random House, 1966), pp. 54-55.

[18] Milton A. Waldor, *Peddlers of Fear* (Newark, N. J.: Lynnross Publishing Co., Inc., 1966), pp. 60-71.

[19] *Ibid.*, pp. 60-61.

[20] Joseph A. King, "Books and Banners: A Case History," *Saturday Review* 46(1963):66.

[21] "Reading in Salinas," *The Nation* 214(1972):453-54.

[22] "Minneapolis Librarians Defeat Censorship Move," *Library Journal* 95(1970):4090.

[23] Everett T. Moore, "Threats to Intellectual Freedom," *Library Journal* 96(1971):3563.

[24] Richard Vahan, *The Truth about the John Birch Society* (New York: Macfadden Books, 1962), pp. 119-20.

[25] *Encyclopedia of Associations*, p. 767.

# CHAPTER 3
# PROTECTION OF INDIVIDUAL RIGHTS

*I realize that there are certain limitations
placed upon the right of free speech. I may
not be able to say all I think, but I am not
going to say anything I do not think.*
—Eugene V. Debs

*On the breast of her gown, in red cloth,
surrounded with an elaborate embroidery
and fantastic flourishes of gold-thread,
appeared the letter A.*
—Nathaniel Hawthorne
*The Scarlet Letter*

## Conventionality vs. Creativity

Many of the promoters of "clean" literature movements demand that
materials in bookstores, libraries, motion pictures, and newspapers conform to
their standards of decency. They often feel that everyone should comply with
prevalent customs and morals and that any "true" or "average" American can
always distinguish between decency and indecency. Other more rational people
realize, however, that absolute conformity and the repression of ideas and
information is never completely successful in any society; it has never been
absolutely effective and probably never will be. The answer to suppression
attempts by pressure groups appears to be an educated citizenry. Theoretically,
public library and school systems of the nation have been committed to the fiat;
however, the success of these institutions has often been somewhat short of the
ideal. Resistance to repression and the maintenance of intellectual curiosity
among the people requires patience and tolerance even in cases of intense
resistance and provocation. A steadfast adherence to the ideals of democracy
should always be our standard, not just an ideal.

If the American culture is to remain productive intellectually, a protective
system must be provided for the thinking, creative, and writing minority,
however erratic, erotic, or zany their ideas may seem to the majority. A
repressive climate of opinion stymies creativity and fossilizes thought. Such a
climate is found not just in authoritarian régimes; it can also be a characteristic
of nations which support giant bureaucracies in which bureaucrats reign with
their often clumsy, rigid, and stultifying rules and regulations. A climate of
opinion sympathetic to the ideas of freedom, replete with legal protections and
numerous channels and modes of expression, has always been the goal of persons

who have promoted intellectual freedom and civil liberties. When our laws insulate the thinking, imaginative, and more passionate individuals among us, we will have taken a greater humanistic step than the one made only a few years ago when man first walked upon the surface of the moon. We will not necessarily cast aside controversial, new ideas in favor of the established order or the true and the tried; new and radical notions and concepts will be allowed a reasonable hearing. Film critic Judith Crist has outlined the effects of censorship by stating:

> I do know . . . what censorship accomplishes, creating an unreal and hypocritical mythology, fermenting an attraction for forbidden fruits, inhibiting the creative minds among us and fostering an illicit trade. Above all, it curtails the right of the individual be he creator or consumer, to satisfy his intellect and his interest without harm. In our law-rooted society, we are not the keeper of our brother's morals—only of his rights.[1]

Great advances which have been made in acquiring and disseminating knowledge in free societies are related to the degree to which the majority of the populace and the government have refrained from forcing conventions or standards upon individuals, especially upon the highly educated minority. From 1949 until 1953, a period in which a number of Americans fell under the spell of McCarthyism, a repressive climate hovered over the nation. McCarthyism demanded conformity as well as an uncritical acceptance of the status quo. The indiscriminate anti-communist hysteria, which was directed so well by Senator McCarthy, capitalized on domestic anxieties related to a fear of communism. In equating the private enterprise system with Americanism, followers of the McCarthy movement also regarded any criticism of our existing political, social, and economic institutions as un-American. Those who critized the established order were labeled "pinkos" or "communist sympathizers." McCarthy and his followers attempted to impose controls and regulations upon those whose thoughts and utterances did not conform to expected norms.

When stringent controls and regulations are levied in the style or manner of McCarthy, there can be no freedom; conversely, when restrictions do not exist or are minimal, creativity, knowledge, ideas, and insights are allowed to emerge freely from diverse, even unexpected, wellsprings. Thus, under free conditions, creativity is more spontaneous and less restricted by inhibiting forces. In so many of the incidents in which nations and states have regulated and censored information, governments have only strengthened authoritarian systems. Frequently, those restrictions have backfired and have resulted in checks on materials of a far less objectionable nature than those left uncensored. In *Purity in Print*, Paul S. Boyer stated: "Censorship, *as actually practiced in American cities today* [emphasis in original], is too often directed against worthwhile publications, while the 'brutalizing' works which the intellectuals rightly deplore are left undisturbed."[2]

Promoters of intellectual freedom have declared emphatically that governments should concern themselves with the accomplishment of only those tasks which private citizens cannot achieve or cannot perform so well. While there are forces in the nation (such as the societies for the suppression of vice and the clean literature groups) which seek governmental protection of the society from "dangers" of obscenity and lust, promoters of intellectual freedom and civil liberties feel that if such "protections" are to be provided at all they should be made operative by such non-government institutions as the family and the church. We are indeed fortunate in the United States that the U. S. Constution limits the government as governments have rarely been curbed before in other countries and that our fundamental laws make the preservation of peace the most important undertaking or charge for our nationally-elected representatives. Extralegal censorship by public officials is expressly forbidden by law; however, no legal guarantee exists to prevent such censorship by private pressure groups or to curb the confining moral codes designed to suppress sexuality. If freedom of inquiry and freedom of speech are to be maintained in our nation, citizens must also have legal protections against extralegal attempts by private groups and individuals. Unfortunately, a legal framework which would prevent such practices has not yet been created other than the guarantees outlined in the Bill of Rights.

## Freedom of Choice

In the recent decade of the sixties, censorship controversies moved from matters of politics to questions of morality and obscenity. In many obscenity controversies, both in and outside the courts, a frequently overlooked yet primary consideration should have been whether freedom of speech—one of our most cherished and explicitly guaranteed constitutional rights—was to be overlooked in preventing the publication and distribution of objectionable materials, not merely whether certain publications were "obscene" or "harmful." Alec Craig, author of *The Banned Books of England*, has pointed out that:

> . . . the claim of policemen, lawyers, and officials to sit in judgment on the works of scholars, men of science, and creative artists is an impertinent tyranny; . . . three hundred years after the publication of Milton's *Areopagitica* it [the judgment] constitutes an anachronism which should be swept away.[3]

Freedom and repression are paired opposites. They form a dichotomy representing the classic conflict between permissiveness and control, between the need in a democracy to exercise some type of restraint so that our social institutions can be intelligently regulated for the protection of citizens' rights and the need for individuals to exercise freedom of choice. The struggle between regulation and freedom of choice, especially in respect to sexual freedom, obscenity, and pornography, demonstrates that our nation is far from resolving the tension. On one hand, an uncomfortable number of Americans, if permitted, would apparently go all out to limit freedoms in the name of law and order; on the other hand, there are some anarchists in our nation who feel no need at all for any controls and who would like nothing more than the eradication of all laws, rules, and regulations. Somewhere between these two extremes lies the democratic ideal—a balance between liberty and control. The achievement of that ideal is perhaps democracy's greatest and most exciting challenge.

Restrictions which our legislators have imposed upon pornography and other sexually-oriented materials have always been very ineffective in consideration of the purposes and aims of those who proposed such legislation. Controls instituted in the past have proved to be unenforceable and ineffectual in short-circuiting the flow of hard-core pornography as well as in protecting citizens' rights to read sexually-oriented publications. In addition to denying the defendant trial by jury in magistrates' courts, repressive legislation has created a vague definition of obscenity. It has helped bring about an atmosphere in which hard-core pornographers have not only increased their production but have reaped unparalleled profits by selling their materials at black market prices. Without a doubt, past repression of materials of a sexual nature and the suppression of sexual activities have contributed to the current exaggerated attention to and emphasis on sex in so many of our communication media, especially in motion pictures, on television programs, and in popular magazines.

The federal courts have been just as unsuccessful as the legislatures in their attempts to control pernicious literature. They have not provided a clear framework for a national policy toward obscenity and pornography—a framework in which state and local governments could operate in forming their own controls of questionable materials. Past attempts to repress pornography by the police and other official agencies have created an atmosphere of ambiguity in which the producers of hard-core pornography have been able to operate with relative ease. A realistic solution to the present obscenity and pornography dilemma has not been achieved by existing legal recourses. At the present time, no one seems to know who, if anyone, is to exercise control. In addition, it is not clear within what framework, with what definitions, and with what philosophical grounds the controls should be regulated, if at all.

When confronted by groups or individuals who attempt to suppress materials by labeling them obscene, morally unacceptable, politically repugnant, or contrary to prevailing customs or convictions, public librarians should challenge the would-be censor if they are convinced that those works deemed objectionable are indeed appropriate and needed in the community. If the content of questionable material is not illegal (not expressly forbidden by law), librarians should not hesitate to purchase and to circulate them if realistic or anticipated needs exist for these works in the community. Librarians cannot develop vital, relevant, and worthwhile collections in an atmosphere of coercion; they cannot permit themselves to be intimidated by various pressure groups or individuals. The removal of materials from library collections because someone feels that certain works are obscene, obnoxious, immoral, depraved, or seditious is contrary to the idea of freedom of choice. What social function will the library perform if its collection is as sterile, innocuous, and tasteless as pablum? What will librarians achieve if they refrain from supplying library users with materials and information concerning subjects and issues which interest them, whether the subject of concern is sexual, political, religious, or whether it deals with realistic life experiences such as drugs and their effects on man, racial problems, ecological issues, or whatever? Librarians must always be on guard against man's inclination to accept the status quo as the norm and to allow narrow community opinions to curb free speech drastically. If public librarians permitted on library shelves only the books and materials which support prevailing morals and established orders, their actions would not only be contrary to the American ideals of individual liberty and freedom of choice, but would also transgress policies recommended by various library professional organizations, particularly the American Library Association.

Public libraries should not be instruments for the regimentation or indoctrination of society. They are not manipulative organizations designed to "condition" library users or to assist citizens in "adjusting." Libraries are organizations of enlightenment through which the individual can obtain access to the great ideas, discoveries, innovations, and even mistakes of mankind. The humanizing influence of our creative writers, artists, philosophers, and teachers is needed today, more than ever, in order to counteract the brutalizing forces of war and destructive social strife with which man in the twentieth century has become so familiar. The public library is one social agency that can provide access to the recorded knowledge which allows that humanizing influence. Through their collections and services, American librarians are in an excellent position to assist library users, as well as the communities that support libraries, to recognize the causes that divide and the goals that can unite our nation, as well as the sources of conflict and the basis for collaboration in our society.

## The Bill of Rights

The Bill of Rights embodied in the first Ten Amendments of the Constitution outlines the basic liberating provisions for freedom in the United States. Prepared by Congress in 1789 and ratified by all the existing states by 1791, these amendments express in clear and simple terms the protections normally assumed under a form of government in which individual rights are taken for granted and are regarded as inalienable. The idea of liberty outlined in the *Magna Carta* in the year 1215 was embodied in the U. S. Constitution in 1789. American citizens are indeed fortunate that at the time the first Ten Amendments to the U. S. Constitution were drafted there was a prevailing desire to include within the new nation's basic legal framework a restraining instrument designed to defend individual rights from gradual government encroachments.

Apparently, those who wanted a written guarantee in 1789 for the preservation of these rights felt, as many now feel, that government should not exist for the sake of government alone and that citizens have a just claim according to the Constitution to change—even to abolish—their form of government if a majority of the people so desire. The First Amendment, which is concerned with free speech, does more than protect the rights of individuals to express their considered views and judgments about vital issues; it also assures a national climate conductive to the attainment of truth, so that citizens can determine their best courses of action as well as carry them out in the most judicious manner. The First Amendment also forbids Congress to pass laws that abridge freedom of the press. Judicial interpretation of the Fourteenth Amendment made that binding also on the individual states. According to J. Shane Creamer, author of *A Citizen's Guide to Legal Rights*, the first Ten Amendments of the Constitution are actually ". . . the Ten Commandments against government—a list of what government can't do to the citizen."[4]

Some of the provisions for freedom of religion, assembly, speech, and the press, in addition to the right to petition the government, have at times been challenged by persons who would like to limit these liberties. While former Attorney General John N. Mitchell apparently acted under the contention that the government had unbridled authority to spy and to eavesdrop on American citizens who espoused radical causes and that internal security matters were too subtle and complex to be left for judges to decide, the Fourth Amendment of the Bill of Rights states otherwise:

> The right of the people to be secure in their persons, houses, papers, and effects, against unreasonable searches and seizures, shall be issued but upon probable cause, supported by oath or affirmation, and particularly describing the place to be searched and the person or things to be seized.

In order to obtain convictions of certain "criminals" or "communists," law-and-order advocates have tended to disregard the Fourth Amendment; they have claimed that the requirement for judge-issued warrants describing the exact scope of the search and the person or materials to be seized is a protection of the law-breaker. The Fourth Amendment is but another example of how the Constitution states what the government cannot do; it is democracy's answer to the totalitarian battle-cry of "law-and-order." The soundness and validity of the Bill of Rights are strongly implanted; attempts to infringe on or to modify them have brought forth such cries of vigorous protest that alterations have been entirely out of the question. Consequently, individual rights protected by the first Ten Amendments are likely to remain undisputable, thus unaltered, in the forseeable future.

In order to promote intellectual freedom in libraries, the American Library Association (ALA) has adopted the *Library Bill of Rights*. ALA's Intellectual Freedom Committee has vigorously promoted and publicized that document since 1948. However, the written principles of the *Library Bill of Rights* do not provide librarians with a legal basis for the practice of freedom of speech and information within libraries. A basis for acquiring and disseminating library materials on all sides of issues is spelled out in the freedom-of-speech provisions contained in the U. S. Constitution. Under those protections, every citizen has the right to express his opinions freely in word, writing, or picture; to circulate them; and to obtain information without restrictions from generally accessible sources. Thus, one of the tasks of our libraries, as well as our educational institutions, is to insure that persons can become enlightened through information and study and that citizens of the United States will have readily available whatever information they need. In an address before the American Library Association, Howard Mumford Jones stated:

> The charter of our freedom is that the people shall have the right freely to receive and freely to discuss ideas regarding themselves and the state to which they belong; and the frail shield which we have to interpose between this hard-won political platitude and the storm of absolutism which is sweeping the world is the thin and perishable leaf of the printed book.[5]

For the protection of individual rights, laws enacted by federal and state legislative bodies should remain tolerant of many "evils" which are condemned by private morality. The separate states of our nation must adjust their judicial and law enforcement agencies in accord with the federal government's tradition of civil liberties and protection of rights outlined in the Bill of Rights. As long as the present U. S. Constitution remains intact, the so-called evils should be recognized for what they are: subjective value judgments, relative both to the situation and to the person perceiving them. The freedom of expression must be viewed in our democracy as an unalterable right when any restrictive laws for the control of information are contemplated or formulated. Consequently, if censorship is to raise its ugly head at all, it ought to be an exception in our nation rather than a rule.

Various pressure groups (religious, political, economic, etc.) which espouse the control (or even the elimination) of certain "evils" have the right to promote their private or group moral standards, causes, and opinions; however, in a free society such activity must take the form of persuasion, attitude change, and propaganda, exercised within the constraints of existing legal structures rather than couched in legislation and controls imposed upon everyone. Matters relating to morality and questions of obscenity and pornography are aesthetic rather than judicial problems. Attempts to legislate morals are thus moot points; they are completely out of the question as long as our rights remain as they are outlined and guaranteed in the U. S. Constitution.

One of the most active groups concerned with safeguarding and promoting civil liberties in the United States is the American Civil Liberties Union (ACLU). Founded in 1920, the ACLU has its national headquarters in New York City. Comprised of 47 state groups, the ACLU's purpose is to champion the rights of man set forth in the Declaration of Independence and in the United States Constitution. These rights include: the freedom of inquiry and expression (speech, press, assembly, and religion); due process of law and fair trial for everybody; and equality before the law, regardless of race, color, national origin, political opinion, or religious belief. The activities of the American Civil Liberties Union include test court cases, the opposition of repressive legislation, and public protests against inroads of citizens' rights. The ACLU maintains committees concerned with academic freedom, church-state relationships, communication media, due process of law, equality, free speech and association, labor and business, and privacy.

In relation to the repressions which take the form of charges of obscenity, the American Civil Liberties Union has declared:

> Any governmental restriction or punishment of any form of expression on the ground of obscenity must require proof beyond a reasonable doubt that such an expression would directly cause, in a normal adult, behavior which has validly been made criminal by statue.[6]

In view of the diverse social events of the 1960s—particularly those relating to civil liberties such as the black civil rights movement, the demands of American Indians, Chicanos, Puerto Ricans, and the Amish, as well as those of various liberation groups such as the Women's Liberation Movement and the Gay Liberation Front—the activities of the American Civil Liberties Union to protect personal and minority rights have become increasingly significant and important toward preserving the freedom and dignity of the American citizen.

## The Library Bill of Rights

The *Library Bill of Rights* outlines in six broad statements the basic freedom-of-access policies governing the services of all libraries. That document is the official policy statement of the American Library Association regarding the rights of library users to read what they wish without intervention from groups or individuals, including the librarian himself. The text of that statement for intellectual freedom was originally written in 1938 and 1939 by Forest Spaulding, who was director of the Des Moines Public Library. Since its adoption in 1939 by the American Library Association, the *Library Bill of Rights* has inspired librarians to recommit themselves to a philosophy of service based on the premise that users of libraries should have access to information on all sides of all issues.[7]

David K. Berninghausen, a library educator and an outspoken advocate of the freedom to read, has asserted that the adoption of the *Library Bill of Rights* and the recognition which it received in and outside the field of librarianship brought about the use of the statement as a ". . . focal point in the education of librarians, trustees, and the public on the question of what should be the guiding principles for the acquisition and dissemination of information through libraries."[8] Although the *Library Bill of Rights* is significant as an ethical guide to conduct in respect to intellectual freedom for American librarians, it does not endow the librarian with any legal rights. It is a standard by which librarians can gauge their day-to-day library practices against professional behavior in the realms of freedom of access to information, freedom of communication, freedom of thought, and freedom of intellectual activity.[9]

## Defending Intellectual Freedom

In a *Library Journal* article entitled "Knights and Windmills,"[10] a state librarian recently suggested that librarians take passive, noncommittal positions in respect to censorship issues. But, on the contrary, librarians cannot afford to wait for the dust of censorship battles to settle, hoping that the victor will be on their side. In a democratic society a free interchange and discussion of ideas is necessary, and he who shies away from ongoing controversies can hardly complain at the end of the conflict that the victor is not sympathetic to his cause.

Librarians do not function in a social vacuum; they are social beings who acquire the means of asserting their identity only when they discover their relationship to library users and to the communities that support libraries. In the opinion-formulating process of a democratic society, each interest group contributes its share to public opinion as a whole. Interest or "pressure" groups perform useful as well as objectionable functions; they are an integral and indispensable part of any democratic community. Some of the advantages of these groups were outlined as follows in 1952 in the proceedings of the First Conference on Intellectual Freedom, held in New York City:

> Their [the pressure groups] role is to help the public generally and government officials particularly to formulate public policy . . . The principal reason for granting groups of people the right of association and freedom to express their opinions is the conviction that such freedom to advocate ideas, such competition for public support and government approval, are best calculated to insure an enlightened public opinion and wise public policy . . . Pressure groups make their greatest contribution to the democratic process by taking an active part in the great competitive arena of ideas, expressions of opinion, and, if you wish, propaganda.[11]

Consequently, public opinion is frequently affected by the interjection of authoritative ideas and judgments of various groups which serve as catalysts. As a special interest group that is capable, when motivated, of applying pressure, librarians should *actively* defend intellectual freedom and express their displeasure over anticipated or real acts of censorship. Librarians cannot apathetically wait until the censors come before they take preventive action in defense of library users' rights. Pleas for inaction expressed in the article "Knights and Windmills" in statements such as "Let us give to intellectual freedom only the attention the censor *forces* us to give it" are analogous to advising someone to wail until the burglar has come before installing locks.

Librarians should be links in a community's information network, and they must be concerned with free communication. The rights of citizens of the United States to free access of ideas and information have been firmly established in theories of library services, and the degree to which librarians are committed to supporting and defending these rights is a socially significant issue. Librarians who give only lip service to the public's right to read—those who do not put into practice the concepts of intellectual freedom as stated in such documents as the *Library Bill of Rights* and the *Freedom to Read* statement[12]—are remiss in their professional obligation. David Berninghausen has commented on the librarian's role in intellectual freedom and on the activities of the Intellectual Freedom Committee (IFC) of the American Library Association as follows:

> During the years of McCarthyism (1945-1953), the IFC made great strides toward persuading the librarians of America that the publicly supported library and the librarians of the nation are living in the political world and cannot divorce themselves from political issues that involve libraries or the freedom to read. An examination of the literature of librarianship before 1938 shows that earlier librarians tended to hold that librarians should be above or aloof from political problems. As the radical right grew bolder and more censorious, however, librarians began to understand that the values of free inquiry, free scholarship, and free dissemination of ideas actually could be and might be lost, and that if lost, librarians could not possibly give honest reference service or circulate books freely to those who wanted to read on all sides of an issue.[13]

Undoubtedly, there have been a number of easily avoidable provocations between librarians and would-be censors. Some of these controversies have received rather sensational treatment in the news media and in professional journals when routine attention would have been appropriate. However, the criticism from librarians who have advocated either appeasement or "hands-off" policies in respect to censorship controversies go far beyond a distaste for sensationalism. Some librarians have taken defeatist outlooks toward censorious attacks. But experience has shown that all unwarranted and illegal attacks of censors and would-be censors require strong reaction lest the censor suspect weakness and mount a stronger and more effective attack. If librarians meekly accept encroachments upon freedom of speech and the right to read, all the more frequently might reactionaries, iconoclasts, and puritan zealots attempt to censor communication media.

Some librarians have also criticized efforts of their cohorts and associates to preserve the anonymity of readers and users of information. Such criticism is particularly disturbing, as some of these librarians apparently believe that if a library user has nothing to hide, an investigation of his reading interests or other activities is acceptable. Obviously, these critics fail to understand that such fishing expeditions by private persons, groups, or agents of the federal government might be used to suppress legitimate dissent or to compile information having no bearing on the maintenance of law and order.

Cries for moderation in carrying out and promoting intellectual freedom from timid, conservative librarians are not dissimilar to the attempts of censors themselves who seek to impose conventionalism and to reject ideas and values which are in conflict with the accepted standard, the established order, or prevailing morals. What librarianship does not need in the 1970s—a time of ferment and change—are voices which cry: "Don't rock the boat" and "Remain silent, librarians, lest someone discover that you exist." Unless librarians guarantee intellectual liberty in libraries and fight their own censorship battles, who is going to do it? Real and anticipated threats to censor library collections are social problems which merit the attention of all American citizens; within the realm of the librarian's professional obligation is the task of bringing such issues into the arena of public attention and discussion.

Thomas R. Asher, a Washington, D. C., lawyer who was president of the Maryland American Civil Liberties Union as well as a member of the ACLU national board, has suggested that librarians should obtain a workable balance between the risks of absolute censorship and the objectives of intellectual liberty. According to the attorney:

It would be most unfortunate if librarians provided reading matter solely in response to community demand merely in order to minimize the danger of loss of job or embarrassing litigation . . . When a librarian refuses to procure a book, or to make available to the public a book which it has already procured, or remove a book from its collection, then the librarian has made a censorship decision.[14]

Librarians should by no means restrict their resistance to censorship to intellectual liberty in libraries. They should also be concerned with all infringements upon the right to read and the free flow of information in our society. The case of the Pentagon Papers, for example, is one that should be of concern to all freedom-loving Americans, especially the professional librarian. The Pentagon Papers decision by the U. S. Supreme Court was not a clear-cut victory for those who struggle to maintain freedom of information. Even though the Court ruled that the Justice Department's action to prevent publication of the Papers on the Vietnam War by *The New York Times* and other newspapers was unconstitutional, the literary community and other thinking Americans are fully aware that under slightly different circumstances, i.e., a Court comprised of more conservative justices, the Supreme Court would have upheld such censorship.[15]

Some comments on the issue of censorship by J. W. Lambert are particularly interesting and ought to be considered carefully by librarians. Lambert, who is literary editor of the *Times Literary Supplement* (London), has offered the view that in the field of the arts and entertainment any form of censorship is undesirable and unnecessary. He feels that if all censorship were suddenly stopped, a country would not be flooded with a torrent of sadism and pornography as many pro-censors have predicted. Lambert has also called for the avoidance of the hypocrisy which bedevils discussion of censorship by statements such as: "Of course, I'm absolutely against any form of censorship, but one must draw the line somewhere." He also warned that

> ... in an increasingly impersonal world we should be increasingly wary of handing over decisions to any form of Authority—not least decisions about what we ourselves, and our children, should be allowed to see, hear, and read.[16]

In consideration of all the forces which appear to be working against the troubled librarian (who, after all, it might be assumed is only attempting to do his or her job as proficiently as possible in compliance with professional recommendations and standards), one might ask what the librarian should do when faced with an actual attempt at censorship. In other words, what methods do librarians have to resist the repressors of information and what professional backing can be expected? In Appendix II, a number of guidelines and statements are provided which might be of help to the librarian. These recommendations are reprinted with the permission of the Office of Intellectual Freedom of the American Library Association; included there is the statement "What the American Library Association Can Do for You to Help Combat Censorship," as well as the Resolution on Challenged Materials. These documents should be periodically reviewed by practicing librarians in anticipation of complaints from would-be censors. A better understanding of intellectual freedom in action might be possible when librarians are thoroughly familiar with policies and procedures approved and recommended by professional organizations.

Another development in the area of the right to read with which librarians ought to be familiar is the Freedom to Read Foundation, which was incorporated in 1969. The purposes of the Foundation were outlined in its articles of incorporation as follows:

To promote and protect freedom of speech and freedom of press as such freedoms are guaranteed by the Constitution and laws of the United States and as such freedoms necessarily involve the public right to hear what is spoken and to read what is written.

To promote the recognition and acceptance of libraries as repositories of the world's accumulated wisdom and knowledge and to protect the public right of access to such wisdom and knowledge.

To supply legal counsel, which counsel may or may not be directly employed by the Foundation, and otherwise to provide to such libraries and librarians as are suffering legal injustices by reason of their defense of freedom of speech and freedom of press as guaranteed by law against efforts to subvert such freedoms through suppression or censorship to the extent such libraries and librarians may request such aid and require it on account of poverty or inability to obtain legal counsel without assistance.

In 1970, the American Library Association's Activities Committee on New Directions recommended a number of measures for the implementation of an effective program which would provide additional support in resisting censorship and in promoting intellectual liberty in libraries. Among the recommendations for action by ALA were the following: 1) workshops for representatives of Intellectual Freedom Committees at state and regional levels, 2) the challenging of every legislative effort to abridge the Freedom to Read, 3) suspension of members from ALA when, as verified by a fair and impartial hearing, their actions have violated the *Library Bill of Rights*, and 4) establishment of a nation-wide program designed to inform the American public about censorship and intellectual freedom issues. While some of these proposals, as well as others which were also recommended, have been partially initiated, considerable work toward insuring a complete climate of freedom in libraries as well as the complete activation of concepts of intellectual liberty still remain to be accomplished. As in other social situations which involve dynamic human interaction, the give-and-take struggle between the suppressed and the suppressor requires constant attention; actual library practices always seem to be slightly short of the desired, recommended goal.

## FOOTNOTES

[1] Judith Crist, *Censorship For & Against* (New York: Hart Publishing Co., 1971), p. 57.

[2] Paul S. Boyer, *Purity in Print; the Vice-society Movement and Book Censorship in America* (New York: Charles Scribner's Sons, 1968), pp. xvii-xix.

[3] Alec Craig, "The Conception of Literary Obscenity and the Freedom of Letters," in *Freedom of Expression: A Symposium*, ed. Herman Ould (Port Washington, New York: Kennikat Press, 1970), p. 140.

[4] J. Shane Creamer, *A Citizen's Guide to Legal Rights* (New York: Holt, Rinehart and Winston, 1971), p. 27.

[5] Howard Mumford Jones, "The Place of Books and Reading in Modern Society," *Bulletin of the American Library Association* 27(1933):585-93.

[6] The *New York Times* (May 28, 1962), 23, cols. 4-5.

[7] David K. Berninghausen, "Bill of Rights, Library," *Encyclopedia of Library and Information Science*, eds. Allen Kent and Harold Lancour (New York: Marcel Dekker, 1969), 2:458.

[8] David K. Berninghausen, "The Librarian's Commitment to the Library Bill of Rights," *Library Trends* 19(1970):21.

[9] American Library Association, *Proceedings of the 87th Annual Conference* (Kansas City, Mo., 1968), p. 22.

[10] Walter Brahm, "Knights and Windmills," *Library Journal* 96(1971): 3096-98.

[11] "Pressure Groups and Intellectual Freedom," in *Freedom of Communication*, Proceedings of the First Conference on Intellectual Freedom, New York City, June 28-29, 1952 (Chicago, American Library Association, 1954), pp. 73-87.

[12] The *Freedom to Read* statement was prepared by the Westchester Conference of the American Library Association and the American Book Publishers Council, May 2 and 3, 1953, and endorsed by the American Library Association Council, June 25, 1953, and the American Book Publishers Council, Board of Directors, June 18, 1953.

[13] Berninghausen, "The Librarian's Commitment to the Library Bill of Rights," pp. 19-38.

[14] Thomas R. Asher, "A Lawyer Looks at Libraries and Censorship," *Library Journal* 95(1970):3248.

[15] "New Wave of Censorship," *Publisher's Weekly* 200(1971):34.

[16] J. W. Lambert, "The Folly of Censorship," *Encounter* 29(1967):60.

CHAPTER 4
BOOK SELECTION IN PUBLIC LIBRARIES

> *On confond toujours l'homme et l'artist sous*
> *prétexte que le hasard les a réunis dans le*
> *même corps. (People always confuse the man*
> *and the artist because chance has united them*
> *in the same body.)*
>
> —Jules Renard

### The Library as a Social Institution

The technology era of "instant" foods, which range from coffee to mashed potatoes, has also created a demand for immediate information. Improvements in the devices and techniques of the mass communications media have played an important role in stimulating this new and immediate quest for information, and, consequently, the public's increasing reliance on its libraries. The transmission of both verbal and visual messages by the mass media, especially television, has apparently contributed to the present interest in and demand for recorded information. The public now turns to libraries almost as soon as the information itself is generated, and in many American cities and communities the public library is the only source of bibliographic information (what is published, source of publications, prices, etc.). As the population of the nation becomes increasingly varied, comprised of many individuals with highly specialized and diverse interests, public libraries are faced with the task of providing facts, statistics, and data about an almost unlimited range of subjects. The question is not whether the public needs information, for we know that an informed citizenry is fundamental to democracy; the issue is whether the books and non-book materials available to library patrons are of the right kind and quantity, of acceptable accuracy, and of appropriate timeliness.[1]

Coupled with the challenge of providing information quickly is the public library's accountability for selection of collections from the vast outpourings of the trade, government, and private presses of the nation. The present publishing situation, sometimes referred to as the "information explosion" or "information overdose," is both a godsend and a dilemma to the librarian. Despite many drastic changes in the book trade and publishing world brought about in the 1960s by mergers, corporate realignments, and shifts in executive editorial positions, the list of new titles available annually has steadily increased.[2] While the range of recorded information has never been greater, the problem of bibliographic control and of developing and maintaining library collections is one which must now be attacked in a thorough, almost scientific, manner. There is a pressing need for prompt and systematic evaluations of new books and audiovisual materials.

In 1970, 36,071 new titles and new editions of books were published in the United States.[3] Not included in this figure are countless state and federal government publications as well as thousands of special reports of private and commercial enterprises. Americans can point with justifiable pride to the fact that more books and various non-book communication media are being produced and distributed in the United States than in any previous time in our nation's history. Greater literacy, an increasing awareness of book reading, and the rising importance of education in our technological society are some of the important factors believed to be responsible for increased publication activities. At any rate, an increase in book and magazine publication creates a greater problem for book selection and bibliographical control for libraries.

Most public library book selection policies are grounded in the review method: reviews of newly-published books and other media in newspapers, magazines, professional journals, and other serials form the backbone of public library acquisition work. Unlike university and other research-oriented libraries (as well as special libraries and information centers), the staffs of which often represent reservoirs of expert subject competence, the public library must depend heavily upon available book review media, whatever their strengths and weaknesses may be. *Library Journal/School Library Journal*, a semi-monthly publication of the R. R. Bowker Company, has an enormous influence upon what Americans find in their public libraries. In 1971 that publication reviewed a total of 8,826 new titles.[4] Although *Library Journal* serves as the most comprehensive professional reviewing service currently available, its coverage is small in comparison to the total annual title output of American publishers.

### What Should the Librarian Purchase?

In view of supply and demand, what kind of collections should public libraries attempt to build? Public libraries cannot limit their collections to books and materials which present an idealistic view of society or which, in the opposite extreme, only document contemporary life's miscellany of illnesses and perplexities; motion pictures, television, and other mass communication media do quite an adequate job of that. A library's collection should contain works allowing understandings and new perspectives on issues that can lead to methods of solving man's personal problems as well as those of his environment. And a public library should furnish ample information containing explanations and clarifications which might help citizens find solutions that are enlightened, endowed with reason, and equitable. In a democratic society citizens must know and appreciate what other people, groups, and minorities of dissimilar perspectives have to offer as well as to share. An ability to exist without suppression and to learn from opposing viewpoints distinguishes free societies from authoritarian regimes; thus, the public libraries of the United States ought to be committed to presenting a true balance of thought and information concerned not only with routine matters of our day-to-day existence but with the essential controversial matters of our contemporary epoch as well.

No books or materials should ever be excluded from library collections simply because the personal opinions of librarians differ from the contents of works, whether they are devoted to political, religious, or moral subjects. In practicing personalized rejection, librarians are defeating the profession's more noble resolves—the commitment to the free exchange of information; the promotion of investigations which allow intelligent and just approaches, perhaps solutions, to problems; the encouragement of active thought and discussion; and the provision of free access to ideas and information. Public librarians can help ease the discomfort resulting from contemporary social changes by creating balanced collections of materials and by maintaining a completely bias-free atmosphere. Only by providing information that can open the way to a clearer comprehension of the mutual relationships occurring among our social sub-cultures—from the arts to technology, to politics, to religion, to education, to the young and the aged, and to the culture itself—can the public library take its place as a viable social institution in communities of the nation. Collections developed with rigid, hidebound selection policies are apt to be stagnant, unimaginative, and in complete support of the status quo.

The social turmoil of the past decade in the United States has wide implications for building library collections; for, when we discover, as was often the case in the 1960s, that the established mores and values of our somewhat aggressive and demanding free-enterprise system conflict or interfere with the more favorable values of human development, self-realization, and emotional stability of persons, we must critically examine the old values and discard those which are disruptive, however painful the process may be. Until fundamental changes are made to reconcile contradictions of our value systems, the goals of our social institutions, including those of our libraries, will become more alienated from the "real world" goals of great segments of our populace. Our institutions have often repressed rather than fostered human fulfillment and happiness. A direct case in point was made recently in *Library Journal* by Mary McKenney in relation to homosexuality and library holdings on that subject:

As social attitudes toward homosexuality—and homosexuals' attitudes toward themselves—become more open, accepting, and free of stereotypical notions, it is only reasonable to expect that library holdings on the subject reflect more than the dying notion that homosexuality is a sickness or a perversion.[5]

At this point, it might be advisable to examine some of the comments on book selection and book rejection of library leaders and practicing librarians. In an article devoted to the question of the rejection of controversial books *versus* the censorship of books, Jerome Cushman pointed out that the librarian must assume the final responsibility of refusing works; however, he emphasized that librarians should not hide behind book selection committees or selection policies in doing so. According to Cushman, "A book selection policy is a guidepost, preferably set out in general terms to be acted upon by reasonable and trained librarians." He emphasized that the collection of a library can be stultified when a selection policy is used as a weapon or as an excuse for rejection: "There is real danger that a dogmatic approach to book selection can result in the error or failure to consider the book as a whole."[6]

Ray Smith, Director of the Mason City (Iowa) Public Library has pointed out that the rejection of books because of their potentiality for becoming controversial ". . . solidly defies the Freedom to Read statement of ALA, which ought to be adopted as a minimum book selection policy by every library board and to be on the agenda of every state association to this end." Smith has also related book rejection to the subjugation of selection policies to pressure group demands; he has stated:

... when a librarian surrenders his right of selection under pressure he becomes only a more or less gracious purveyor—not an intellectually desirable role, and one with a growing shadow across the community.[7]

Mortimer Adler suggested in *How to Read a Book* that books should be read three times and in three ways: structural, interpretive, and critical. Under structural considerations, Adler listed as important criteria the subject matter, an understanding of what the book is attempting to state, a knowledge of how it is divided into parts, and a recognition of the problems the author is trying to solve. Under interpretive considerations, Adler included the following: the recognition and interpretation of the book's most important words, sentences, and paragraphs, as well as a recognition of those problems solved by the author and those which were left unresolved. Critical considerations noted by Adler included: a respect for the difference between knowledge and opinion or the areas in which the author is uninformed, misinformed, illogical, or wherein an analysis or account is incomplete.[8]

Pierce Butler's *Introduction to Library Science*, an apparent attempt to formulate a theory of librarianship, points out that librarians who possess an ". . . evolutionary theory of literary history" will consider any book or piece of literature as valuable if it is significant in the line of progress. Butler suggested that such a librarian will prefer books that are perceived as very influential in the development of literature in its historical aspects, and he also argued that the rewriting of the record of human activities is important for the transmission of our culture, even from decade to decade.[9] Carter and Bonk suggested in *Building Library Collections* that a knowledge of the library's community is important for book selection if the library is to acquire those books which will be useful to their clientele. Book selection policies should also be reviewed from time to time, according to these authors, since the nature of any community is subject to change as time progresses. Carter and Bonk emphasize that unless librarians are alert to community changes, library collections might not contain what the community needs.[10]

In *A Technical Services Manual for Small Libraries* John Corbin discussed some recommended criteria for considering the value of gift books; he suggested that the same criteria should be applied to gift books as those applied to purchased works, that there should be no special stipulations or "strings" attached to gifts, and that worn or outdated editions of publications should not be accepted when better material is still in print.[11]

In additional published statements on book selection in libraries, May Hill Arbuthnot stressed in *Children and Books* a number of principles which ought to be followed in building collections for children, including the purchase of works which children themselves like to read; the selection of works that will contribute to the emotional, intellectual, and moral competencies of young people; and a realization that in order to label a book as a "good" one for children, it must be a work which is enjoyed by them. Conversely, she suggested that a book is "bad" for children if it cannot be understood by them or if it bores them, even though it might be considered a classic by adults.[12] *The Library Reaches Out*, compiled and edited by Kate Coplan and Edwin Castagna, demonstrates that libraries are frequently attempting to bolster good citizenship within communities and that librarians attempt to accomplish that by raising the sights of readers and by providing information which will assist the public in performing better on their jobs or learning more about their professions, providing books and materials to help them pass their leisure hours and in facing the day-to-day problems of life.[13] Eric Moon has recommended, in his introduction to *Book Selection and Censorship in the Sixties*, a balance theory for library collections—i.e., the notion that a library's collection should represent all points of view on controversial questions.[14] And Jesse Shera's social function theory of librarianship, which is included in an article about libraries in the *International Encyclopedia of the Social Sciences*, states that a library is effective only if its collection and services coincide with or are closely related to the communication patterns established by the society which uses or is supposed to use the records contained in the library collection.[15] In *Introduction to Reference Work*, Hutchins stresses the importance of direct, personal aid to users of libraries, for whatever purpose the user may have, and the idea that reference services should be guided by an operating principle which stresses making information as easily available as possible.[16] Wilson has stressed the fact that a book selection policy must be based upon the idea that any specialization within a collection must be supplemented with materials in closely related fields,[17] and Ashworth has stressed two principles of acquisition: the establishment of a collection or the extension of the collection into other subject areas and the maintenance of an up-to-date collection by the addition of new publications and by being aware of new and forthcoming works.[18]

Despite the foregoing documented statements, which could understandably give the impression that all librarians practice rational and well-thought-out selection policies, research in this area of librarianship has demonstrated that such is not always true in practice. Those persons within the library profession who argue that librarians always follow these recommended practices and that they have not performed intramural censorship must be reminded of the activities of a few librarians of the past who not only practiced repression of information but also carried on active crusades designed to hinder or to forbid the reading of certain "objectionable" books. James M. Hubbard, an employee of the Boston Public Library, labeled a collection of books "The Inferno" in that library. Books in "The Inferno" were available only to adults, and they apparently failed to meet Hubbard's personal moral standards. It should be stated that the administration of the Boston Public Library became very disenchanted with Mr. Hubbard's narrow views, and, with the support of the local newspapers, the head librarian was able to effectively combat his staff member's zealous attempts to purify the collection and to suppress certain types of books. In another event from the past, F. B. Perkins, librarian of the San

Francisco Public Library, wrote a publication in 1885 entitled *Free Libraries and Unclean Books* in which he criticized a patron for wanting to read Henry Fielding's *The History of Jonathan Wild the Great.* Mr. Perkins also attacked readers of books which he believed to be in bad taste and to which he voiced objections on moral grounds; he called those who read such materials "dirt-eaters." Perkins obviously felt obligated as a librarian to protect innocent readers from books containing ideas or images that he beleived were unclean and unwholesome.

In more recent times, Marjorie Fiske has documented widespread intramural censorship in certain California public and school libraries. The results of Fiske's research, which dealt with library book selection practices, will be discussed at length in a later section of this chapter. In other events, the Conservative Library Association was established in 1965 with the purpose of cleansing libraries of "tasteless, socialistic, subversive, and pornographic" materials. Although very little has been heard from that organization since its aims were attacked as a form of book burning by Charles Reid, a former president of the American Library Association, we must remain aware of the fact that within the ranks of American librarianship there are some librarians who apparently would like nothing more than to set their personal, social, moral, and political standards as norms and who would limit library collections to materials which do not conflict with or which do not challenge the established order. Bill Katz has pointed out in *Library Journal*:

> Neither all laymen nor all librarians would agree that censorship is necessarily evil. Many, in fact, strongly believe that a certain degree of censorship is advisable, particularly where the establishment's morality is threatened ... The profession says the librarian should select material based on positive criteria. No librarian should reject for the sake of rejection. The problem comes from the librarian who sincerely believes he knows what is best for all readers. This librarian is satisfied to believe that his own attitudes are equivalent to the 'proper' ones ... librarians consider pressures to change not only illegitimate but dangerous.[19]

### Controversial Works

In the final analysis, then, what is the librarian to do when faced with a controversial book or material *for which a need is felt or anticipated in a community?* Based on a careful examination of existing recommended policies, published statements of leaders within the profession, and authorities in the area of library acquisitions, the following criteria are proposed as guidelines and are listed in the order of their deemed priority for the selection or the rejection of questionable materials (books, periodicals, films, microforms, pamphlets, newspapers, phonograph or tape recordings, works of art, etc.):

1. Is the work honest?
2. If the work is indeed factual, is the information accurate and has it been verified? If the work is fictional, does it contribute to human understanding or happiness?

3.  If the work contains more opinion than fact, are the thoughts and ideas contained therein rational and logically deduced?
4.  Does the author or producer of the work in question achieve what he hoped to accomplish with the material?
5.  Does the work contribute to existing information, offer new insights, or present new perspectives?
6.  If the work meets *any* of the above criteria, it should be selected for inclusion in the library's collection; if the librarian still feels, however, that despite a work's lack of any of the above suggested qualities it would be of some use or value to library users, the final question should then be:
7.  Is the work protected by the Constitution of the United States (The Bill of Rights) and other laws in light of prevailing interpretations by the United States Supreme Court? If the work under consideration meets these legal standards, it should be added to the collection; if not, it should then, and only then, be rejected.

A very useful anthology of book selection policies of representative school, public, and college libraries has been compiled by Calvin Boyer and Nancy Eaton. The compilation, entitled *Book Selection Policies in American Libraries*,[20] can be used by librarians as a guide and a source book for creating, reviewing, or revising policies for the selection of library materials. Selection criteria used by a number of public libraries for controversial materials are contained in the work.

## FOOTNOTES

[1] J. Nehnevjsa, "Information Needs of Society: Future Patterns," *Proceedings of the 31st Congress of the International Federation for Documentation* (Washington, 1965), p. 161.

[2] H. Raymont, "Book Trade Upset by Changes in Ownership, Size, and Staff," The *New York Times*, March 4, 1968, Sec. C, p. 28.

[3] Janice Johnson and Frank L. Schick, eds., *The Bowker Annual of Library and Book Trade Information 1971* (New York: R. R. Bowker, 1971), p. 70.

[4] *Ibid.*, p. 93.

[5] Mary McKenney, "Gay Liberation," *School Library Journal* 97(1972): 733.

[6] "Book Rejection: Is It Censorship?" *Library Journal* 89(1962):2299.

[7] *Ibid.*, p. 2302.

[8] Mortimer Adler, *How to Read a Book* (New York: Simon & Schuster, 1940).

[9] Pierce Butler, *An Introduction to Library Science* (Chicago: The University of Chicago Press, 1933), p. 86.

81

[10] Mary Duncan Carter and Wallace J. Bonk, *Building Library Collections* (Metuchen, N. J.: Scarecrow Press, 1969), pp. 13-14.

[11] John Corbin, *A Technical Services Manual for Small Libraries* (Metuchen, N. J.: Scarecrow Press, 1971), p. 39.

[12] May Hill Arbuthnot, *Children and Books*, 3d ed. (Chicago, Scott, 1964).

[13] Kate Coplan and Edwin Castagna, eds. *The Library Reaches Out* (Metuchen, N. J.: Scarecrow Press, 1969).

[14] Eric Moon, ed., *Book Selection and Censorship in the Sixties* (New York: R. R. Bowker, 1969), p. 13.

[15] Jesse Shera, "Libraries," in *International Encyclopedia of the Social Sciences*, David L. Sills, ed. (New York: The Macmillan Co., 1968), 7:314.

[16] Margaret Hutchins, *Introduction to Reference Work* (Chicago: American Library Association, 1944).

[17] Louis Round Wilson, *The University Library; the Organization, Administration, and Functions of Academic Libraries*, 2d ed. (New York: Columbia University Press, 1956).

[18] Wilfred Ashworth, *Handbook of Special Librarianship and Information Work*, 3d ed. (London: Aslib, 1967).

[19] Bill Katz, "The Pornography Collection," *Library Journal* 96(1971): 4061.

[20] Calvin J. Boyer and Nancy L. Eaton, *Book Selection Policies in American Libraries; An Anthology of Policies from College, Public, and School Libraries* (Austin, Texas: Armadillo Press, 1971).

# CHAPTER 5
# FACING THE CHALLENGE

*The will of the people is the only legitimate foundation of any government, and to protect its free expression should be our first object.*

—Thomas Jefferson

## The Public Librarian and Censorship

Public librarians in the United States are in a position to foster and to encourage freedom of speech and the freedom to read, both of which are essential to a democratic way of life. By virtue of their involvement in the dissemination of information and in the communication of ideas, they can play significant roles in the communication networks of American cities and communities. But ideas have sometimes incited controversies, which, in turn, have provoked attempts at official and unofficial control of the dissemination by libraries of books and other communication media. It is not surprising, therefore, that public libraries have at times been confronted with censorship problems. The issue of obscenity has been paramount in recent years in confrontations with the forces of censorship; consequently, public librarians have been increasingly involved with the censor.

No community appears to be immune to censorship, and reports indicate that the pressures of would-be censors have been exerted on public libraries by groups, organizations, and individuals who have lacked faith in the public's discrimination. Censors or would-be censors have apparently acted under the assumption that the unrestricted reading of books and periodicals might lead to the deterioration of personal morality, cultural values, and the security of our democratic form of government. On the other hand, it is generally agreed within the library profession that public librarians should resist the encroachment on and suppression of the public's freedom to read by challenging the censor as a danger to the very freedoms on which American democracy is based.

Censorship has been defined by political scientist Harold D. Lasswell as:

the policy of restricting the public expression of ideas, opinions, conceptions and impulses which have or are believed to have the capacity to undermine the governing authority or the social and moral order which that authority considers itself bound to protect.[1]

Lasswell has also pointed out that censorship may be exercised by political or religious authorities, or even by individuals who assume a quasi-official position in respect to the enforcement of anticipated prohibitive policies.[2] Although censorship activity has most generally been associated with governmental control, Henry J. Abraham has written in the *International Encyclopedia of the Social Sciences* that censorship as an activity of private groups having both religious and secular interest is becoming more common.[3]

As applied to libraries the term "censorship" is operationally defined as "the rejection by a library authority of a book (or other material) which the librarians, the library board, or some person (or persons) bringing pressure on them holds to be obscene, dangerously radical, subversive, or too critical of the existing mores."[4]

Librarians use the term "intellectual freedom" as the antithesis of censorship. The term denotes the freedom claimed by persons to have access to books and information without restraint from public or private interests. Academic freedom, which protects educators from pressures in their scholarship and in their teaching, might be classed as a type of intellectual freedom under this generic usage of the term; however, intellectual freedom within the library profession usually means the library user's right to read, to watch, or to listen to what he wants to read, to see, or to hear, respectively, without supervision or restraint from public officials, public opinion, institutional repression, or private groups or individuals. Implicit in the library science concept of intellectual freedom is the conviction that freedom and ease of access to library collections are imperative if library users are to exercise their rights.

Censorship pressures of varying intensities have been applied to public libraries especially during times of national crisis and social tension. A somewhat spectacular example of such pressures resulted from the McCarthy-led anti-communist hysteria of the 1950s. As reported in Blanshard's book *The Right to Read*, a newspaper campaign was conducted by *Boston Post* editor John Fox against the Boston Public Library. Blanshard states in his book:

> For twenty-eight consecutive days, with only four exceptions, the *Post* carried anti-library stories, sixteen of them on the front page. The editor boldly asserted: WE BELIEVE that we are in a fight to the death ... WE BELIEVE that to permit pro-Communists to circulate their poison among our people is sheer stupidity.[5]

The Boston Public Library won its long struggle against the censorship campaign, but the margin was very narrow. The determination of the librarian, bolstered by support from other newspapers in Boston, helped save the library in its defense of the public's right to read. It is not surprising that a reaffirmation sprung up among librarians of the commitment to intellectual freedom as a result of the repressive spirit of McCarthyism during the 1950s.[6]

Although there have been many incidents in other libraries of similar censorship attempts in which the librarian's public defense of freedom of access has received recognition and acclaim, a number of leaders within the profession have expressed doubt as to whether freedom-to-read principles are always being supported in public libraries in proportion to the increased activities of censors. There are published reports of a number of episodes in which public libraries have meekly yielded to censorship pressures and have removed from their collections books or other materials which were opposed on political, religious, or moral grounds. The American Library Association's *Newsletter on Intellectual Freedom* has reported incidents in which some public librarians have hastily withdrawn "objectionable" books from the shelves of their libraries, putting into practice their own form of intramural censorship.

Robert Downs has emphasized the truth that although more reading materials of all kinds are available today than ever before, freedom of access to reading materials cannot be looked upon in a matter of fact fashion or be taken for granted.[7] The commitment to the public's right to read must go beyond the verbalization stage, in which many librarians readily give lip service to the library user's right to inquiry. A true commitment to freedom of access to books and information should progress from the realm of abstract conceptualization to functional operation in the day-to-day activities of the librarian, especially in the event that a library is confronted with censorship pressures.

The recommended stand for the public librarian in regard to controversial materials has been outlined in standards adopted by members of the Public Library Association of the American Library Association. Principle number 34 of *Minimum Standards for Public Library Systems* states that "library collections should contain opposing views on controversial topics" and that "the public library does not promote particular beliefs or views [but] provides a resource where the individual can examine issues freely and [make] his own decision."[8] According to the ALA approved standards, the public library which does not provide the means and information resources that would allow the exploration of all sides of issues is failing in one of its unique roles. The principle directly related to outside pressures for inclusion or removal of controversial materials is reprinted here from the standards:

> Materials of the required quality, serving the purpose of the library and relating to an existing need or interest will not be removed from the collection nor will materials lacking these qualities be added because of pressure by groups or individuals. Care must be taken that parts of the community do not unduly influence the collections, either positively or negatively. Selection must resist efforts of groups to deny access to other segments of the community. Libraries must also resist efforts to force inclusion of materials representing political, economic, moral, religious, or other vested positions when these materials do not conform to the institution's selection policies.[9]

The following statement, taken from a large metropolitan library's book selection policy as typical of declarations in other written selection policies, clearly reflects the philosophy of freedom of access to information and ideas that has become ingrained in theories which underlie public library services in the United States:

> Freedom of speech and freedom of the press are rights of our heritage guaranteed by the Constitution and defended by our courts. Since the meaning of these doctrines is determined finally by the attitude of the American people, it follows that the Enoch Pratt Free Library must provide free access to all points of view on public questions.[10]

One of the significant guides for accomplishing library book selection, *Building Library Collections*, makes some strong points in support of the idea of the public library as a social institution with the responsibility for representing the democratic ideal of tolerance. Mary Carter and Wallace Bonk, authors of the work, believe that librarians should not play passive roles in the communities which support their institutions but that the force of the library should be used to help preserve free access to reliable and unbiased information.[11]

## The Public Librarian and the Freedom to Read

The rights of citizens of the United States to freedom of access to ideas and information have been firmly established in theories of public library service; the degree to which librarians are committed to supporting and defending these rights is indeed a socially significant issue. In a society which values and protects intellectual freedom, the individual can read what he pleases rather than what someone believes he ought to read. Thus the public librarian should not think that his role is to protect his public from unorthodox views or from controversial and unpopular subjects. Rather, the librarian should serve in a spirit and in reality as a provider of the widest diversities of views and expressions.

As public librarians are constantly involved in the selection of new books and other sources of information for a diversity of publics, and as it seems inevitable that there will always be controversial subjects, it is likely that the librarian will remain in the arena of public scrutiny by those citizens or groups who advocate repressive measures on reading and free communication. In his book *The Public Library in the United States*, Robert D. Leigh has pointed out that the public library has a responsibility for avoiding censorship and that, as an agency of municipal or county governments, the library cannot neglect the fact that it is accountable either for careful qualitative selection or for asserting a very broad area of free communication.[12]

In a democratic society in which sovereignty resides in the people, a book selection policy that is based on an equalitarian philosophy and allows the purchase of only "harmless" books of such a general nature as to offend no one is certainly contrary to the idea of freedom of choice. The question of whether a library should adopt such a policy is indeed a moot one. Carter and Bonk point out in *Building Library Collections* that a librarian's lack of faith in the people's judgment is paradoxical, and the authors ask: "If the people cannot be trusted to read and react intelligently, what can they be trusted with?"[13] According to Edwin Castagna, a past president of the American Library Association and a former chairman of its Intellectual Freedom Committee, the caution exercised by some public librarians to avoid controversial materials is often the result of timidity or ignorance. While that type of behavior cannot be labeled censorship in the general sense of the term, it is an intramural, restrictive practice, and the effect, as Castagna points out, is the same. Castagna also feels that the attitudes of librarians should be receptive and liberal, and that those responsible for libraries should accept and even seek out controversial material which might jar complacency and present an opportunity for people to examine contradictory ideas.[14]

When a public library follows a negative selection policy based on the avoidance of controversial materials, the collection which results is often devoid of any ideas and information dealing with many contemporary social, political, religious, and economic issues. Such a policy might produce a collection containing no works on civil rights; no books dealing with pressing social problems of urban areas; no information about social innovations and changes such as communal living; no information dealing with sex education, abortion, or homosexuality; no materials on drugs, narcotics, and drug addiction; no books dealing with anti-war movements and demonstrations; and no underground newspapers or periodicals. As unreasonable as that kind of situation might appear, past research dealing with censorship and book selection in libraries has revealed that some librarians have pursued, with varying intensity, non-controversial or non-offensive selection policies.

Suspicions about negative and non-offensive selection policies of some libraries have been voiced by leaders in the library profession. Wheeler and Goldhor have speculated in *Practical Administration of Public Libraries* that libraries are probably not subjected to a great deal of censorship pressures because librarians have acted as self-censors and have avoided controversial books.[15] Oliver Garceau also supports that suspicion; in his study of the relationship of the public library to the political process, the following statement concerning intramural censorship appears:

> The censorship of library holdings does not often become a public issue, largely because it is an intramural activity. As a member himself of the white collar middle class that uses his library, the librarian has a green thumb for cultivating those books that will be popular and an equal knack for weeding out what will be considered dangerous.[16]

### Intramural of Self-Imposed Censorship

While attempts to censor library collections do become public issues from time to time, and while a number of librarians have fought vigorously for the public's right to read when faced with censorship pressures, there is certainly substantial evidence that compromise with censors and voluntary censorship are practiced in some public libraries. The literature of librarianship contains numerous reminders that librarians are far from being unanimous in their opinions about the freedom to read. In *The Library Reaches Out*, Albert C. Lake voiced the suspicion that some librarians pay lip service to the right to inquiry and the freedom of access to books and information as abstract concepts but ignore their application in libraries.[17] In her study of the professional development of librarians, Elizabeth W. Stone discovered that many professional librarians recognize intellectual freedom, but only as a matter to which they have rarely paid attention. She found that the 1956 graduating class of library schools accredited by the American Library Association ranked intellectual freedom as an important professional matter, yet she also found that they devoted little attention to it.[18]

Robert H. Haney asserts in *Comstockery in America* that much of the censorship practiced today is of a subtle nature. He states: "Within the last hundred years, we Americans have developed various methods—crude and precise, official and unofficial, obvious and surreptitious—for controlling what is read, seen, and said."[19] If that statement truly reflects contemporary censorship practices, the library profession must determine whether librarians have developed their own sophisticated type of control—the methods of repression being more subtle, but the results being the same. In the controversy over positive book selection as opposed to intramural censorship in libraries, Lester Asheim has stated that repression of the freedom to read is undertaken by librarians when they, in the exercise of their own judgment, decide not to purchase a book which has every lawful justification to be included in the library's collection.[20]

The National Book Committee's study,[21] concerned primarily with problems of censorship and with the freedom to read books, underscored the fact that little was known about the extent to which censorial pressures affect the attitudes and behavior of librarians. The study also indicated that librarians were increasingly seeking to avoid public controversy by voluntarily curtailing the purchase and circulation of certain types of books. Despite the adoption of the *Library Bill of Rights* by the Council of the American Library Association, there are strong indications that some librarians endorse literary freedom statements, but that, when confronted with actual or anticipated censorship pressures, they react in a manner contrary to the principles of these same statements.

In 1962, the editors of *Library Journal* conducted a national survey to determine how many of 20 selected controversial novels were included in public library collections. Many of the books on the checklist distributed for the survey were deemed to be "problem" fiction, including such works as *Lolita, Wayward Wife, Tropic of Cancer, The Goddam White Man, Lady Chatterly's Lover,* and *The Carpetbaggers.* As a result of data compiled from returned checklists, the editors of the periodical concluded that readers in the Northeast could expect the widest range of controversial novels to be available on the shelves of public libraries. In the Midwest, on the other hand, book selection policies were labeled the most rigid, since Midwestern public libraries owned only 7.5 of the 20 controversial titles. The South followed with only 9.1 of the titles included in collections. As the sample of public libraries used in the study was neither random nor proportional in respect to all public libraries in the United States, the results of this study cannot be considered completely reliable;[22] however, they do heighten the suspicion that some librarians are avoiding controversial books.

## The Fiske Censorship Study

In 1959, Marjorie Fiske's report on book selection and censorship activities in school and public libraries of selected California communities was published. It was the result of a rigorous two-year study conducted between 1956 and 1958. Sociologist Fiske and her associates sought to determine whether censorship restrictions were being placed upon libraries or whether librarians were imposing limitations on themselves that threatened the citizen's right to easy access to adequate collections of books and materials. The study was made possible by a grant from the Fund for the Republic and was sponsored by the School of Librarianship of the Univeristy of California at Berkeley. It has had far-reaching effects on librarianship in the 13 years since its results were first published; for the findings were surprising (even shocking) to many people, both in and outside the library profession. Data collected for the study showed conclusively that many of the California librarians who served as respondents were themselves the most active censors of the contents of their libraries. The methodology employed by Fiske and her associates was carefully planned and executed, and only tested social science survey research techniques were used. Every effort was apparently made by the investigator to proceed at all steps of the research with scholarly caution in order to obtain objective data. *Book Selection and Censorship*[23] is the published report of Fiske's research.

The Fiske study found a surprising lack of actual censorship pressure for the removal or inclusion of books in selected school and public libraries in California; however, it showed that in the selection process librarians had so carefully screened their purchases beforehand that books likely to have caused complaints from patrons or school administrators were not added to collections. In other words, a conclusion was reached in the Fiske study that librarians were generally following the principle that the best way to avoid censorship controversies or pressures in libraries was to avoid purchasing controversial books. The study also revealed that there was strong evidence that many of the librarians acquiesced in favor of the complainant when confronted with objections to library materials from individuals or groups.

Nearly two-thirds of the librarians interviewed in California who were involved in book selection reported instances when a controversy about a book or author resulted in a decision not to purchase a work.[24] The report also showed that nearly one-fifth of these book selectors habitually avoided buying any controversial materials or books which they felt might become controversial.[25] The study uncovered various restrictions placed on the circulation or distribution of controversial books in 82 per cent of the 91 circulating library units used for the study.[26]

Fiske refrained from generalizing the findings of her study to libraries and librarians over the nation. As a matter of fact, she did not say that her findings were typical of California libraries. Findings and conclusions were limited to those libraries actually included in the sample; however, one cannot help suspecting that similar attitudes and actions prevail in school and public libraries in other states. The need for further research into library book-selection practices and the attitudes of librarians toward censorship and intellectual freedom has long been recognized within the profession. Replication of the Fiske study is needed in other geographic areas to determine whether librarians sometimes lack their profession's avowed dedication to the freedom to read and are limiting in various ways complete access to library collections. If a large number of librarians are discovered to be timid, voluntary censors of their collections and if they are too prone to compromise, too cautious, and do not speak out in strong defense of the library patron's right to inquiry and freedom to read, drastic measures in the areas of professional education and training of librarians and in library administration would appear to be in order.

The gravity of the censorship issue has been stated very well by Marie Jahoda. Writing in the book review selection of *The Public Opinion Quarterly*, Miss Jahoda made the following comment about the Fiske report:

> ... it raised the more fundamental problem of the public library as a democratic institution whose policies and practices require constructive thought if the principle of freedom to read is to become more than a slogan.[27]

The findings of the Fiske study in California raise two questions important to librarianship: 1) what causes some librarians to conform to convention rather than risk possible contention and 2) are there personality traits which are associated with censorship on the part of librarians? Without a doubt, no single psychological incentive could be selected as the salient influence causing such rigid adherence to conventional values. Daniel Katz, former president of the Society for Psychological Study of Social Issues, has cautioned behavioral scientists about the great error of oversimplification when a single cause is ascribed to given types of attitudes. He has stated that a number of motivational forces must be taken into account in the consideration of attitudes and behavior, and that an attitude can have a different basis in different people.[28]

The study of attitudes toward censorship and intellectual freedom which follows in Part II attempts to examine by means of survey research the opinions of a relatively large population of public librarians in the Midwest. It was based upon a doctoral dissertation at Indiana University by the author of this book.

## FOOTNOTES

[1] Harold D. Lasswell, "Censorship," in *Encyclopedia of the Social Sciences* (New York: Macmillan Co., 1930), 3:290.

[2] *Ibid.*, p. 291.

[3] Henry J. Abraham, "Censorship," in *International Encyclopedia of the Social Sciences* (New York: Macmillan Co. and the Free Press, 1968), 2:356.

[4] Robert D. Leigh, *The Public Library in the United States* (New York: Columbia University Press, 1950), p. 117.

[5] Paul Blanshard, *The Right to Read: The Battle Against Censorship* (Boston: Beacon Press, 1956), p. 64.

[6] Kenneth F. Kister, "Educating Librarians in Intellectual Freedom," *Library Trends* 19(1970):159.

[7] Robert B. Downs, "Freedom of Speech and Press: Development of a Concept," *Library Trends* 19(1970):18.

[8] American Library Association, Public Library Association Standards

Committee and Subcommittee, *Minimum Standards for Public Library Systems, 1966* (Chicago: American Library Association, 1967), p. 38.

[9] *Ibid.*, pp. 38-39.

[10] Marion E. Hawes, ed., *How Baltimore Chooses: Selection Policies of the Enoch Pratt Free Library* (Baltimore: Enoch Pratt Free Library, 1968), p. 5.

[11] Mary Duncan Carter and Wallace John Bonk, *Building Library Collections* (Metuchen, N. J.: Scarecrow Press, 1969), p. 155.

[12] Leigh, *The Public Library in the United States*, pp. 116-17.

[13] Carter and Bonk, *Building Library Collections*, p. 152.

[14] Edwin Castagna, "Nature and Development of Library Collections," *Local Public Library Administration*, ed. Roberta Bowler (Chicago: International City Manager Association, 1964), pp. 180-81.

[15] Joseph L. Wheeler and Herbert Goldhor, *Practical Administration of Public Libraries* (New York: Harper & Row, 1962), p. 461.

[16] Oliver Garceau, *The Public Library in the Political Process* (New York: Columbia University Press, 1949), p. 132.

[17] Charles Albert Lake, "Library Book Selection—Its Challenges and Responsibilities," in *The Library Reaches Out*, ed. Edwin Castagna (Dobbs Ferry, N. Y.: Oceana Publications, Inc., 1965), p. 196.

[18] Elizabeth W. Stone, *Factors Relating to the Professional Development of Librarians* (Metuchen, N. J.: Scarecrow Press, 1969), p. 140.

[19] Robert H. Haney, *Comstockery in America: Patterns of Censorship and Control* (Boston: Beacon Press, 1960), p. 1.

[20] Lester Asheim, "Not Censorship but Selection," *Wilson Library Bulletin* 28(1953):63.

[21] Richard McKeon and Robert K. Merton, *The Freedom to Read: Perspective and Program* (New York: R. R. Bowker Co., 1957).

[22] "'Problem' Fiction," *Library Journal* 87(1962):487.

[23] Marjorie Fiske, *Book Selection and Censorship: A Study of School and Public Libraries in California* (Berkeley: University of California Press, 1959).

[24] *Ibid.*, p. 64.

[25] *Ibid.*

[26] *Ibid.*, p. 69.

[27] Marie Jahoda, Review of *Book Selection and Censorship: A Study of School and Public Libraries in California*, by Marjorie Fiske, *The Public Opinion Quarterly* 25(1961):150-52.

[28] Daniel Katz, "The Functional Approach to the Study of Attitudes," *The Public Opinion Quarterly* 24(1960):167.

# PART II

# ATTITUDES OF
# MIDWESTERN PUBLIC LIBRARIANS
# TOWARD INTELLECTUAL FREEDOM
# AND CENSORSHIP: A STUDY

## CHAPTER 6
# INTRODUCTION TO THE STUDY AND METHODOLOGY

*Opinions cannot survive if one has no chance to fight for them.*

—Thomas Mann

### Purpose of the Study

Under the rubric "Opinion Survey of Midwestern Public Librarians," an opinion poll was conducted in 1970 among 3,253 public librarians in Illinois, Indiana, Michigan, Ohio, and Wisconsin for the following purposes: 1) to determine the extent to which librarians accept intellectual freedom principles of the *Library Bill of Rights* and the *Freedom to Read* statement, 2) to determine the attitudes of librarians toward censorship, 3) to determine the relationship of librarians' censorship attitudes to their attitudes toward selected authoritarian beliefs, and 4) to determine the relationship between librarians' intellectual freedom and censorship attitudes. By means of survey research among a random sample of public librarians, which was stratified and selected from the population, data were collected concerning attitudes by means of a questionnaire containing an intellectual freedom "test," a censorship attitude scale, and the F scale on authoritarianism. The selected sample of 900 librarians was approximately 28 per cent of the population size, and 76 per cent of the distributed questionnaires were returned. The data for the study reported in Part II of this book are based on 624 usable questionnaires, or 69 per cent of the total distributed to public librarians.

Questions relating to the magnitude of the practice of intramural censorship documented in the Fiske study in California and questions pertaining to the psychological motives underlying these voluntary repressive measures on intellectual freedom in libraries provoked the opinion research in this investigation. Since the findings of the Fiske study cannot be generalized to the entire population of public librarians in the United States, there exists a need to conduct further research about library book-selection practices and the attitudes of public librarians toward censorship and intellectual freedom.

The study reported here did not make use of the same methodology employed by Fiske, as it was not the investigator's purpose to examine actual book-selection practices. This study did attempt to measure the attitudes and opinions about censorship and intellectual freedom held by public librarians in five Midwestern states. It also correlated these findings with certain syndromes of authoritarianism with the use of the F scale, an indirect measure of anti-democratic trends. Adorno's work, *The Authoritarian Personality*,[1]

93

provided a strategy for the analysis of at least one aspect of personality, and it seems particularly germane to an inquiry into the opinions of librarians about repressivism in view of conclusions of the Fiske report.

An individual possessing an authoritarian personality has been described as:

> One who craves unquestioning obedience and subordination. This is the defining quality, but various other qualities are believed to be generally associated with it such as a servile acceptance of superior authority, scorn for weakness, rigidity, rejection of out-groups, conventionality, desire to have everything clearly marked off and determined . . .[2]

On the other hand, Adorno has pointed out that in contrast to the bigot of the older style the authoritarian type of man:

> . . . seems to combine the ideals and skills which are typical of a highly industrialized society with irrational or antirational beliefs. He is at the same time enlightened and superstitious, proud to be an individualist and in constant fear of not being like all the others, jealous of his independence and inclined to submit to power and authority.[3]

The Adorno study of the authoritarian personality also revealed that the authoritarian is driven by the fear of being weak, that he displays an intolerance of ambiguity, that he is uncomfortable when faced with complex or uncertain situations which do not easily yield to understanding or to control, and that he suffers from anxiety if and when he deviates from conventional moral standards. In the present study, however, an investigation of antidemocratic attitudes of librarians was undertaken in order to determine the relationship of pro-censorship attitudes to authoritarian ideas and beliefs.

While the study was undertaken with the expectation that attitudes of librarians toward censorship, intellectual freedom, and authoritarianism would be positively related and that certain independent variables such as size of the community and librarians' ages and sexes would be closely associated with attitudes, the five hypotheses postulated for the study were stated as the opposite of what the investigator expected, i.e., negatively in the form of null hypotheses. Numerical precision and testability are more readily obtained in testing null hypotheses than in testing positive ones; based on the rule of negative inference in logic, null hypotheses can be proved or disproved more easily than their positive counterparts. The following five hypotheses were established for this study of censorship and intellectual freedom attitudes among Midwestern public librarians:

1. There is no significant relationship between the attitudes of librarians toward intellectual freedom and the attitudes of librarians toward censorship.

2. There is no significant relationship between the attitudes of librarians toward intellectual freedom as expressed in the *Library Bill of Rights* and the *Freedom to Read* statement and the following variables: (a) age, (b) sex, (c) size of the community of employment, (d) position of the librarian in the library, (e) state in which employed, and (f) educational attainment level.

3. There is no significant relationship between the attitudes of librarians toward censorship and the variables (a-f) listed in Hypothesis 2.

4. There is no significant relationship between the attitudes of librarians toward characteristic authoritarian beliefs contained in selected F scale items of the authoritarian personality test and the attitudes of librarians toward censorship.

5. There is no significant relationship between the attitudes of librarians toward characteristic authoritarian beliefs contained in the F scale items from the authoritarian personality test and the variables (a-f) listed in Hypothesis 2.

## Selection of the Sample and Development of the Questionnaire

The research methodology and the various procedures used to obtain data for the support or rejection of the hypotheses of this study were developed after the general purpose and scope of the investigation had been delineated. These methods and procedures included: (a) identification of the population to be surveyed; (b) determination of the type of sample to be selected; (c) choosing the dependent variables and the pertinent independent variables of the opinion research; (d) development of the questionnaire, including its format and the logistical techniques to be used in distributing the instrument; and (e) determination of the procedures to be used in analyzing the collected data.

Survey research techniques were chosen as the means of collecting data in this opinion research, since this method allowed the investigation of the opinions of a large population comprised of 3,253 public librarians. A complete enumeration of the population of Midwestern public librarians would have required more time and financial support than was available for the project. Instead, a sample, selected by a purely random process, was used to obtain essentially the same data as could have been obtained by a study of the entire population, and the research was conducted at considerably less expense but with appropriate efficiency and accuracy. The selection from the population of a sample of public librarians and the analysis of the attitudes of these librarians allowed an examination of the relative incidences, distribution, and interrelations of sociological and psychological variables of all public librarians in the east north-central states.

## The Population

The Midwest has frequently been referred to as the heartland of the North American continent, both geographically and functionally. Illinois, Indiana, Michigan, Ohio, and Wisconsin, the five east north-central states from which the population of this study was selected, comprise a major portion of the Midwestern region and approximately 15 per cent of the total land area of the United States. Rank orders by population of the five east north-central states in comparison to the other 50 states are as follows: Illinois, 4; Indiana, 12; Michigan, 7; Ohio, 6; and Wisconsin, 16.[4] As can be seen in Table 1, 70.7 per cent of the population of the east north-central states is concentrated in urban areas. This is very close to the national average of 69.9 per cent of the population in urban areas. The per cent of growth of the east north-central states during the period 1900 to 1960 is also provided in Table 1. These states experienced a growth percentage of 128.4, and during the same period the per cent of growth of the United States was 135.5, a similar but slightly greater rate.

While the states from which the population of this study was selected form a distinct geographic area, and while there are a number of population characteristics which could be recognized as representative of the nation as a whole, these factors were not the most important criteria in the selection of an area from which to draw a population of librarians. A more important reason for selecting respondents from the Midwest for this study was the fact that an indigenous American culture has been recognized in the region. The following explanation of the development of Midwestern culture is contained in *The North American Midwest, A Regional Geography*:

> It has been said many times that if a distinctive American culture is to evolve it will develop in the Midwest. Today, in the core of the continent at the very center of the nation, is a distinctive Midwestern culture. Not a blatant sectionalism or even state pride, for many see nothing spectacular or even interesting about the Midwest; it is a way of life based upon an unprecedented continental position and boundless natural wealth which views world order in a different fashion from that of the seaboards. Remote from the sea yet readily accessible, the Midwest developed in terms of itself rather than as an adjunct to Europe or a gateway to some other part of the world . . . . Without the restrictions of tradition and separated from the centers of origin by restrictive physical barriers, Midwestern culture is the result of the impact of a rigorous people on an entirely new natural environment, the potential of which has been slow to be understood and appreciated. Akin to all yet comparable to none, Midwestern culture is truly the indigenous American culture.[5]

In consideration of factors relevant to population and cultural characteristics, and in view of the fact that the Midwestern states contained a manageable population of public librarians whose attitudes toward censorship and the freedom to read could be obtained within the financial and time limitations available for this study, the population for this investigation was identified as public librarians employed in the east north-central states.

In addition to the requirement of residence and employment in one of the east north-central states, respondents identified in the frame for this survey had to be employed in municipal or county tax-supported public libraries. Another prerequisite for inclusion of librarians in the population was employment in one of the five job classifications established for the survey. Each classification was assigned a code designation (A-E), and they were as follows: (A) director or chief administrator of a public library; (B) assistant director or administrative assistant; (C) branch librarian; (D) head of a public service department; and (E) head of a subject, extension, or technical service department. The decision to include librarians who were in job classifications B through E along with

96

## TABLE 1

## POPULATION CHARACTERISTICS, EAST NORTH-CENTRAL STATES[1] AND NUMBER OF PUBLIC LIBRARIANS BY STATES INCLUDED IN THE SAMPLE[2]

| State | Total Population 1960 | Rank Order by Population | Per cent Urban | Per cent Growth 1900-1960 | Number Public Librarians | Per cent of Population | Number Selected in Sample | Usable Question-aires Returned |
|---|---|---|---|---|---|---|---|---|
| Illinois | 10,081,158 | 4 | 80.7 | 109.1 | 773 | 24 | 216 | 133 |
| Indiana | 4,662,498 | 12 | 62.4 | 85.3 | 490 | 16 | 144 | 94 |
| Michigan | 7,823,194 | 7 | 73.4 | 223.1 | 722 | 22 | 198 | 142 |
| Ohio | 9,706,397 | 6 | 73.4 | 133.4 | 787 | 24 | 216 | 159 |
| Wisconsin | 3,951,777 | 16 | 63.8 | 91.0 | 481 | 14 | 126 | 96 |
| Totals | | | | | 3,253 | 100 | 900 | 624 |
| East North-Central States | 36,225,024 | — | 70.7 | 128.4 | | | | |
| U.S.A. (48 states) | 179,323,175 | — | 69.9 | 135.5 | | | | |

[1] U.S. Census of Population, 1960.
[2] Sample size was 900, or 27.6 per cent of the total population of public librarians in the East North-Central States (3,253).

directors or heads of libraries was based on the assumption that a truly representative expression of opinions about censorship and intellectual freedom among Midwestern public librarians could not be obtained by surveying chief librarians alone. Implicit in this assumption is the conviction that heads of departments and services help formulate and implement the institution's programs and services, including book selection; work with children and young people; circulation work; reference, bookmobile, extension, and audiovisual services; public relations; and reader's advisory programs. Consequently, the inclusion of all librarians who were in charge of or directing these programs and activities represents an attempt in the design of the sample to minimize bias and maximize the reliability of collected data.

The identification of librarians employed in public libraries in the east north-central states was made by using the 1968-69 *American Library Directory*[6] and current state library and library association lists and directories for the five Midwestern states. Several supplementary lists were also secured from state library associations, and they were used to update previously published directories.

## Determination of the Type of Sample

In 1968, Charles J. Adams, librarian of the LaPorte (Indiana) Public Library, conducted a statewide survey of selection practices in regard to controversial books in Indiana public libraries. As a result of the research, Adams concluded that the size of the population served was "of overriding importance as a determining factor in attempting to predict whether a given library unit might tend to be permissive (positive) or rigid (negative) in its approach to political *and* sexual writings."[7] While size of population served by a library and size of population of the city in which a library is located may not necessarily be the same, there is a high positive correlation between these two variables.

The size of the population of towns and cities proved to be an important variable insofar as attitudes of librarians were concerned in the final pre-test of the questionnaire prepared for the present investigation. Because public libraries are located in very small communities as well as medium-sized and large cities, and because there was evidence that the attitudes of librarians are affected by this variable, a decision was made to stratify the population according to population-size categories or strata. Categorization of libraries by size of communities is shown in Table 2. The criterion for dividing the universe according to stratification variables was the size of the community or city in which librarians were employed. The frame was divided into homogeneous strata consisting of the seven population-size categories shown in Table 2. Authority for the determination of the populations of all communities, towns, and cities was the 1960 *Census of the Population of the United States.*[8] The stratification of the population was based on a table of population as a guide to public library size as listed in "Quantitative Guides to Public Library Operation."[9] Stratum I consisted of librarians employed in communities of under 5,000 inhabitants, and the librarians were further subdivided into increasing population increments up to stratum number VII, in which librarians employed in Chicago, the largest city,

## TABLE 2

### NUMBER OF LIBRARIANS IN THE POPULATION OF THE STUDY AND IN THE SAMPLE AND PERCENTAGE OF QUESTIONNAIRE RETURNS ACCORDING TO POPULATION-SIZE CATEGORY

| Category | Description | Population Range | Number Librarians in Category | Per cent Librarians in Category | Number Librarians Selected in Sample | Usable Question-naires Returned | Per cent of Returns* |
|---|---|---|---|---|---|---|---|
| I | (a) very small | under 5,000 | 1,000 | 31 | 276 | 156 | 62 |
| II | (b) very small | 5,000-14,999 | 534 | 16 | 147 | 116 | 79 |
| III | (c) very small | 15,000-34,999 | 446 | 14 | 125 | 91 | 73 |
| IV | small | 35,000-99,999 | 498 | 15 | 137 | 107 | 78 |
| V | medium | 100,000-399,999 | 372 | 12 | 102 | 80 | 78 |
| VI | large | 4,000,000-1,200,000 | 258 | 8 | 73 | 43 | 59 |
| VII | very large | above 1,200,000 | 145 | 4 | 40 | 22 | 55 |
| Totals | — | — | 3,253 | 100 | 900 | 624 | 69 |

[1] 684 questionnaires were returned, of which 624 were usable. The overall rate of return was 76 per cent; usable rate of return was 69 per cent.

were classed. Some examples of the classification of libraries into strata follow: librarians in Fennimore, Wisconsin, with a 1960 census population of under 5,000 were placed in stratum I; librarians in Lorain, Ohio, with a population falling between 35,000 and 99,000 were classed in category IV; and librarians in Chicago, with a population of more than 1,200,000, were classed in category VII.

After the population had been divided into homogeneous subparts or strata, a simple random sample was drawn from each stratum for each state. In order to make the subsamples proportional, their sizes were determined according to the percentage of librarians in the population in each of the strata. For example, 74 Wisconsin public librarians fell within the parameters of the population of this study and were classed in population-size category IV. That number represents 15 per cent of all the librarians in Wisconsin falling within the parameters and counted in the state's population of librarians for the purpose of this investigation. Consequently, 15 per cent, or 19, of the 126 librarians selected in the Wisconsin sample were chosen from population-size stratum IV.

In order to obtain a proportional sample in respect to the varied population-size categories in which public librarians were employed, a stratified probability sample was chosen as the means for selecting respondents. The selection of a random probability sample from the universe insured that each individual in the group being studied had an equal chance of being selected.

## Choosing the Sample

Separate cards were prepared for each librarian in order to select a probability sample from the population numbering 3,253. All names and addresses of librarians were entered on the cards, along with identifying codes consisting of numbers and letters indicating state, population-size category, and job classification. The cards were separated by states and further subdivided within state groupings according to population-size categories. This was done in order to facilitate the use of a stratified random-sampling technique.

Although a sample of 20 per cent would normally have been adequate for a population of the size of this study, a sample size of more than that number was decided upon in order to compensate for the fact that some of the librarians selected would have changed positions or terminated their employment as listed in available directories. A decision was made to select 900 librarians in the sample, a number which comprised 27.6 per cent of the total population. A breakdown of the number of librarians according to states included in the population and in the sample is provided in Table 1.

## The Variables

Although the population comprised a relatively homogeneous group of librarians who were all employed in municipal libraries in Midwestern states, several qualitative and quantitative independent variables were identified and used in the analysis of data. Qualitative independent variables were sex, state

100

where employed, and position held by each respondent in the library of employment. Quantitative independent variables were age, educational attainment level, and size of the community in which librarians were employed. Age was broken down in the demographic section of the questionnaire into nine categories, ranging from a 19- to 21-year-old category to a 43- to 45-year-old increment. Respondents in the over 45-year-old bracket were placed in a category so designated without further differentiation on the assumption that, if age was of significance as an independent variable, a differentiation among the opinions of respondents would be evident within the ten age categories provided. In addition to this reason, the age categories were not expanded beyond 45 years in order to keep the demographic section as brief as possible and to avoid the possibility of offending those individuals who might be sensitive about revealing their age.

Four major educational attainment levels were established into which respondents were placed: (1) high school, (2) junior college, (3) four-year college, and (4) fifth-year library science degree. A fifth category for respondents who had attended but had not completed college was further subdivided during the scoring process into four brackets: (1) one to 30 credit hours, (2) 31 to 60 credit hours, (3) 61 to 90 credit hours, and (4) more than 91 credit hours. These categories approximate the number of credit hours generally completed by college freshmen, sophomores, juniors, and seniors, respectively.

## The Questionnaire

The problem in this investigation of attitudes in a sensitive subject area was not that of making a decision to ask librarians questions. It was, however, the structuring of a questionnaire which would measure exactly what it proposed to measure—attitudes toward censorship and the freedom to read. By necessity, the questionnaire had to replace face-to-face interviews, which would have been conducted with respondents had time and more financial support been available. It was necessary, consequently, to devise a set of questions or items and to put them into a printed questionnaire in order to elicit respondents' opinions. Efforts were made to structure an instrument which would measure with high degrees of reliability and validity the librarians' existing predispositions to respond to the concept of intellectual freedom and free access to books and ideas. Opinions of librarians about restrictive outside censorship pressures also had to be determined, as well as attitudes toward intramural censorship. In other words, the purpose of the questionnaire was to obtain a measure of respondents' agreement with abstract concepts of intellectual freedom as expressed in the *Library Bill of Rights* and the *Freedom to Read* statement, as well as a measure of their agreement with these concepts when they were made operational through situational and other dispositional variables and set down in statements or questions in a formal questionnaire.

The specific manifestations of intellectual freedom and censorship matters in relation to public libraries were already known. In a theoretical context, the ideal behavior of librarians in regard to intellectual freedom has been established in philosophies of library service, and this behavior should function as a guideline for the practicing librarian. Consequently, the questionnaire was not designed to determine whether librarians could recall acceptable practice or ideal behavior. Its purpose was to obtain from a permissive-repressive intellectual freedom scale a quantitative index of each librarian's attitude toward censorship. In other words, since the desired and acceptable attitudes of librarians toward intellectual freedom and censorship have already been established, the questionnaire's purpose was to determine the respondents' agreement or disagreement with these attitudes. These considerations precluded the need for open-ended questions; therefore, items incorporated into the questionnaire were structured for fixed-alternative responses.

Another factor contributing to the rejection of open-ended questions was the idea of a strong possibility that a study of censorship attitudes (a relatively sensitive area of inquiry) would elicit irrelevant and unpredictable responses, many of which might be of an emotional nature. Responses to issues perceived by some respondents as "touchy" would undoubtedly have made coding and analysis of written comments difficult if not impossible. Likert-type attitude scales with fixed alternative responses provided a method for stating and delineating issues in items which were as precisely worded as possible. A numerical ranking for each fixed response was devised on a scale containing predetermined units of measurement. Quantitative values of the units were completely reversed among the items in order to obtain more flexibility in stating questions. It was possible, therefore, to slant the statements in items of the questionnaire both positively and negatively.

Two criteria were established in devising items to be included in the censorship portion of the questionnaire: 1) the items had to be designed to elicit responses that were psychologically related to a librarian's attitude toward censorship, and 2) the scaled items had to show a differentiation among respondents who might have varying views toward censorship, or whose views would be at different points along a continuum ranging from a position of opposition to censorship to one of approval of censorship. The following item from the censorship scale illustrates the use of the first criterion: "Librarians should be especially watchful to see that books containing unorthodox views are kept from their collections." In fulfilling the second criterion of discriminating among respondents who might differ slightly, fixed-alternative responses to items permitted the expression of various degrees of agreement and disagreement with each item. An example of this can be seen in the following item and the provided fixed-alternative responses:

Item 8. Since librarians are in a position to recognize dangerous ideas in books and other printed materials, they should carefully control their circulation to the general public.

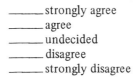

_____ strongly agree
_____ agree
_____ undecided
_____ disagree
_____ strongly disagree

This juxtaposing of the attitude objects of this investigation (censorship and repressive measures on reading) in hypothetical situations described in items of the questionnaire represented an attempt to determine the attitudes of librarians toward the freedom to read, in accord with the use of the term "attitude" in the behavioral sciences. In this investigation, the use of the term corresponds with Milton Rokeach's definition which follows:

> An attitude is a relatively enduring organization of interrelated beliefs that describe, evaluate, and advocate action with respect to an object or situation, with each belief having cognitive, affective, and behavioral components. Each one of these beliefs is a predisposition that when suitably activated results in some preferential response toward the attitude object or situation, or toward others who take a position with respect to the maintenance or preservation of the attitude itself. Since an attitude object must always be encountered within some situation about which we also have an attitude, a minimum condition for social behavior is the activation of at least two interacting attitudes, one concerning the attitude object and the other concerning the situation.[10]

Intramural or self censorship on the part of the public librarian is normally a rather sensitive subject, so that some of the items devised to measure relevant attitudes were indirect, allowing respondents to project questions to other people. For example, items 21 and 34 of Part I of the questionnaire allowed respondents to transfer the issue to another party:

Item 21. If a person or group in the community complains about a book in a library's collection because of an objectionable sexual theme or because of frank terminology, the librarian should attempt to absolve himself by claiming that sexual themes and four-letter words are included in most present-day novels.

Item 34. Library users who want to read erotic novels like *Return to Peyton Place, The Carpetbaggers, God's Little Acre, Candy,* and *Fanny Hill* should not expect to find them in the public library but should buy their own.

The questionnaire was divided into three major parts. The cover page dealt with demographic information from which pertinent facts about the independent variables could be extracted for each respondent. The three numbered parts contained the various items or questions designed to measure the sought-after opinions. They were as follows: Part I, 18 items about censorship and 18 items about intellectual freedom interspersed on pages two through five; Part II, items on page five of the questionnaire which were not part of the three attitude scales but were concerned with unresolved issues about which no conclusive evidence has been established; and Part III, 18 items from the F scale of the authoritarian personality test listed on pages six and seven. A copy of the questionnaire is provided in Appendix I.

Items included in Part II dealt with parental responsibility for children's reading, the relationship between reading pornography and juvenile delinquency, the permissiveness or restrictiveness of present laws dealing with obscenity in books and other printed matter, and judgments about reading tastes. The four items in Part II were included in a separate section because they were not scored as a part of the attitude scales; however, the opinions of librarians about these unresolved issues were solicited in order to obtain additional information germane to the respondents' feelings toward censorship and the freedom to read.

The F scale of the authoritarian personality test was listed separately in Part III of the questionnaire because items in the scale were uniquely different from the censorship and intellectual freedom items. Listing the F scale items in a separate section allowed respondents to consider them in a specific order and as a related entity, in addition to enhancing the internal consistency of the instrument as a whole.

Censorship is any activity related to the prohibition of expression or communication. Because it is often in effect an attempt to impose conventionalism and to reject ideas and values which are in conflict with the conventional, the established order, or prevailing morals, it appears to be very closely related to an underlying authoritarian belief system. Despite the fact that Adorno and his associates admitted that the F scale does not yield an accurate estimate of fascist receptivity at the personality level, the highly discriminatory items from the scale were used in order to determine whether they correlated significantly with pro-censorship attitudes which were measured by the censorship attitude scale constructed for the present investigation.

Eighteen items from the F scale on authoritarianism were used in Section III of the questionnaire. These items were taken from the revised Forms 45 and 40 prepared by Adorno and his associates in their attempt to measure antidemocratic trends. The items used in the present investigation had demonstrated high degrees of discriminatory power in a number of tests in authoritarian personality studies. Items from the test which were no longer timely or which have been shown to have low discriminatory power were not used in this opinion research.

### Pre-Testing the Questionnaire

The first draft of the questionnaire contained 33 items, all pertaining to censorship. It was devised by the investigator in 1968 and was pre-tested, revised, and subsequently tested again a number of times in preparation for the present investigation. Since items for measuring respondents' attitudes toward intellectual freedom were taken almost verbatim from the *Library Bill of Rights* and the *Freedom to Read* statement, they were not included in any of the pre-tests. Four pre-tests of the censorship portion of the questionnaire were conducted prior to the final mailing; however, eight major revisions of the instrument had been made before the final draft was completed. Prior to the first pre-test, the questionnaire was scrutinized by a number of librarians and by library educators, all of whom made suggestions for deleting, adding, or revising items.

Revisions were based on pertinent suggestions, and the questionnaire was then pre-tested on two additional groups: 1) a composite group of both graduate and undergraduate library science students, and 2) a group of seven library science doctoral students. As a result of the first two pre-tests, the original items designed to measure censorship attitudes were decreased in number to 27.

The subsequent pre-test proved to be useful in restructuring the question-naire, in rephrasing some censorship items, and in allowing the elimination of additional items shown to be irrelevant. The exploratory study was conducted in December 1968 among all students in the Master of Library Science degree program of the Indiana University Graduate Library School. A total of 135 questionnaires was distributed to students, and 96 usable ones were returned. The questionnaire also included the F scale from the authoritarian personality test. Results of the opinion research among students were included in an article entitled "Student Attitudes Toward Censorship and Authoritarianism."[11]

As a result of the previously described pre-test, a t-test was performed on all items in the attitude scale in order to eliminate those which did not differentiate between high- and low-scorers. Five of the items showed either low or no differentiation and were eliminated from the questionnaire. The phraseology of several additional items was altered to clarify item or single-word ambiguities with which some students had expressed difficulty. Several new statements were devised and added as replacements for those eliminated items that contained problems or issues about which a measure of attitudes was needed. Further consultations with public librarians and library educators were held, and these resulted in additional revisions based on suggestions.

A final pre-test was conducted in the spring of 1970 among a randomly selected group of 40 public librarians in Iowa, Minnesota, and Missouri. These states were not included in the population of the present study; however, they are immediately west of three of the states which were included. Since these states selected for the pre-test were in close proximity to the states from which the final sample was taken, an assumption was made that the attitudes of librarians in these two areas would not differ significantly.

Twenty-eight of the questionnaires were returned in the final pre-test. Additional t-tests were performed on items, and two more questions were eliminated. A few minor changes were also made in the phraseology of items, and the censorship items were reduced in number to 18. These 18 items, along with items from the *Library Bill of Rights, Freedom to Read* statement, and the F scale of the authoritarian personality test, were brought together in a four-part questionnaire containing 58 items, not including nine demographic questions listed on the cover of the questionnaire. The final draft of the instrument was then prepared for reproduction for the present opinion research.

## Organization of the Measuring Instrument

A cover letter was attached to the seven-page instrument. Typed on printed letterhead stationery designed especially for the survey, the letter identified the investigator, gave his address, justified the study in rather general terms, informed the respondent that a name was not required on the questionnaire, and promised both personal and institutional anonymity of returned replies. Care was taken in the wording of the cover letter to conceal the specific purpose of the opinion research. This was done by merely stating: "The survey is an attempt to determine how librarians feel about a number of library issues and socially important topics . . . ." The exact purpose of the survey was shielded in order to avoid, insofar as possible, the effect of saliency, which results when respondents realize that their attitudes about a particular subject, object, or issue are being measured and that they are expected to have certain opinions about the topic. This recognition could have caused a tendency on the part of librarians to express those attitudes toward censorship and intellectual freedom which they deemed acceptable to professional librarians, their membership group. Although some of the respondents might have ascertained or suspected the general purpose of the research, care was taken in introducing the study and in presenting the questionnaire not to specify that the instrument was contrived to measure censorship and intellectual freedom attitudes. To have done so would have allowed respondents to predict the attitudes reflected by their responses; hence, the effects of saliency on attitude scores would have been greater.

The 18 items constituting a measure or test of a librarian's attitude toward censorship were designed to determine the extent of tolerance allowed for repressive measures on freedom of access to books and information. These items were dichotomous questions requiring a response of either "agree" or "disagree," to which were also appended "strongly agree" and "strongly disagree." An "undecided" response alternative was also included for those librarians who could not decide about a question. These five fixed-alternative responses for each of the 18 items served as an index of the respondents' degrees of tolerance for censorship activity. In terms of degrees of agreement or disagreement each librarian was asked to indicate on a scale the response which most closely expressed his or her view about each item. Provided below are two items, with directions, from Section I of the questionnaire:

**DIRECTIONS**: Please read all statements carefully and decide for each whether you strongly agree, agree, are undecided, disagree, or strongly disagree.

Item 2. There is a place in public libraries for periodicals which contain "left wing" articles such as *Ramparts, Evergreen Review, Liberation,* and *Avant Garde.*

| Strongly agree (1) | Agree (2) | Undecided (3) | Disagree (4) | Strongly disagree (5) |
|---|---|---|---|---|

Item 14. A censorship controversy over a single book or magazine is not worth the adverse public relations which it could cause for the library.

| Strongly agree (1) | Agree (2) | Undecided (3) | Disagree (4) | Strongly disagree (5) |
|---|---|---|---|---|

Numbers under each scale position indicate the scoring system used, but they were not included in the questionnaire. All responses to items were scored according to one of the two methods indicated, depending on whether the response was favorable or unfavorable toward censorship.

To enhance the validity of the measures being sought, all issues and problems contained in items of the questionnaire were based on one or more of the following: a) remarks about censorship from the literature of librarianship made by recognized leaders in librarianship, and b) editorial comments contained in the *Newsletter on Intellectual Freedom*. David K. Berninghausen's monograph on the teaching of a commitment to intellectual freedom was also of particular help in preparing the original items for the questionnaire.[12] *Research Methods in Social Relations*[13] by Claire Selltiz was used as a guide for writing items and for structuring the questionnaire. Weighting of censorship items was separately checked against independent criteria such as the *Library Bill of Rights* and the *Freedom to Read* statement as well as by jury opinion obtained in consultation with public library leaders and library educators.

### Mailing and Return of the Questionnaires

Under the rubric "Opinion Survey of Midwestern Public Librarians," the questionnaires were mailed to respondents in the summer of 1970. The complete mailing consisted of the seven-page questionnaire, a cover letter, and a pre-addressed, stamped envelope. Respondents were urged to return the questionnaire within ten days. After a two-week period had passed, the first follow-up letter encouraging participation was sent to respondents who had not replied. Enclosed with the letter was a postal card on which respondents were asked to indicate the status of their questionnaire or whether or not they wished to participate in the survey. By the end of August 1970, 71 per cent of the questionnaires had been returned. Although the rate of response was considered to be rather high, far surpassing initial expectations, a second follow-up letter, which made a final plea for participation, was mailed on October 1, 1970. Since it was the investigator's intention to obtain maximum participation in the survey research, a second copy of the questionnaire was also enclosed with the last follow-up letter. As a result of the final letter, the total response rate was increased to 76 per cent. Copies of the questionnaire, cover letter, follow-up letters, and the postal card are provided in Appendix I.

Of the 900 questionnaires mailed to respondents, 684 were returned, a response rate of 76 per cent of the total. Sixty of the instruments were either incomplete or improperly filled out and were discarded as unusable. The final data in this study, consequently, were based on the replies of 624 public librarians, and that number represents a total response rate of 69.3 per cent from the sample.

## FOOTNOTES

[1] T. W. Adorno, et al. *The Authoritarian Personality* (New York: Harper & Brothers, 1950).

[2] Horace B. English and Ava Champney English, *A Comprehensive Dictionary of Psychological and Psychoanalytical Terms: A Guide to Usage* (New York: David McKay Co., 1962), pp. 53-54.

[3] Adorno, *The Authoritarian Personality*, p. ix.

[4] U. S. Bureau of the Census, *Statistical Abstract of the United States: 1969* (Washington: Government Printing Office, 1969), p. 12.

[5] John H. Garland, *The North American Midwest: A Regional Geography* (New York: John Wiley & Sons, Inc., 1955), pp. 15-16.

[6] F. Steiner-Prag, comp., *American Library Directory 1968-69* (New York: R. R. Bowker Company, 1968).

[7] Charles J. Adams and Clayton Shepherd, "Censorship or Selection? in Hoosier Libraries," *Focus on Indiana Libraries* 22(1968):58.

[8] U. S. Bureau of the Census, *U. S. Census of Population: 1960*, vol. 1, Characteristics of the Population (Washington: Government Printing Office, 1963).

[9] Charles E. Rockwood and Ruth H. Rockwood, "Quantitative Guides to Public Library Operation," *Occasional Papers*, University of Illinois Graduate School of Library Science 89(1967):14.

[10] Milton Rokeach, "The Nature of Attitudes," in *International Encyclopedia of the Social Sciences* (New York: The Macmillan Company and the Free Press, 1968), 1:457.

[11] Charles H. Busha, "Student Attitudes toward Censorship and Authoritarianism," *Journal of Education for Librarianship* 11(1970):118-36.

[12] David K. Berninghausen, "Teaching a Commitment to Intellectual Freedom," *Library Journal* 92(1967):3601-3605.

[13] Claire Selltiz, et al., *Research Methods in Social Relations* (New York: Holt, Rinehart and Winston, 1961).

# CHAPTER 7
# ANALYSIS OF THE DATA

*You can spot the bad critic when he starts*
*by discussing the poet and not the poem.*
                                        —Ezra Loomis Pound

## Some Characteristics of the Sample

Eighty-one per cent, or 508, of the respondents were females, and 19 per cent, or 116, were males. Fifty-one per cent of both the male respondents and the female respondents were over 45 years old. Among the respondents, 330 had completed the fifth-year library science degree, and of these 107 were males and 222 were females. Without the fifth-year library science degree were 295 respondents; however, 99 of that group had earned degrees from four-year colleges. Respondents without either the fifth-year library science degree or a degree from a four-year college totaled 196, but, among that number, 21 were graduated from junior colleges, and an additional 87 had earned some college credits. Those respondents who had earned college credits but had not attained degrees from either a junior or a four-year college fell into the following categories: 1) 29 had completed between one and 30 credit hours, 2) 27 had completed between 31 and 60 credit hours, 3) 20 had completed between 61 and 90 credit hours, and 4) 11 had completed more than 91 credit hours. Eighty-one of the respondents had no formal education beyond high school, and six of the respondents were not graduated from high school.

In respect to type of positions into which responding librarians fell, 311 of the librarians who returned questionnaires were either directors, head librarians, or chief administrators of public libraries. Twenty-six of the respondents were assistant directors or administrative assistants. The total number of branch librarians responding was 106, and another 65 of them were heads of subject, extension, or technical services departments. Heads of public service departments totaled 116.

Sixty-two per cent (representing 133 respondents) of the questionnaires sent to librarians in Illinois were returned. Questionnaires returned from Indiana totaled 94 or 65 per cent of the number sent. Michigan librarians returned 142 questionnaires, or 72 per cent of the number mailed. One hundred fifty-nine questionnaires were returned by Ohio librarians, that number representing 74 per cent of the total number of instruments mailed to librarians in that state. Ninety-six questionnaires were returned by Wisconsin librarians, and that number represents 76 per cent of the instruments mailed to librarians in that state. The overall return rate of usable questionnaires was slightly more than 69 per cent of the total distributed.

109

Table 2 in Chapter 6 contains the number and percentages of questionnaires returned according to population-size categories. As can be discerned from data displayed in the table, the highest rate of return was from librarians working in communities with populations between 5,000 and 14,999. Seventy-nine per cent of the questionnaires mailed to these librarians were returned. The second highest rate of return was obtained from librarians in cities with populations which fell between 35,000 and 399,999; 78 per cent of the total number of questionnaires mailed to librarians in categories IV and V were returned. Fifty-five per cent was the lowest rate of return from any single population-size category; that category was VII (more than 1,200,000).

The greatest number of questionnaires distributed to librarians in any single population-size category was 173, and that category was I, into which librarians employed in the smallest towns and communities were placed and from which the rate of return was 63 per cent. Only 29 of the responding librarians from population-size category I had obtained a fifth-year library science degree. That number represents approximately 16 per cent of the 173 librarians in the smallest communities who responded in the opinion survey. Fifty-six of the 173 librarians in population-size category I had not obtained formal education beyond the high school level. A more detailed analysis of sample characteristics will be provided in subsequent sections of this report which deal with the relationship of independent variables to attitude scores.

## Scoring and Coding of Item Responses

After the incompleted and improperly marked questionnaires had been eliminated, the usable 624 instruments were scored, and the data were manually coded prior to being keypunched on machine-readable cards at the Indiana University Research Computing Center. In order to insure accuracy of data keypunching, the cards were all verified, and corrections were made when necessary. Many of the calculations performed with the data deck during the course of this study were made by a computer; however, some statistical computations were done manually in order to conduct reliability and validity tests which were not included in the standardized computer programs used.

The first step in analyzing the data consisted of manual scoring of responses to all items of the questionnaire. Scores for each of the 624 respondents on the three attitude tests were keypunched on cards. Scoring procedures for the censorship and intellectual freedom attitude scales were explained in the section of Chapter 6 devoted to construction of the attitude tests. Scoring of F scale items was slightly different. Each respondent was given an authoritarian score based on the assignment of one point for a response with low authoritarian content, two points for a response with moderate authoritarian content, four points for a response with high authoritarian content, and five points for a response having a very high authoritarian content. Unlike the two other attitude tests used in the study, the F scale on authoritarianism did not contain a "don't know," "uncertain," or "undedided" response alternative. Scoring of item responses of the F scale on authoritarianism were accomplished according to the numerical values shown for the following item:

Item 12. People can be divided into two distinct classes: the weak and the strong.

| Strongly agree (5) | Agree (4) | Disagree (2) | Strongly disagree (1) |
|---|---|---|---|

The summated ratings (scores) for the three attitude tests were rated as either low, intermediate, or high. In a normal distribution of scores, two-thirds of the scores can be expected to fall between one standard deviation above and one standard deviation below the mean. On the assumption that the scores of respondents on the three attitude tests were normally distributed, scores which were more than one standard deviation from the mean were classified as high; those which were less than one standard deviation from the mean were classified as low. From a possible range of scores between 18 and 90 points for each test, ranges for low, intermediate, and high scores were computed as follows using the mean scores and standard deviations as shown in Table 3:

**Intellectual Freedom**

Low scores ........................................ 18-24
Intermediate scores ............................... 25-39
High scores ...................................... 40-90

**Censorship**

Low scores ........................................ 18-29
Intermediate scores ............................... 30-52
High scores ...................................... 53-90

**F scale on authoritarianism**

Low scores ........................................ 18-34
Intermediate scores ............................... 35-56
High scores ...................................... 57-90

TABLE 3

MEAN SCORES, STANDARD DEVIATIONS, AND RELIABILITY
COEFFICIENTS FOR EACH ATTITUDE TEST

| Measure | Attitude Test | | |
|---|---|---|---|
| | Intellectual Freedom | Censorship | F scale on Authoritarianism |
| Mean | 31.75 | 40.74 | 45.44 |
| Standard deviation | 7.14 | 11.09 | 10.12 |
| Cronbach alpha coefficient | .87 | .91 | .86 |

Classification ranges for low-, intermediate, and high-scoring respondents were established in order to group these librarians with similar attitudes into descriptive categories. These categories have no direct relationship to the testing of the five hypotheses; hypothesis testing was accomplished as a result of data qualification and computation, not by employing the more qualitatively-determined classification categories of low, intermediate, and high.

Table 4 contains the percentages of Midwestern public librarians with high, intermediate, and low censorship scores who rated high, intermediate, or low in intellectual freedom. In Table 4 are also displayed the percentages of the same librarians who obtained high, intermediate, and low censorship scores in comparison with their high, intermediate, or low scores on the F scale on authoritarianism.

More than one-half of the respondents (55 per cent to be exact) obtained intermediate scores on both the censorship and the intellectual freedom attitude tests. The attitudes of respondents whose scores caused them to be in the intermediate category could be said to be neither highly favorable toward intellectual freedom nor highly unfavorable to censorship activities. Nine per cent of the respondents made both low censorship and low intellectual freedom scores, an indication that the attitudes of those librarians are both definitely pro-intellectual freedom and anti-censorship.

Somewhat paradoxical was the finding that nine per cent of the respondents obtained scores in the intermediate category for intellectual freedom and at the same time obtained high scores in censorship. Scores of that nature indicate a general agreement with principles of intellectual freedom, yet generally above-average agreement with censorship activities. Immediately apparent from an examination of Table 4 is the fact that attitudes of librarians tended to be more favorable toward intellectual freedom principles than they tended to be unfavorable toward censorship.

As can be discerned from Table 4, slightly more than nine per cent of the respondents whose censorship attitude scores were high also obtained high scores on the F scale on authoritarianism. Sixty-one per cent of them obtained attitude scores for both censorship and authoritarianism which fell within the intermediate scoring bracket. Less than six per cent of the respondents' scores were classed as both low on censorship and low on authoritarianism. Almost six per cent of the 624 respondents obtained high authoritarianism scores and intermediate censorship scores. When the data as total individual scores were plotted in a bivariate graph with censorship scores on one axis (variable two) and authoritarianism scores on the other axis (variable three), a revealing graphic pattern was formed. The pattern indicated a high, positive relationship between censorship and authoritarianism attitude scores of respondents. An examination of the graph demonstrated a trend of an increase in variable three for each unit increase in variable two. Although the data do not progress unit for unit, the plotted points would fall near, but not directly on, a straight line if one were drawn diagonally from the lower left-hand to the upper right-hand corner of the scatter diagram.

## TABLE 4

**PERCENTAGE OF ALL RESPONDENTS WITH HIGH, INTERMEDIATE, AND LOW CENSORSHIP SCORES WHO RATED HIGH, INTERMEDIATE, OR LOW ON INTELLECTUAL FREEDOM AND ON AUTHORITARIANISM**

| Censorship Score | Intellectual Freedom Score | | | | F Scale on Authoritarianism Score | | | |
|---|---|---|---|---|---|---|---|---|
| | Low (18-24) | Intermediate (25-39) | High (40-90) | (Number) | Low (18-34) | Intermediate (35-36) | High (57-90) | (Number) |
| Low (18-29) | 9.0 | 5.6 | 0.0 | (94) | 5.8 | 9.1 | 0.0 | (93) |
| Intermediate (30-52) | 9.0 | 55.0 | 7.2 | (444) | 4.3 | 61.1 | 5.9 | (445) |
| High (53-90) | .2 | 9.0 | 5.0 | (86) | 0.0 | 4.7 | 9.1 | (86) |
| Total for each group | 18.2 | 69.6 | 12.2 | — | 10.1 | 74.9 | 15.0 | — |
| Grand Total | | 100.0 | | (624) | | 100.0 | | (624) |

## Measures for Central Tendency and Variability

Since there is a tendency in most distributions for scores to be centrally dispersed, mean scores and standard deviations for the censorship, intellectual freedom, and F scale attitude tests were computed. As indicators of central tendency and variability, these values were determined by machine tabulation, and they are shown in Table 3. Using these determined points of central tendency and indications of variability, the standard errors of the means were computed in order to obtain indexes of the reliability of the attitude scores of the sample Midwestern public librarians.

After having computed the standard error of mean scores and having determined population parameters for scores at the .01 level of confidence, a prediction was made that in 99 out of 100 cases the entire population of Midwestern public librarians would obtain mean scores falling within a plus or minus 2.55 standard error of the mean scores made by respondents in the sample. The population mean score for the intellectual freedom test can be estimated between 31.02 and 32.50 at the .01 level of confidence; the population mean censorship score can be estimated between a score of 39.71 and a score of 41.77; and the population mean score on the F scale on authoritarianism can be estimated within the bracket 44.41 and 46.47.

Because the observed mean scores equalled the true scores plus errors and as the observed variance equalled the true score variance plus error variances, a reliability index of the three tests was obtained by computing the Cronbach alpha coefficients of internal consistency, which are shown in Table 3. The formula used for obtaining the coefficients was a generalization of a standard reliability test, the Kuder-Richardson Formula 20 for dichotomous items. The use of the formula has been explained by Cronbach.[1] When the Cronbach formula is used as a reliability test, a perfect degree of reliability among the items of a scale is represented by an obtained coefficient of *one*. The Cronbach alpha coefficients obtained for the attitude tests of this study were as follows: .87 for intellectual freedom, .91 for censorship, and .86 for the F scale on authoritarianism. These coefficients revealed a relatively high degree of internal consistency in the three attitude tests, especially the censorship attitude scale.

## Censorship Item Analysis

A distribution of total item responses expressed in percentages was obtained by subjecting the data card deck to computer analysis. Table 5 provides the means, standard deviations, and coefficients of correlation for all items in each of the attitude tests. Mention will not be made in this section, therefore, of total responses to all items: only highly discriminatory items as indicated by total responses will be discussed. These highly discriminatory items seem particularly worthy of attention and will be discussed in four separate groups: those from 1) the censorship test, 2) the intellectual freedom test, 3) the authoritarianism test, and 4) items in Section II which were not included in the three attitude tests.

The lowest standard deviation computed for any one item in the censorship

# TABLE 5

## MEANS, STANDARD DEVIATIONS, AND CORRELATIONS FOR EACH ITEM OF THE QUESTIONNAIRE

| | Intellectual Freedom Test (Part I) | | | | Censorship Attitude Scale (Part II) | | | | F Scale on Authoritarianism (Part III) | | |
|---|---|---|---|---|---|---|---|---|---|---|---|
| Item Number | Mean Score | Standard Deviation | Correlation with the Scale Sum | Item Number | Mean Score | Standard Deviation | Correlation with the Scale Sum | Item Number | Mean Score | Standard Deviation | Correlation with the Scale Sum |
| 1 | 1.9 | .9 | .53 | 7 | 1.6 | .8 | .36 | 1 | 2.8 | 1.2 | .60 |
| 2 | 2.1 | .8 | .59 | 10 | 1.8 | .9 | .35 | 2 | 2.9 | 1.1 | .59 |
| 3 | 2.6 | 1.2 | .63 | 13 | 1.5 | .6 | .49 | 3 | 2.9 | 1.1 | .56 |
| 4 | 2.5 | 1.3 | .67 | 16 | 1.8 | .8 | .47 | 4 | 2.4 | 1.0 | .48 |
| 5 | 1.8 | .8 | .71 | 18 | 2.3 | 1.0 | .35 | 5 | 3.1 | 1.1 | .38 |
| 6 | 1.9 | .9 | .65 | 19 | 1.6 | .5 | .49 | 6 | 2.6 | 1.1 | .34 |
| 8 | 2.0 | 1.0 | .69 | 20 | 1.7 | .6 | .43 | 7 | 2.4 | 1.1 | .49 |
| 9 | 1.8 | .9 | .70 | 22 | 1.7 | .7 | .45 | 8 | 3.3 | 1.1 | .42 |
| 11 | 2.0 | .7 | .52 | 23 | 1.8 | .7 | .63 | 9 | 1.9 | .8 | .50 |
| 12 | 2.8 | 1.2 | .60 | 24 | 1.4 | .5 | .46 | 10 | 2.4 | 1.0 | .47 |
| 14 | 2.6 | 1.1 | .61 | 27 | 1.9 | .8 | .47 | 11 | 2.3 | 1.0 | .40 |
| 15 | 2.1 | .9 | .64 | 28 | 2.1 | .9 | .32 | 12 | 2.1 | .9 | .47 |
| 17 | 3.0 | 1.1 | .60 | 29 | 1.8 | .7 | .53 | 13 | 2.3 | 1.1 | .61 |
| 21 | 2.5 | .9 | .28 | 30 | 2.0 | .7 | .44 | 14 | 2.5 | 1.0 | .50 |
| 25 | 2.0 | .9 | .57 | 32 | 1.6 | .6 | .30 | 15 | 1.9 | .7 | .54 |
| 26 | 2.4 | 1.0 | .51 | 33 | 1.9 | .8 | .24 | 16 | 2.2 | 1.0 | .62 |
| 31 | 2.3 | .8 | .60 | 35 | 1.6 | .5 | .47 | 17 | 2.2 | .9 | .40 |
| 34 | 2.5 | 1.0 | .49 | 36 | 1.6 | .7 | .52 | 18 | 3.3 | 1.2 | .27 |

attitude test was .7, and the highest for an item was 1.3. In Table 5, the standard deviations for censorship items are displayed. Standard deviations for items numbered 3, 4, 6, 8, 12, 14, 21, 26, and 34 were the highest, ranging from .9 to 1.3. Five of those items dealt with the topic of sex, and total responses indicated a reluctance on the part of a number of librarians to treat books and materials dealing with that subject in accord with the overall rather liberal views toward intellectual freedom expressed by most respondents. In other words, a general disparity between permissive and repressive attitudes was noted when respondents were presented questions or problems relating to sex. A number of examples of respondent unwillingness, as indicated by attitudes, to deal with sexual subject matter in accord with liberal ideas toward the freedom to read as expressed by almost all librarians in the study will be discussed in subsequent paragraphs. The item analysis in those paragraphs will not distinguish between responses of "strongly agree" and "agree," both of which will be combined and considered as "agrees." Likewise, "disagree" and "strongly disagree" response alternatives will be grouped together and considered as "disagrees." In all other sections of this study in which scores were quantified and subjected to statistical analysis, differences between the two positive and the two negative response alternatives are considered, as each response alternative was assigned a numerical value.

Respondents were asked in item number 17 whether *The 120 Days of Sodom*, a book by the French libertine novelist the Marquis de Sade, should be on the open shelves of any public library. The book was described in the questionnaire item as a work "which contains numerous episodes of sexual perversion combined with cruelty." Thirty-six per cent of the librarians thought that it should not be in any public library. In contrast to that view, the same number of respondents, 36 per cent, were of the opinion that the book should be included. Twenty-eight per cent, or 175 out of 624, of the librarians were undecided about the question. According to 29 per cent of the participants of this study, another controversial book with a sexual theme, *Portnoy's Complaint*, does not belong on the open shelves of any public library. Item number three of the instrument described the novel as a book containing descriptions of exhibitionism, voyeurism, autoeroticism, and oral coitus, but 62 per cent of the librarians did not object to including the book in public library collections. A decision to include or to exclude the book could not be resolved, however, by ten per cent of the respondents.

In answer to item number 34, 61 per cent of the respondents felt that library users who want to read "erotic novels" should purchase their own copies and should not expect to find them in the public library, while only 21 per cent disagreed. In order to provide an index of the type of novels being considered "erotic," several books were designated as examples; however, the publications were listed (by design) because they were not particularly erotic in view of current standards. They were: *Return to Peyton Place, The Carpetbaggers, God's Little Acre, Candy,* and *Fanny Hill.* Seventeen per cent of the librarians were undecided as to whether librarians should purchase such novels.

Complaints from library users about books and materials dealing with sexual topics or themes was the subject of item number 21. In response to the item, 21 per cent of the respondents felt that when confronted with such complaints a librarian should attempt to absolve himself or herself by claiming that sexual themes and four-letter words are included in most present-day novels. Approximately 64 per cent of the librarians disagreed with that approach to the problem, while 17 per cent were undecided about the question.

Twenty-six per cent of the respondents agreed with item number four, which stated a definite need in our society for efforts of civic-minded and religious groups which endeavor to keep our libraries free of "filth." On the other hand, approximately 59 per cent saw no need for that type of censorship, and 13 per cent of the librarians were undecided on the issue. The word "filth" was used purposefully because it is commonly used in the vernacular to identify a wide range of objectionable subject matter, particularly materials dealing with sexual topics.

Closely related to the sexual issue was item number 26, which was concerned with the problem of book labeling and was stated as follows: "Books which may offend standards of taste should be starred as a guide to those library users who wish to avoid these types of works." According to 21 per cent of the librarians, offensive books should be starred; approximately 63 per cent disagreed. Undecided about the starring or labeling of books were 16 per cent of the respondents. In contrast to the attitude toward the labeling of books, a policy with which 21 per cent agreed and with which 16 per cent were undecided, was the overall response to item number 30, a statement against labeling taken verbatim from the *Freedom to Read* statement and included in the intellectual freedom attitude test. Eighty-seven per cent of those completing the questionnaire indicated their disapproval of book labeling as a means of forcing a pre-judgment on the reader; however, in response to item number 26, 21 per cent agreed that books should be starred and 16 per cent were undecided about the issue.

In response to item number 12, which stated "No matter how much librarians talk about intellectual freedom, there are just some controversial books in public libraries that should be kept off the open shelves and in restricted rooms or cabinets," 36 per cent checked either "agree" or "strongly agree." On the other hand, 49 per cent checked either "disagree" or "strongly disagree." Undecided about the question were 15 per cent of the respondents. In their answers to item number 14, 22 per cent of the respondents were also undecided as to whether a censorship controversy over a single book or magazine was worth the adverse public relations which it could cause for the library. Responses of the 25 per cent who checked either "agree" or "strongly agree" apparently indicated that those librarians felt that a controversy over a single publication is not worth the effort. Responses from 53 per cent of the respondents indicated that over half of the librarians surveyed thought that a controversy was justified even though it could cause adverse public relations.

## Intellectual Freedom Item Analysis

Because each of the three attitude scales contained 18 items and since the possible scores on each test ranged from a low of 18 to a high of 90 points, a quantitative comparison can be made among the attitude scores. A low score on intellectual freedom indicated agreement with freedom-to-read and freedom-of-access principles. The higher a respondent's score, for example, the less liberal did he appear with respect to intellectual freedom. Likewise, a low score on the censorship attitude scale indicated non-agreement with censorship, while the higher a score the more the respondent accepted or tolerated censorship practices. The same held true for scores on the F scale, where a low score indicated non-agreement with certain authoritarian attitudes. The average intellectual freedom score was by far the lowest of the three average mean attitude scores.

The mean intellectual freedom attitude score shows that attitudes of the typical respondent-librarian in this survey are in complete agreement with the principles of the *Library Bill of Rights* and the *Freedom to Read* statement. Statements were worded so that agreement would indicate approval of the freedom to read and that disagreement would indicate opposition to that freedom. Mean scores for each of the 18 items in the intellectual freedom attitude test are shown in Table 5, and they fall either within the "agree" or "strongly agree" categories. Standard deviations computed for each item of the test were very low, ranging from only .5 to 1.0. Most of the deviations clustered near the mean score. Several examples of definite liberality expressed by respondents in their acceptance of intellectual freedom principles will be considered next, in a section dealing with an analysis of total responses to selected items from that test.

Three intellectual freedom principles were completely accepted or agreed with by 96 per cent of the 624 respondents: 1) public libraries should not exclude materials because of the race or nationality or the social, political, or religious views of the author; 2) there would be a conflict with the public interest if librarians established their own political, moral, or aesthetic views as the sole standards for determining what books should be published or circulated; and 3) it is the responsibility of publishers and librarians to give full meaning to the freedom to read by providing books that enrich the quality of thought and expression.

Ninety-nine per cent of the respondents agreed that there is no need for publishers and librarians to endorse every idea or presentation contained in books which are produced and made available in libraries and that librarians should provide books and other materials presenting all points of view concerning the problems and issues of our times. One hundred per cent of the respondents felt that the rights of an individual to the use of a public library should not be denied because of age, religion, national origins, or social or political views.

Ninety-eight per cent of the respondents agreed to item number 35, which stated: "Publishers and librarians have a profound responsibility to give validity to the freedom to read by making it possible for readers to choose freely from a variety of offerings." Ninety-seven per cent felt, as stated in item number 20, that "As an institution of education for democratic living, the library should welcome the use of its meeting rooms for socially useful and cultural activities and discussions of current public questions." Ninety-three per cent of the respondents felt, as stated in item number 23, that "It is in the public interest for publishers and librarians to make available the widest diversity of views and expressions, including those which are unorthodox or unpopular with the majority." Ninety-four per cent agreed with item number 36: "The suppression of ideas is fatal to a democratic society," and 90 per cent felt, as stated in item number ten, that "Materials should not be proscribed or removed from libraries because of partisan or doctrinal disapproval."

There was also a very high rate of agreement with additional intellectual freedom items; however, those items will not be discussed in this analysis. The concensus of agreement among respondents to items already discussed and the low mean score obtained by respondents on the intellectual freedom attitude test clearly demonstrate that intellectual freedom as an abstract concept was almost universally accepted by librarians who completed the questionnaire. All librarians in this survey apparently agreed that intellectual freedom in libraries was a good concept.

## F Scale Item Analysis

As shown in Table 5, the mean scores for individual items in the F scale on authoritarianism were higher than similar scores on the other two attitude tests; as a consequence, the mean score obtained by the 624 respondents on that attitude test was the highest of the three mean attitude test scores. An investigation of the antidemocratic attitudes of respondents in this study was not made in order to identify and to label certain Midwestern public librarians as authoritarians. It was undertaken in order to correlate the expressed attitudes of these librarians about censorship activities with their agreement with authoritarian attitudes. The relationship between these two types of attitudes will be examined more closely in a subsequent section of this report; in this section an analysis will be made only of certain noteworthy total responses to items in Section III, which contained the F scale on authoritarianism. As mentioned earlier, a neutral response was not included as one of the response alternatives to F scale items. Apparently, the authoritarianism test was constructed so as to force respondents to agree or to disagree with items. Questionnaires of respondents which were returned incompleted, even for the omission of one F scale item response, were among those instruments mentioned earlier as unusable.

According to the expressed attitudes of 39 per cent of the respondents, "Obedience and respect for authority are the most important virtues children should learn," but approximately 61 per cent of the librarians disagreed. Responding to another item about young people, 44 per cent of the librarians agreed that "Young people sometimes get rebellious ideas, but as they grow up they ought to get over them and settle down." Forty-four per cent of the respondents agreed that "If people would talk less and work more, everybody would be better off," but approximately 56 per cent disagreed.

In response to item number five, "Science has its place, but there are many important things that can never possibly be understood by the human mind," 54 per cent of the librarians agreed. Twenty-eight per cent of them also agreed with item number seven: "Most people don't realize how much our lives are controlled by plots hatched in secret places." Seventy-two per cent disagreed. Sixty-four per cent of the respondents felt, as stated in item eight, that "Human nature being what it is, there will always be war and conflict"; however, 36 per cent disagreed. In response to item 16, 19 per cent of the respondents agreed that "Nowadays when so many different kinds of people move around and mix together so much, a person has to protect himself especially carefully against catching an infection or disease from them." Almost 81 per cent did not agree with that statement. Most of the librarians in this survey, 62 per cent to be exact, agreed with item number 18: "More and more people are prying into matters that should remain personal and private." Only 38 per cent disagreed with that statement. Some of the librarians who agreed with item number 18 also commented in statements penciled in on the survey instrument that the questionnaire used for this opinion survey was an example of an intrusion into the privacy of individuals.

## Item Analysis of Section II

Section II of the questionnaire dealt with issues related to, but not necessarily directly pertaining to, censorship and intellectual freedom. Because of the controversial and unresolved nature of the issues included in the items, they were not included as part of the attitude tests of the study. The four items in Section II pertained to issues for which there presently appears to be little or no agreement, even among the concerned specialists and authorities, and total responses to them warrant attention as indicators of the opinions of a sizable group of public librarians.

Responses to the first item in Section II revealed that 75 per cent of the librarians felt that a child's reading should be more the responsibility of parents than booksellers and librarians. Nineteen per cent felt, on the other hand, that what a child reads should not be primarily the responsibility of the parents; only six per cent of the librarians were undecided on this issue. Concerning the issue in item number two of the relationship between reading pornography and juvenile delinquency, 15 per cent of the respondents felt that there was a causal relationship, 57 per cent were undecided about the causality, and 28 per cent saw none. When asked in item number three for their opinions about the permissiveness or repressiveness of present laws dealing with obscenity in books and other printed matter, 25 per cent felt that the laws were too permissive, but 49 per cent did not feel likewise. Twenty-six per cent of the librarians apparently had no definite opinion on the question as they checked the "undecided" response alternative. The public's judgment of reading material was the fourth item. Twelve per cent of the respondents felt that most people have little critical judgment of what they read and are inclined to select the bad rather than the good or the inferior rather than the superior. Seventy-three per cent, on the other hand, disagreed, and 15 per cent had no opinion about the public's ability to discriminate qualitatively among reading materials.

## Testing of the Null Hypotheses

In this study the five hypotheses all included statements of "no difference" between two or more pertinent variables; each hypothesis could thus be stated as $\mu_1 - \mu_2 = 0$. As stated earlier, the hypotheses represented the contrary of predictions from related theories and from expectations of the investigator, who anticipated that there would be a difference between and among the variables and that the difference in the sample means would be sufficiently large to warrant the rejection of the hypotheses in favor of alternatives. These alternatives, consequently, could be stated as $\mu_1 - \mu_2 > 0$. To insure that the results of the attitude study would carry conviction to others, a fairly large random sample of librarians was selected, and a high level of significance (one per cent) was established to justify a categorical decision to reject or to retain the hypotheses. Reliability testing at the .01 level of significance decreased the probability of a Type I error, which is the rejection of a hypothesis when it is indeed true. If, in fact $\mu_1$ was found to be equal to $\mu_2$, the probability would be only one chance in one hundred that a hypothesis would be rejected in favor of an alternative.

Insofar as the relationship between librarians' attitudes toward censorship and intellectual freedom is concerned, Fiske's research in the area of book selection, as well as theories of a number of library leaders as discussed in Chapter 5, led to a prediction in this study that the collected data would indicate an agreement in a theoretical context among librarians with intellectual freedom principles but that librarians' attitudes might not correspond entirely with these principles when they were operationalized, i.e., applied to "real" or simulated censorship situations in libraries.

Relationships between repressive or permissive attitudes and several independent variables were hypothesized negatively in order to facilitate the testing of differences by means of accepted statistical techniques. In order to determine the relationship between respondents' intellectual freedom and censorship attitudes (Hypothesis 1) and between censorship and authoritarian attitudes (Hypothesis 4), it was first necessary to determine whether the sample means obtained in the attitude tests were indeed no different from the population means at a designated level of confidence. No significant difference existed between these means, as was demonstrated earlier in this chapter. Throughout this study, the .01 level of significance was used to test all hypotheses, and the sample size N = 624 was used in statistical computations.

Hypothesis 1 stated that there would be no significant relationship between the attitudes of public librarians toward intellectual freedom and the attitudes of public librarians toward censorship. The following steps were taken to test the hypotheses: 1) a coefficient of correlation between the attitude scores of respondents on the censorship test and on the intellectual freedom test was computed, 2) the coefficient of correlation was normalized, and 3) the reliability of the obtained coefficient was tested. The relationship between censorship and intellectual freedom scores of the 624 respondents produced a positive coefficient of .5975, or .60. Reliability of the obtained coefficient was then tested at the .01 level of significance.

Using the book *Introduction to Mathematical Statistics*[2] by Paul G. Hoel as a guide for the reliability testing of both Hypothesis 1 and Hypothesis 4, a decision was made that the hypothesis could be rejected at the .01 level of confidence if the z values of the scores were greater than 2.55. In other words, if the z values of the scores were greater than two and one half standard deviations from the mean scores, the sample coefficients of correlation would be sufficiently different from zero to indicate that the mean scores of the population would almost certainly be different from zero. A logarithmic transformation of the coefficient of correlation was first made in accord with procedures outlined by Hoel. The logarithmic transformation was made in order to normalize the data by reducing it to a normal curve. The following computations were made:

$$z = \frac{1}{2} \log_e \frac{1 + .5975}{1 - .5975} = \frac{1}{2} \log_e \frac{1.5975}{.4025}$$

$$= \frac{1}{2} \log_e 3.9689 = \frac{1}{2} \log_e 3.97$$

$$= \frac{1}{2} (1.37877) = .689$$

$$z = \frac{1}{\sqrt{624 - 3}} = .40$$

$$\left| \frac{0 - .689}{.040} \right| = 17.225$$

Had the null hypothesis been correct, a difference as large as 17.225 would not have occurred as often as once in 100 trials. The obtained results fall within the region of rejection at the .01 level of confidence. Hypothesis 1 was therefore rejected, since 17.225 was significant beyond the .01 level of 2.55, or two and one half standard deviations beyond the mean. Having rejected Hypothesis 1, the opposite of the hypothesis was tentatively accepted, i.e., that there was a real relationship between the attitudes of Midwestern public librarians toward censorship and their attitudes toward intellectual freedom. The relationship or correlation between these two types of attitudes was not perfect; however, it was positive, and it was significant.

Hypothesis 4 of the study stated that there would be no relationship between the attitudes of librarians toward characteristic authoritarian beliefs contained in the F scale and the attitudes of librarians toward censorship. Steps taken to test Hypothesis 4 were identical with those used in testing Hypothesis 1. A positive coefficient of correlation of .7307, or .73, was found to exist between the 624 pairs of scores on censorship and authoritarianism. Computations for normalizing the coefficient of correlation and for testing its reliability were as follows:

$$z = \frac{1}{2} \log_e \frac{1 + .7307}{1 - .7307} = \frac{1.7307}{.2697}$$

$$= \frac{1}{2} (1.85942) - .92971$$

$$\left| \frac{0 - .92971}{.040} \right| = 23.24$$

The test for reliability of the coefficient of correlation at the .01 level of confidence revealed that the probability of obtaining a coefficient of .73 by chance alone would be only one per cent out of 100 per cent. In other words, if Hypothesis 4 had been correct, a difference as large as that observed would not have occurred as often as one time in one hundred trials. Hypothesis 4 was rejected as false. The numerical relationship of the change in variable two (censorship) in relation to the change in variable three (authoritarianism) was a positive .73, indicating that the pairs of attitude scores changed in the same direction and at a fairly high proportional ratio. As depicted in the scatter diagram in Appendix II, a distinct graphical relationship existed in the plot format of the censorship and authoritarianism attitude scores.

### Relationship of Variables to Attitude Scores

The three remaining hypotheses, Hypothesis 2, Hypothesis 3, and Hypothesis 5, stated that there woule be no relationship between the attitudes of librarians toward intellectual freedom, censorship, and authoritarianism (the three attitude test scores) and the following variables: age, sex, size of community of employment, position of the librarian in the library, state in which employed, and educational-attainment level of the respondent. Statistical procedures outlined in *Statistics in Research*[3] by Bernard Ostle for an analysis of variance were used as a guide for testing the differences between and among the obtained attitude scores and the independent variables. As variance is the arithmetic average of the squared deviations of scores from their mean, or the square of the standard deviation, it is determined by summing the squared deviations of scores from the grand mean.

The Multiple Range Test BMD07V for automatic computation was used to perform six analyses of variance with the independent variables and the three attitude scores of respondents. The procedures for the analysis of variance used in the BMD07V computer program closely follow those outlined in Ostle's work cited earlier as well as those contained in *Introduction to Statistical Analysis*[4] by W. J. Dixon. The Multiple Range Test is explained in detail in *BMD Biomedical Computer Programs*, which was also edited by Dixon.[5] The program performs multiple range tests on two kinds of input data: 1) data about one variable with unequal group sizes and 2) sample size, group means, standard deviations, and group labels. Two articles written by D. B. Duncan, "Multiple Range and Multiple F tests"[6] and "Multiple Range Tests for Correlated and Heteroscedastic Means,"[7] provided additional guides for arranging the raw data in preparation for machine computation and for interpreting the results produced by the computer for the statistical tests.

Among-groups variance and within-group variance was determined by comparing the three attitude scores obtained by the 624 respondents with each of the variables *a* through *f* listed in Hypothesis 2. The rationale of this comparison was based on the realization that the within-group variance and the among-groups variance are estimates of the population variance. Computation of variance revealed, for example, whether the mean scores obtained by librarians in the nine educational attainment levels (samples) varied around the grand mean more than the individual scores varied around the sample means. For each variable deemed to be important in this study an analysis of variance was computed in relation to the three attitude scores.

### Educational-Attainment Level

The first variable considered in relation to the three attitude scores was the educational-attainment level of respondents. Respondents were classed into nine educational-attainment levels as follows: (Level 1) 330 respondents had obtained both a four-year college degree and a fifth-year library science degree or its equivalent; (Level 2) 99 respondents had obtained only a four-year college degree; (Level 3) 11 respondents were non-college graduates but had earned 91 or more credit hours of college work; (Level 4) 20 respondents had earned between 61 and 90 credit hours of college work; (Level 5) 21 respondents had graduated from junior colleges; (Level 6) 27 respondents had earned between 31 and 60 credit hours of college work; (Level 7) 29 respondents had earned less than 30 credit hours of college work; (Level 8) 81 had no formal education beyond high school; and (Level 9) six respondents had not obtained high school diplomas.

The $F$ ratio was then computed to determine for each variable the size of the within-group variance as compared with the among-groups variance. $F$ ratios are measures of the association between independent and dependent variables, and they do not indicate cause and effect. The sums of squares and means of squares, in both among- and within-group, as well as the $F$ ratios, are displayed in Table 6. The determined $F$ ratios were compared with $F$ values for 623 degrees of freedom (N-1) for both within-group and among-groups variances, which were found in Fisher's *Statistical Tables for Biology, Agricultural and Medical Research.*[8] The $F$ ratios computed exceeded the $F$ criterion values; therefore, Hypothesis 2-f, Hypothesis 3-f, and Hypothesis 5-f, which stated that there would be no relationship between educational-attainment levels and attitude scores of respondents, were rejected at the .01 level of significance.

The analysis of variance of mean censorship scores obtained by respondents grouped according to educational-attainment levels allowed identification of three subsets (levels) of respondents who obtained similar scores. The scores of these homogeneous subsets of respondents did not differ by more than the shortest significant range for a subset of that size, and they are as follows:

(1) Subset 1 – Librarians with a fifth-year library science degree or its equivalent and non-college graduates who had earned more than 91 credit hours.

(2) Subset 2 – Non-college graduates who had earned 91 or more credit hours, non-college graduates who had earned between 61 and 90 credit hours, non-college graduates who had earned between 31 and 60 credit hours, non-college graduates who had earned between one and 30 credit hours, junior college graduates, and high school graduates.

(3) Subset 3 – College graduates, non-college graduates who had earned more than 91 credit hours, non-college graduates who had earned between 61 and 90 credit hours, and non-college graduates who had earned between 31 and 60 credit hours.

# TABLE 6

## RANK ORDER OF MEAN SCORES OBTAINED BY RESPONDENTS ON ATTITUDE TESTS ACCORDING TO LEVEL OF EDUCATION

| Level of Education | Attitude Test | | | | | |
|---|---|---|---|---|---|---|
| | Intellectual Freedom | | Censorship | | F Scale | |
| | Rank Order | Mean Score | Rank Order | Mean Score | Rank Order | Mean Score |
| 1 | 1 | 30.0 | 1 | 36.8 | 1 | 42.5 |
| 2 | 2 | 31.5 | 2 | 40.9 | 3 | 44.5 |
| 3 | 3 | 32.3 | 3 | 43.0 | 4 | 47.7 |
| 4 | 6 | 34.9 | 4 | 43.7 | 6 | 50.1 |
| 5 | 5 | 33.6 | 7 | 47.9 | 2 | 43.7 |
| 6 | 4 | 33.4 | 5 | 43.9 | 5 | 50.0 |
| 7 | 8 | 37.3 | 6 | 47.1 | 7 | 50.6 |
| 8 | 7 | 34.8 | 8 | 48.6 | 8 | 53.4 |
| 9 | 9 | 37.7 | 9 | 65.3 | 9 | 61.3 |
| Analysis of Variance $F$ Ratio | 8.46 | | 21.02 | | 16.94 | |

When mean authoritarianism scores of the same educational-attainment levels were analyzed, five homogeneous subsets were identified as follows:

(1) Subset 1 — Librarians with fifth-year library science degrees, junior college graduates, four-year college graduates, and non-college graduates who had earned 91 or more credit hours.

(2) Subset 2 — Non-college graduates who had earned 91 or more credit hours, non-college graduates who had earned between 31 and 60 credit hours, non-college graduates who had

earned between 61 and 90 credit hours, non-college graduates who had earned less than 30 credit hours, and high school graduates.

(3) Subset 3  —   Junior college graduates, non-college graduates who had earned 91 or more credit hours, non-college graduates who had earned between 31 and 60 credit hours, non-college graduates who had earned between 61 and 90 credit hours, and non-college graduates who had earned less than 30 credit hours.

(4) Subset 4  —   Non-college graduates who had earned between 31 and 60 credit hours, non-college graduates who had earned between 61 and 90 credit hours, non-college graduates who had earned less than 30 credit hours, high school graduates, and non-high school graduates.

(5) Subset 5  —   Junior college graduates, four-year college graduates, non-college graduates who had earned more than 91 credit hours, and non-college graduates who had earned between 61 and 90 credit hours.

In Table 6, the rank orders of mean scores obtained by the nine educational-attainment groups on the attitude tests show differences among scores. The general decrease in mean scores as educational-attainment levels increase is evident in the tabular data. That progression is particularly apparent in the rank order of censorship attitude mean scores as shown in Table 6, where the lowest mean score for level one is 36.8 and the highest mean score for level nine is 65.3.

In the ranking of educational-attainment levels according to attitude scores as shown in Table 6, level number five, which contained the 21 junior college graduates, appears to be slightly out of order; in the plot of attitude scores shown in Graph 1, there also appears a rather abrupt increase in scores from level four to level five and a subsequent sharp decline to level six. This was probably caused by the fact that the respondents of educational-attainment level five, by virtue of having been graduated from junior colleges, had completed approximately the same number of credit hours of college work as those respondents at the lower limits of level four or as those respondents at the upper limits of level six. Level five as an exclusive category for junior college graduates should probably have been eliminated and the respondents should have been placed in either level four or six; however, the exact number of hours completed by these respondents was not known. Had junior college graduates been placed in one of the two adjacent categories and had level five *per se* been eliminated, the rank orders for levels four and six would most probably have been more systematic, and the sharp increase in the line graph representing the three attitude scores would most probably have been considerably smoother.

There was a definite relationship between a librarian's educational-attainment level and his or her scores on each of the attitude tests. This relationship can be stated operationally as follows: librarians who possessed more formal education had more liberal views in respect to intellectual freedom; they were also more opposed to censorship practices; and they also disagreed with more of

126

the authoritarian ideas contained in the F scale. Likewise, as the amount of formal education obtained by librarians decreased from level one, (fifth-year library science degrees) to level nine (non-high school graduates), the attitudes became more restrictive of intellectual freedom, more receptive to censorship, and more authoritarian. Graph 1 contains a plot of the three attitude scores in relationship to educational-attainment levels.

## Population-Size Categories

The next variable taken into consideration and compared with attitude scores was size of the community in which librarians were employed. When respondents were grouped according to seven population-size categories, there was not a considerable difference in attitudes toward intellectual freedom from category to category. Table 2 in Chapter 6 contains the number of librarians who responded from each population-size category, and Table 7 contains a rank ordering of mean intellectual freedom scores obtained by respondents in the various sized town and cities. Librarians in population-size category VII (more than 1,200,000 inhabitants) obtained the lowest mean scores on intellectual freedom, and librarians in category I (under 5,000) obtained the highest. The difference between the lowest and the highest mean scores on intellectual freedom was only 5.5 points.

The $F$ ratio obtained from the analysis of variance for intellectual freedom and population-size categories was low, as can be seen in Table 7; however, the $F$ ratio did indicate a significant difference among the scores of the various categories. While homogeneity is apparent among the intellectual freedom attitudes of librarians in towns and cities of more than 5,000 inhabitants, there was a slight tendency for librarians to reject intellectual freedom principles as community size decreased. A large rejection occurred, however, only among librarians classed in population-size category I (very small towns).

Table 7 contains a listing of the various population-size categories and their rank orders according to mean scores obtained on the three attitude tests. The lowest mean scores were obtained by librarians in categories IV, V, and VII; however, there was little difference between the scores of librarians in these categories and the scores of librarians in categories I, III, and IV. In fact, the censorship attitude scores of librarians in categories I, II, III, IV, V, and VI placed those respondents in a homogeneous subset; no pair of categories in that subset differed by more than the shortest significant range for a subset of that size. A distinctive difference in censorship attitude scores was evident, however, in category I, which included librarians employed in very small communities. The mean score obtained on the censorship attitude test by the 166 librarians in population-size category I was 7.2 points higher than the mean score obtained by the next highest-scoring group, category VI. The difference between the lowest and highest mean scores for any group, with the exception of Group I, was only 3.4 points. It was evident that librarians in very small communities were the most conservative in their opinions; they tended to look upon censorship practices more favorably than other librarians did. An analysis of variance produced an $F$ ratio of 17.81, as shown in Table 7, which indicated that

# TABLE 7

## RANK ORDER OF POPULATION-SIZE CATEGORIES ACCORDING TO MEAN SCORES OBTAINED BY RESPONDENTS ON ATTITUDE TESTS

| Size Category | Attitude Test | | | | | |
| :---: | :---: | :---: | :---: | :---: | :---: | :---: |
| | Intellectual Freedom | | Censorship | | F Scale | |
| | Rank Order | Mean Score | Rank Order | Mean Score | Rank Order | Mean Score |
| I | 7 | 34.2 | 7 | 47.6 | 7 | 50.3 |
| II | 5 | 31.6 | 5 | 39.5 | 6 | 44.7 |
| III | 4 | 31.1 | 4 | 38.4 | 4 | 44.2 |
| IV | 3 | 30.1 | 2 | 37.0 | 2 | 42.3 |
| V | 2 | 30.1 | 1 | 37.0 | 3 | 43.8 |
| VI | 6 | 31.9 | 6 | 40.4 | 5 | 44.3 |
| VII | 1 | 28.8 | 1 | 37.0 | 1 | 41.0 |
| Analysis of Variance $F$ Ratio | 5.72 | | 17.81 | | 10.45 | |

there was a significant overall relationship between the size of the community in which librarians were employed and the attitudes of those librarians toward censorship. That relationship is also graphically depicted in Graph 2.

Ranges of mean scores on authoritarianism in relation to population-size categories were strikingly similar to the attitudes of librarians toward censorship. A difference of 9.3 points in mean F scale attitude scores existed among librarians in population-size category I and librarians in category VII. Table 7 contains the $F$ ratio computed in an analysis of variance. The ratio, significant at the .01 level of confidence, indicates that there was a significant difference among the scores of librarians in various sized towns and cities but that the difference was by no means as large as that found among the scores of librarians classified according to educational-attainment levels. Because the $F$ ratios computed for the size of community variables and the attitude scores are

128

**GRAPH 1**

**DISTRIBUTION OF SCORES
BY
EDUCATIONAL ATTAINMENT LEVELS**

**GRAPH 2**

**DISTRIBUTION OF SCORES
BY
POPULATION-SIZE CATEGORIES**

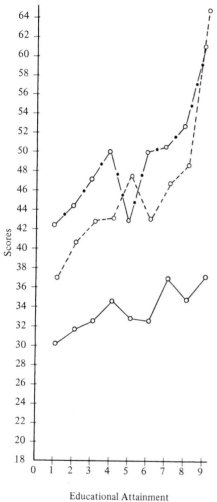

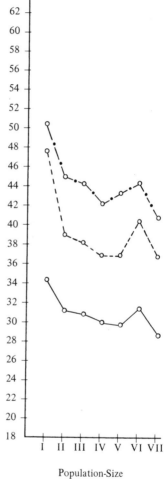

Educational Attainment
Level

Population-Size
Category

KEY: o———o Intellectual freedom
o— — —o Censorship
o—•—•—o F-scale on authoritarianism

129

significant at the .01 level of confidence and because they indicate degrees of differences among the attitudes of librarians toward the attitude objects of this study, Hypothesis 3-c, Hypothesis 4-c, and Hypothesis 5-c, which stated that there would be no difference among these variables, were rejected as false. The collected data revealed that there was a significant difference between the attitudes of librarians in various sizes of communities in the Midwest toward intellectual freedom, censorship, and beliefs included in the F scale on authoritarianism. The differences were small for various population groups with the exception of population-size category I, where the attitude scores were found to be markedly higher.

### Age Groups

An analysis of variance of intellectual freedom attitude scores by age groups did not reveal a relationship between respondents' ages and their attitudes toward the principles contained in the *Library Bill of Rights* and the *Freedom to Read* statement. Respondents were classed into nine age groups as shown in Table 8, and these age groups were then ranked in order of mean intellectual

TABLE 8

AGE GROUPS AND NUMBER OF RESPONDENTS IN EACH GROUP

| Age Group Number | Inclusive Ages of Group | Number of Respondents in Each Group |
|:---:|:---:|:---:|
| 1 | 22 - 24 | 9 |
| 2 | 25 - 27 | 24 |
| 3 | 28 - 30 | 33 |
| 4 | 31 - 33 | 23 |
| 5 | 34 - 36 | 20 |
| 6 | 37 - 39 | 14 |
| 7 | 40 - 42 | 45 |
| 8 | 43 - 45 | 32 |
| 9 | over 45 | 424 |

freedom scores of each group as shown in Table 9. A difference of only 2.8 points between the lowest- and the highest-scoring age groups was found. The $F$ ratio of 1.4107 listed in Table 9 was not significant at the .01 level of confidence, and Hypothesis 2-a could not be rejected, since there appeared to be no relationship between the ages of Midwestern public librarians and their attitudes toward intellectual freedom.

Hypothesis 3-a, which stated that there would be no relationship between censorship attitudes of Midwestern public librarians and their ages, can be rejected, since the $F$ ratio was significant at the .01 level of confidence. A

TABLE 9

## RANK ORDER OF AGE GROUPS ACCORDING TO MEAN SCORES OBTAINED BY RESPONDENTS ON ATTITUDE TESTS

| Age Group | Attitude Test | | | | | |
|---|---|---|---|---|---|---|
| | Intellectual Freedom | | Censorship | | F Scale | |
| | Rank Order | Mean Score | Rank Order | Mean Score | Rank Order | Mean Score |
| 1 | 5 | 30.1 | 6 | 37.2 | 2 | 40.1 |
| 2 | 1 | 29.5 | 1 | 33.4 | 5 | 40.7 |
| 3 | 4 | 29.9 | 2 | 33.5 | 4 | 40.2 |
| 4 | 3 | 29.7 | 3 | 33.7 | 3 | 40.2 |
| 5 | 2 | 29.5 | 5 | 35.4 | 6 | 41.6 |
| 6 | 6 | 31.4 | 4 | 34.4 | 1 | 39.6 |
| 7 | 7 | 31.6 | 7 | 37.4 | 7 | 44.6 |
| 8 | 8 | 32.3 | 8 | 40.2 | 8 | 44.7 |
| 9 | 9 | 32.3 | 9 | 43.1 | 9 | 47.0 |
| Analysis of Variance $F$ Ratio | 1.41 | | 9.41 | | 5.46 | |

difference of ten points between the lowest and highest-scoring age groups was evident. The mean censorship score of respondents in age group one was 37.2, and the rank order of that group's mean score was number six. Although the mean score was relatively high in comparison to the other scores of age groups, it should be remembered that only nine out of 624 respondents were included in the 22- to 24-year-old age group. With the exception of group one, there was a steady increase in mean censorship attitude scores as respondents' ages increased, but the increase was slight. There was approximately a three-point difference between the mean score on censorship of the 32 respondents in group eight (43-45 years) and the mean score of the 424 respondents in group nine (over 45 years). Among the 424 librarians over 45 years of age, there was very little variance in censorship attitude scores. The $F$ ratio shown in Table 9 was significant at the .01 level of confidence; therefore there was a significant relationship between the ages of Midwestern public librarians and their attitudes toward censorship.

Age as a factor in the attitudes of librarians toward authoritarian ideas was of some statistical significance, but it was apparently not an exceedingly important factor in view of the results of an analysis of variance. The data presented in Table 9 reveal a difference of only 7.5 points between the highest- and lowest-scoring age groups of the F scale test. The highest scores were obtained by respondents in the lowest age groups. Table 9 contains the results of an analysis of variance of age and F scale scores of respondents, and the $F$ ratio obtained was significant at the .01 level of confidence. The relationship between attitude scores and age is also clearly evident in Graph 3. Hypothesis 5-a was therefore rejected; there was a relationship between the ages of Midwestern public librarians and their attitudes toward authoritarianism.

### Sex of Respondents

When scores were analyzed according to sex of respondents, males had lower mean scores on all three attitude tests. Table 10 provides a rank ordering of male and female scores as well as data obtained from an analysis of variance based on sex of respondents and attitude scores. Mean scores of female respondents averaged 4.8 points greater than the mean scores of males on the intellectual freedom, censorship, and authoritarianism attitude tests.

As can be seen by examining the $F$ ratios provided in Table 10, means of males and females on each attitude test differ significantly at the .01 level of confidence. The high $F$ ratios obtained on each analysis of variance test allow the rejection of Hypothesis 3-b, Hypothesis 4-b, and Hypothesis 5-b since there was a significant difference between the attitudes of male and female librarians. Male librarians agreed more with intellectual freedom principles than did female librarians; male librarians were more opposed to censorship than were female librarians; and male librarians were less authoritarian than female librarians.

### State Where Employed

In order to determine whether librarians in each of the five Midwestern states held significantly different attitudes, the respondents were grouped

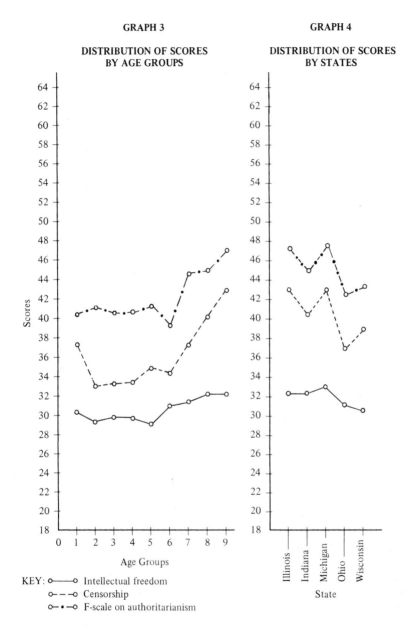

GRAPH 3

**DISTRIBUTION OF SCORES
BY AGE GROUPS**

GRAPH 4

**DISTRIBUTION OF SCORES
BY STATES**

Scores

Age Groups

State

KEY: o———o  Intellectual freedom
o – – –o  Censorship
o—•—o  F-scale on authoritarianism

133

# TABLE 10

## MEAN ATTITUDE SCORES AND RANK ORDERS OF MALE AND FEMALE RESPONDENTS

| | Attitude Test | | | | | |
|---|---|---|---|---|---|---|
| | Intellectual Freedom | | Censorship | | F Scale | |
| | Rank Order | Mean Score | Rank Order | Mean Score | Rank Order | Mean Score |
| Male | 1 | 29.3 | 1 | 35.4 | 1 | 42.2 |
| Female | 2 | 32.3 | 2 | 42.0 | 2 | 46.2 |
| Analysis of Variance *F* Ratio | 17.02 | | 34.98 | | 14.62 | |

according to the state of employment. Table 1 in Chapter 6 provides a list of the number of usable questionnaires returned by librarians from each state. Ranges of mean attitude scores of respondents grouped according to state of employment are provided in Table 11. As can be seen in that table, small differences existed in the intellectual freedom attitudes among librarians in the five states. An analysis of variance of the scores with state of employment as a variable revealed that no relationship existed between state of employment of responding librarians and scores on the intellectual freedom attitude test. The $F$ ratio of 1.85, shown in Table 11 and obtained from an analysis of variance, did not allow the rejection of Hypothesis 2-3. There appeared to be no significant relationship at the .01 level of confidence between Midwestern public librarians' attitudes toward intellectual freedom and state of employment. The plotted scores in Graph 4 also illustrate quite clearly that geography had little relationship to librarians' attitudes toward intellectual freedom.

As displayed in Table 11, the $F$ ratios computed with censorship and authoritarian attitude scores and state of employment of respondents were 6.15 and 6.65, respectively. Both $F$ ratios were significant at the .01 level of confidence, and Hypothesis 3-e and Hypothesis 5-e were rejected; there was a significant relationship between the state in which librarians were employed and attitudes toward censorship and authoritarianism. An examination of the rank ordering of attitude scores in Table 11 will reveal a difference in mean scores of 5.2 points on the censorship attitude test and 4.9 on the F scale on authoritarianism between librarians in the low-scoring and high-scoring states. Graph 4

# TABLE 11

## RANK ORDER OF STATES ACCORDING TO MEAN SCORES OBTAINED BY LIBRARIANS ON ATTITUDE TESTS

| State | Attitude Test | | | | | |
|---|---|---|---|---|---|---|
| | Intellectual Freedom | | Censorship | | F Scale | |
| | Rank Order | Mean Score | Rank Order | Mean Score | Rank Order | Mean Score |
| Illinois | 4 | 32.1 | 4 | 43.0 | 4 | 47.4 |
| Indiana | 3 | 32.0 | 3 | 40.4 | 3 | 45.4 |
| Michigan | 5 | 33.0 | 5 | 43.0 | 4 | 47.4 |
| Ohio | 2 | 31.0 | 1 | 37.9 | 1 | 42.9 |
| Wisconsin | 1 | 30.8 | 2 | 39.4 | 2 | 43.6 |
| Analysis of Variance $F$ Ratio | 1.85 | | 6.15 | | 6.65 | |

also shows that the attitude scores of librarians on both the censorship and authoritarian tests were uniformly different when plotted by states but that the differences were not very great. In the ranked scores of librarians according to states, Indiana librarians were in the center of each ranking. Wisconsin and Ohio librarians remained at the lower-scoring end of the distribution, and Illinois and Michigan librarians were consistently at the high-scoring end. Librarians in Michigan obtained the highest scores on all three attitude tests; however, as previously pointed out, the differences between scores of librarians grouped according to states was only a few points.

## Job Classification

In order to determine the relationship between the librarians' attitudes and their positions in libraries, respondents were grouped according to the job classifications discussed in Chapter 6. There was no significant relationship between the attitudes of librarians toward intellectual freedom and the kinds of library positions which they held. Table 12 provides a rank ordering of the mean intellectual freedom attitude scores of respondents grouped according to job classifications. The analysis of variance, the results of which are also displayed in Table 12, with these two variables produced an $F$ ratio of 2.94, and it was not statistically significant at the .01 level of confidence. Hypothesis 2-d could not be rejected because no relationship was found between a librarian's job classification and his or her attitude toward the principles of the *Library Bill of Rights* and the *Freedom to Read* statement.

On the other hand, there was a relationship at the .01 level of confidence between a librarian's position in a library and his or her attitude toward censorship, and Hypothesis 3-d was rejected. Table 12 contains the results of an analysis of variance of the two variables, and the $F$ ratio (6.83) was significant at the .01 level of confidence. The rank order of censorship attitude scores according to various job groups is also provided in Table 12. The ranking of scores from lowest to highest according to jobs revealed that directors or head librarians obtained a mean score which was approximately five points more than

TABLE 12

**MEAN SCORES AND RANK ORDERS OF RESPONDENTS GROUPED ACCORDING TO POSITIONS HELD IN LIBRARIES**

| Job Code | Attitude Test | | | | | |
|---|---|---|---|---|---|---|
| | Intellectual Freedom | | Censorship | | F Scale | |
| | Rank Order | Mean Score | Rank Order | Mean Score | Rank Order | Mean Score |
| A | 5 | 32.4 | 5 | 42.8 | 5 | 47.3 |
| B | 3 | 31.6 | 2 | 37.5 | 2 | 42.7 |
| C | 4 | 32.3 | 4 | 40.1 | 3 | 44.2 |
| D | 1 | 29.9 | 1 | 37.2 | 1 | 42.7 |
| E | 2 | 31.1 | 3 | 39.4 | 4 | 44.4 |
| Analysis of Variance $F$ Ratio | 2.94 | | 6.83 | | 6.83 | |

# GRAPH 5

## DISTRIBUTION OF SCORES
## BY POSITIONS IN LIBRARIES
## HELD BY RESPONDENTS

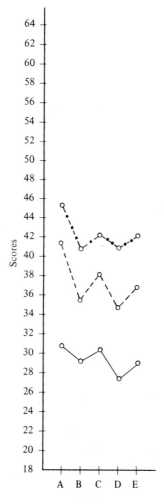

Positions

KEY: o———o Intellectual Freedom
o– – –o Censorship
o—•—o F-scale on authoritarianism

the lowest-scoring group according to job classification. The lowest-scoring group consisted of heads of public service departments.

An analysis of variance of attitudes toward authoritarian ideas of the F scale with job classifications of respondents produced an $F$ ratio of 6.08, which was significant at the .01 level of confidence. Data obtained in the analysis of variance are listed in Table 12 along with a rank ordering of mean F scale scores according to the various job classifications. As was the case with censorship attitudes in comparison with jobs, different employment groups of librarians had significantly different attitudes toward authoritarianism. Hypothesis 5-d was rejected because of those differences.

Directors and head librarians obtained the greatest mean scores on all three of the attitude tests, and heads of public service departments obtained the lowest mean scores. Directors and head librarians obtained a mean censorship score which was approximately five points more than the same score obtained by heads of public service departments. Because age proved to be statistically significant as a variable insofar as censorship and authoritarian attitudes were concerned, and since most of the respondents classed as heads of libraries in this study were over 45 years of age, higher agreement among this group of respondents with authoritarianism could quite possibly be a correlate of their age more so than of their job.

# FOOTNOTES

[1] Lee J. Cronbach, "Coefficient Alpha and the Internal Structure of Tests," *Psychometrika* 16(1951):297-334.

[2] Paul G. Hoel, *Introduction to Mathematical Statistics* (New York: John Wiley and Sons, Inc., 1962), pp. 166-68.

[3] Bernard Ostle, *Statistics in Research: Basic Concepts and Techniques for Research Workers* (Ames: The Iowa State University Press, 1963), pp. 278-88.

[4] Wilfrid J. Dixon and F. J. Massey, *Introduction to Statistical Analysis* (New York: McGraw-Hill, 1957), pp. 145-52.

[5] Wilfrid J. Dixon, ed., *BMD Biomedical Computer Programs* (Berkeley: University of California Press, 1970), pp. 572-85.

[6] D. B. Duncan, "Multiple Range and Multiple F Tests," *Biometrics* 11(1955):1-42.

[7] D. B. Duncan, "Multiple Range Tests for Correlated and Heteroscedastic Means," *Biometrics* 13(1957):164-76.

[8] Ronald Aylmer Fisher and Frank Yates, *Statistical Tables for Biological, Agricultural and Medical Research* (London: Oliver and Boyd Ltd., 1938), pp. 33-35.

# CHAPTER 8
# SUMMARY AND CONCLUSIONS

> *I am mortified to be told that, in the United States of America, the sale of a book can become a subject of inquiry, and of criminal inquiry, too.*
>
> —Thomas Jefferson

## Purposes and Procedures of the Study

The two major purposes of this study were, first, to investigate the extent to which public librarians in the east north-central states of the United States accept the intellectual freedom principles and concepts of the *Library Bill of Rights* and the *Freedom to Read* statement and, second, to determine the attitudes of these librarians toward censorship practices. As a correlate of these purposes, the study was also designed to ascertain the relationship between librarians' attitudes toward censorship and their attitudes about certain characteristic beliefs of authoritarianism.

By means of survey research among a stratified random sample of 900 individuals, selected from a population of 3,253 public librarians in Illinois, Indiana, Michigan, Ohio, and Wisconsin, the study sought to quantify Midwestern public librarians' attitudes toward censorship, intellectual freedom, and certain beliefs contained in selected items from Adorno's F scale. The sample size was approximately 28 per cent of the population size. A mailed questionnaire was used to collect the necessary data. Approximately 70 per cent, or 624, of the instruments were returned as usable. That number represents approximately 19 per cent of the total population of public librarians in the east north-central states.

The questionnaire used to gather the data contained the following tests: 1) a group of statements taken almost verbatim from the *Library Bill of Rights* and the *Freedom to Read* statement, designed to measure whether librarians' attitudes were in accord with the principles of intellectual freedom adopted by the American Library Association; 2) a censorship attitude scale constructed by the investigator to measure whether librarians were opposed to, approved of, or were neutral to censorship activities; and 3) 18 items taken from the F scale on authoritarianism designed to measure the potential of an individual to accept fascist ideology.

Item responses from the returned usable questionnaires were tabulated, and percentages of answers to each fixed-alternative response were calculated. Scores on the three tests were correlated in order to determine the relationships among attitudes. The standard error for each mean score was ascertained, and population parameters for attitude scores were computed in order to obtain reliability indexes of internal consistency of the attitude tests. Five null hypotheses were then tested at the .01 level of confidence by comparing the three attitude scores, which were the dependent variables, with five pertinent demographic and sociological characteristics of the respondents, which were the independent variables. An analysis of variance with scores and independent variables was then computed in order to determine $F$ ratios (relationships) which existed between attitude scores and the independent variables.

This survey research was basically exploratory and descriptive, since prior to this study, very little investigation had been made of the attitudes of librarians toward the freedom to read and the freedom of access to books and information. Before the Fiske study of book selection and censorship in California, an assumption was apparently generally made within the library profession that librarians, as collectors and disseminators of various print and non-print media, would be unlikely to condone or to practice the censorship of books and other communication media. This concluding chapter will summarize what the findings of the present study indicate about the relationships among the attitudes of Midwestern public librarians toward intellectual freedom, censorship, and authoritarianism. The reader is reminded that the results of this research have not been generalized to any librarians other than those included in the population selected.

## Reliability of the Censorship Scale

Because of the lack of an appropriate attitude scale with which to measure censorship attitudes among librarians, as valid an instrument as possible had to be constructed for that purpose. Certain time and financial limitations posed restrictions, and an attempt had to be made to determine the reliability of the instrument before indexes of attitudes of Midwestern public librarians about censorship could be established. The censorship attitude scale prepared was the product of several months of investigation to determine what attitudes public librarians should and should not have toward censorship if their opinions were to be in conformity with the standards, principles, and concepts adopted by the American Library Association. That search involved the examination of hundreds of professional journal articles dealing with censorship and the concept of intellectual freedom in order to tabulate the frequently-occurring statements of opposition to the censorship of books and information. These statements included both theoretical and practical statements made by librarians and library educators, as well as by experts in the area of censorship who were outside the field of librarianship.

Although the censorship scale constructed for this opinion research was prepared by the investigator who conducted the study, it is based upon the opinions of experts. The choice of wording of items and the weighting of fixed-alternative responses were based upon jury opinion. While advice about the construction of the tests used was sought from and freely given by library educators, practitioners, and library science doctoral students in the Indiana University Graduate Library School, and while the scale was subjected to a number of pre-tests, the altering, addition, and elimination of items during the process of construction was essentially the responsibility of one person—the investigator. The scale was considered as exploratory in this study; that factor should be taken into account in considering its reliability and validity as a device for determining censorship attitudes.

A Cronbach alpha coefficient for the censorship attitude scale, computed as an index of the scale's reliability, was .91. Because a perfect reliability index or coefficient would be the value *one*, .91 indicates a high degree of internal consistency among the items. The reliability index for the censorship scale was actually the highest computed for the three attitude tests used in this study. It was .05 points higher than the coefficient of reliability computed for the F scale and .04 points higher than the index computed for the intellectual freedom test. Used as an exploratory probe in this investigation, the censorship attitude scale was deemed to be a reliable instrument, and the measures it provided were accepted as valid quantification of librarians' attitudes toward censorship.

## Pro- and Anti-Censorship Librarians

Taking the evidence from results of the measurement of censorship attitudes, some general conclusions can be drawn about the characteristics of Midwestern public librarians who predominantly approved of the repression of books and materials and other suppressive acts. It should first be pointed out that high-scoring respondents on censorship were classified as being pro-censorship, and low scorers were classified as being anti-censorship. The majority of pro-censorship librarians (73 per cent) were employed in communities with populations of less than 35,000, whereas only 59 per cent of those librarians who responded were from communities of the same size. Sixty-two per cent of the librarians with pro-censorship attitudes were directors or heads of public libraries, whereas only 50 per cent of those librarians responding were in the same position. Ninety-three per cent of those who obtained high censorship scores (53-90) were over 45 years of age, whereas 68 per cent of the total number of librarians who responded were of the same age. Among the pro-censorship librarians, 92 per cent were women, the ratio of female to male high scorers having been eleven-to-one as opposed to the overall female to male ratio of four-to-one in the sample. The educational-attainment of the group of librarians with pro-censorship attitudes was considerably lower than that achieved by librarians who were strongly opposed to censorship: 20 per cent of the pro-censorship librarians had obtained a Master's degree in library science or its equivalent, whereas 74 per cent of those librarians with anti-censorship attitudes had obtained a fifth-year library science degree. In addition, 29 per cent of the librarians who expressed pro-censorship attitudes had no formal education beyond high school, whereas only 13 per cent of the total number of librarians had not continued their education beyond high school.

An analysis of the characteristics of pro-censorship Midwestern public librarians allowed the construction of a profile or composite of the typical public librarian who could be expected to look favorably on repressive measures toward the freedom to read and the freedom of access to information. The findings of this study suggest that the Midwestern public librarian most likely to approve strongly of censorship—either within or outside of the library—would be a female head librarian in a community of less than 35,000 inhabitants. She would in all probability be over 45 years of age and would most likely not have earned a degree from a four-year college, even though she might have acquired some college credits.

One hundred thirty-nine, or 22 per cent, of the 624 respondents in the survey obtained low censorship scores (18-32). These librarians, whose attitudes were classified as anti-censorship, were found to be dispersed in communities of all sizes; however, several population-size categories contained heavier concentrations of low scorers on censorship: 24 per cent of the low scorers were employed in cities with populations between 5,000 and 14,999; 20 per cent were in cities with populations between 100,000 and 399,999; 19 per cent were from cities with populations between 35,000 and 99,999; and 15 per cent were from cities with populations between 15,000 and 34,999.

Forty-four per cent of the anti-censorship respondents were employed in libraries as directors or heads; 34 per cent were directors or members of public service departments; 16 per cent were branch librarians; 12 per cent were heads of subject, extension, or technical service departments; and four per cent were assistant directors. Seventy per cent of the librarians with strong anti-censorship attitudes were females, and 30 per cent were males. The ratio of female to male librarians who were strongly opposed to censorship practices was 2.3 to one; however, that fact should be considered in relation to the overall ratio of four females to one male respondent in the random sample.

Whereas most of the pro-censorship respondents were in the three highest age brackets used for classifying librarians in this study, 51 per cent of the anti-censorship librarians were over 45 years old, and the remaining librarians fell into the other eight age brackets as follows: two per cent were from the 22-24 age bracket, nine per cent were from the 25-27 bracket, 12 per cent were from the 28-30 bracket, five per cent were from the 31-33 bracket, four per cent from the 37-39 bracket, nine per cent from the 40-42 bracket, and four per cent from the 43-45 bracket.

In comparison with the pro-censorship respondent-librarians, those classed in a group as anti-censorship had completed more years of formal education. Seventy-four per cent of those librarians who expressed strong anti-censorship feelings had obtained a fifth-year library science degree, i.e., a Master of Library Science degree or its equivalent; 12 per cent were graduated from four-year colleges; four per cent had earned some college credits, although they were not graduated from colleges; and only five per cent had not advanced their formal education beyond high school.

It is more difficult to construct a profile of the typical public librarian in the Midwest whose attitudes would most likely be definitely anti-censorship. The characteristics of low-scoring (anti-censorship) respondents did not fall as neatly at one or the other end of the series of repressive-permissive categories as did those of the high-scoring (pro-censorship) respondents. The most critical differential between pro- and anti-censorship respondents appeared to be the respondents' educational-attainment levels; the chances appear to be about three to one that librarians strongly opposing censorship would have earned a degree

142

from a four-year college in addition to a fifth-year library science degree. In view of the overall findings of the study as discussed in Chapter 7 and in consideration of the characteristics of librarians who expressed strong anti-censorship attitudes in the three preceding paragraphs, a characterization of the Midwestern public librarian who would be most likely to disapprove strongly of censorship can be made only in a more general manner and with more qualifications. In approximately 6.5 cases out of ten, for example, the anti-censorship librarian would be employed in a city containing more than 15,000 inhabitants. In 5.6 cases out of ten the anti-censorship librarian would be in a position other than that of head librarian. If the librarian were not the head or director of a library, 4.5 times out of ten he or she would be a head or a member of a public service department and three times out of ten a head of a branch library. Although more women than men obtained low censorship scores, the ratio being two to one, it should be remembered that the overall ratio of female to male respondents in the survey was four-to-one. It appears, consequently, that insofar as sex is concerned neither would have an edge over the other, since there would be a 50/50 chance for a member of either sex to have strong feelings against censorship. Likewise, there also appears to be a .50 chance that the typical anti-censorship librarian would be under 45 years of age.

In this attempt to characterize the typical anti-censorship Midwestern public librarian, it became apparent that he or she cannot often be described using those characteristics which are just the opposite of the pro-censorship librarian. Neither sex was noticeably more likely to be against censorship; the chances were almost equal that he or she would be over 45 years of age; librarians who are very much opposed to repression might be employed in a Midwestern community of almost any size and in almost any kind of position.


## Relationship of Attitudes to Variables

All five of the null hypotheses were rejected, with the exception of three sub-parts of Hypothesis 2, which dealt with the attitudes of librarians toward intellectual freedom in relation to the independent variables (characteristics of librarians). The hypotheses will be discussed in this section in numerical order.

Hypothesis 1, which stated that there is no significant relationship between the attitudes of Midwestern public librarians toward intellectual freedom and the attitudes of librarians toward censorship, was rejected at the .01 level of confidence because a fairly high and statistically significant coefficient of correlation was computed between the 624 pairs of intellectual freedom and censorship scores. The coefficient of correlation was a positive .60; thus, the two dependent variables or attitudes changed together generally in approximate magnitude and in the same direction. In other words, the degree to which respondents rejected censorship measures was approximated by the degree to which they accepted intellectual freedom principles.

Because the interrelation between Midwestern public librarians' attitudes toward intellectual freedom and censorship was positive and statistically significant, the opposite of the hypothesis—that there is a relationship between the two attitudes—was tentatively accepted. Librarians who approved of intellectual freedom principles of the *Library Bill of Rights* and the *Freedom to Read* statement also disapproved of censorship to an approximately corresponding degree; however, the degree of disapproval was not in direct proportion to the degree of approval of intellectual freedom principles. A librarian's expression of agreement with these liberal principles did not completely preclude his or her disagreement with all censorship measures and practices, for the coefficient of correlation was not a perfect positive one. Some librarians' attitudes about the freedom to read and the right to inquiry were in complete agreement with the letter and the spirit of intellectual freedom, but their attitudes toward censorship indicated, at the same time, a tolerance for restraints on book reading.

Three sub-parts of Hypothesis 2, that is, 2-a, 2-b, and 2-d, could not be rejected because age, sex, and position of employment were found to have no significant relationship at the .01 level of confidence with librarians' attitudes toward intellectual freedom. On the other hand, there were significant relationships between the other three independent variables and librarians' attitudes toward intellectual freedom. These variables were: 1) the size of the community in which the librarian was employed, 2) the state where librarian was employed, and 3) the amount of formal education completed. Because relationships between these independent variables and attitudes toward intellectual freedom were positive at the .01 level of confidence, inasmuch as the $F$ ratios were significant, Hypothesis 2-c, 2-3 and 2-f were rejected.

Summarizing the findings in relation to the intellectual freedom attitudes of Midwestern public librarians, then, one could state that some statistical relationship was found, on the one hand, between librarians' attitudes toward concepts in the *Library Bill of Rights* and the *Freedom to Read* statement and the state in which librarians were employed, the size of the community of employment, and the amount of education completed by librarians. On the other hand, no relationships were found between librarians' attitudes toward intellectual freedom and their age, sex, and job classification.

It became clear in the analysis of the data that variations among the attitudes of Midwestern public librarians toward intellectual freedom were indeed small, even though there were some significant relationships among attitude scores and three of the independent variables. The group mean intellectual freedom score for all respondents was rather low; responses to items in the intellectual freedom test, which were all taken almost verbatim from the *Library Bill of Rights* and the *Freedom to Read* statement, were distinctly favorable, as most librarians either agreed or strongly agreed with each of them. Furthermore, the statistical analysis made to predict population parameters for the three attitude scores revealed that at the .01 level of confidence an estimated mean score on the intellectual freedom test of between 31.02 nad 32.50 could be made for the entire population of Midwestern public librarians. The range of 1.48 between these estimated limits is indeed very low, and the lowest limit is only .8 below the sample mean intellectual freedom score. The data show that Midwestern public librarians definitely approve, with very few exceptions, of the statements of intellectual freedom included in the *Library Bill of Rights* and the *Freedom to Read* statement. In other words, when it comes to the concept of intellectual freedom, almost all Midwestern public librarians are for it.

Among the most revealing results of this opinion research was the close correspondence found between librarians' attitudes toward censorship and the five independent variables considered. The collected data allowed the complete and profound rejection of Hypothesis 3, which stated that there is no relationship between librarians' attitudes toward censorship and age, sex, size of community of employment, position in the library, state where employed, and amount of formal education completed. A positive and proportional relationship was found between age and censorship attitudes: as the ages of librarians increased there was a tendency for librarians to look more favorably on repressive censorious acts. The only exception found among the age groups was within group one, which contained only nine respondents between the ages of 22 and 24 years, and with group six, which contained only 14 respondents between the ages of 37 and 39 years. Since the number of respondents represented in the sample within these two age groups was relatively small in comparison with the number in other groups, these exceptions did not appear to be indicative. There was an overall positive, significant relationship between the ages of librarians and their attitudes toward censorship at the .01 level of confidence.

Sex of librarians was found to be a very significant differentiating criterion in relation to classifying librarians on a repressive-permissive continuum. The mean censorship attitude score obtained by male librarians was 6.6 points lower than the mean censorship score obtained by female librarians; thus, men looked less favorably at repression than did women. The standard deviation of 9.5 computed for male librarians for the censorship attitude test was also lower than the standard deviation of 11.1 computed for female librarians. That difference indicated a somewhat smaller variation in the attitudes of men than of women. At the .01 level of confidence there was a significant difference between the attitudes of male and female librarians toward censorship. The data indicate that male public librarians in the Midwest are less likely to approve of censorship than are female librarians.

When sizes of communities in which librarians were employed were considered in relation to attitudes toward censorship, the data indicated an inverse relationship between community size and the degree to which librarians approved of repressive measures on the freedom to read and the freedom of inquiry; thus, as community size increased, attitudes of librarians working within them tended to become less tolerant of censorship practices. Librarians employed in Chicago, the largest city from which respondents were selected, were very unfavorable toward censorship because they obtained the lowest mean censorship attitude score, but librarians employed in the smallest communities (under 5,000 population) obtained the highest mean censorship score. Size of community in which librarians were employed was seen to be statistically significant as an independent variable in relation to pro- and anti-censorship attitudes.

The evidence collected in the study also indicated a significant relationship between the position held by a librarian and his or her attitudes toward censorship. Heads of public service departments obtained the lowest mean censorship score, and library directors obtained the highest mean censorship score. Perhaps the day-to-day confrontation of library users and their informational problems helps liberalize public service librarians in respect to access to information.

When formal education obtained by librarians was compared with attitudes toward censorship, the data indicated an inverse relationship, since censorship attitude scores decreased proportionately almost unit for unit as the amount of obtained formal education increased. Contrary to the null hypothesis, which predicted no relationship between these two variables, a statistically significant connection was determined. The group of respondents with very anti-censorship attitudes was comprised of librarians who had obtained fifth-year library science degrees. The lowest-scoring group of librarians obtained a mean score which was 29 points less than the score obtained by the highest-scoring group, comprised of six librarians who had not completed high school. The findings clearly indicated that the more formal education librarians had obtained the less likely they were to be disposed to accepting censorship practices. Even within the group of librarians who had earned some college credits but were not college graduates, attitudes became less favorable toward censorship as the number of earned credit hours increased.

The data suggest, therefore, that formal education mattered greatly as a liberalizing influence on the attitudes of librarians toward the freedom to read and the freedom of access to information.

Hypothesis 4, which stated that there would be no relationship between Midwestern public librarians' attitudes toward censorship and their attitudes toward the 18 items of the F scale on authoritarianism, was rejected on the evidence obtained from the opinion research. A coefficient of correlation of .73 was computed between the 624 pairs of scores for each respondent on censorship and on authoritarianism. Consequently, there was a statistically significant relationship between the attitudes of Midwestern public librarians toward authoritarian beliefs and their attitudes toward censorship. Because of the rejection of Hypothesis 4, its opposite is tentatively accepted as true: librarians who tend to accept or to agree with authoritarian beliefs contained in the F scale on authoritarianism will also tend, very strongly, to accept or to agree to censorship measures at the operational level; librarians who do not agree with these beliefs will be rather uniformly unsympathetic with censorship activities.

Not only was there a high correlation between censorship and authoritarian attitudes of librarians, but all the important variables in which high- and low-scoring respondents on censorship differed were found to be identical to those which mattered for authoritarianism. Hypothesis 5 was thus rejected at the .01 level of confidence. The hypothesis stated that there would be no relationship between the attitudes of librarians toward characteristic authoritarian beliefs contained in the F scale and the same independent variables or characteristics of librarians used in Hypothesis 2 and Hypothesis 3. Statistically significant differences in attitudes with those variables were obtained when the data were analyzed. The relationships observed were close parallels with the relationships found between censorship attitude scores and the independent variables.

The data revealed that the greater the age of a librarian, the more he or she would tend to agree with authoritarian beliefs. In addition, female librarians' attitudes tended to be more authoritarian than those of male librarians, and the attitudes of directors of libraries tended to be more sympathetic to authoritarianism than librarians employed in other library positions. When the respondent-librarians were grouped by states where employed according to the rank order of their authoritarian scores from lowest to highest, the following order was found: 1) Ohio, 2) Wisconsin, 3) Indiana, 4) Illinois, and 5) Michigan. There was a statistically significant relationship between authoritarian scores and the state where librarians were employed. Also apparent from the collected data was the fact that as the amount of formal education obtained increased, librarians rejected authoritarian beliefs.

## Conclusions and Recommendations

The most significant result of this study, in the opinion of the investigator, is that the data show a marked disparity between the attitudes of many librarians toward intellectual freedom as a concept and their attitudes toward censorship as an activity. Theoretically, librarians would be expected to be unanimous in their opposition to restraints on the freedom to read and the freedom of access to library materials. This study revealed, however, that the attitudes of 14 per cent of the public librarians in the east north-central states were predominantly sympathetic toward censorship and that the attitudes of only 22 per cent of these librarians were strongly opposed to censorship practices. The findings also suggest that the attitudes of the remaining 64 per cent of Midwestern public librarians were somewhat neutral, neither highly favorable nor unfavorable toward censorship. The attitudes of librarians whose scores placed them in this middle-of-the-road position regarding censorship activities appear to be inconsistent with the favorable attitudes expressed by almost all of these same librarians toward the liberal freedom-to-read and intellectual freedom principles contained in the *Library Bill of Rights* and the *Freedom to Read* statement.

## Implications of the Study

The data collected for this opinion research were not based on a national random sample forming a heterogeneous cross-section of all public librarians in the United States; thus, the selection of a representative sample for all public librarians was beyond the means of this study. Rather, the data collected here were obtained from a stratified random sample of public librarians in a large section of the Midwest containing the states of Illinois, Indiana, Michigan, Ohio, and Wisconsin. As was pointed out in Chapter 6, these east north-central states have some population characteristics which closely parallel those of the nation as a whole: a population which is 70.7 per cent urban as compared with a national urban population of 69.9 per cent, and a population growth rate for the years 1900 to 1960 of 128.4 as compared with a total national increase of 135.5 for the same period.

However, these broad similarities between the region studied and the entire United States do not justify conclusions about the attitudes of all American public librarians; thus, the findings based on the random sample selected in the present study are generalized only to Midwestern public librarians. Certain relationships between independent and dependent variables appeared with regularity and uniformity, however, in the data collected from all five of the states in this investigation, and a few justifiable implications warrant attention.

The association found between the amount of formal education completed by respondents and their attitudes toward censorship may have implications for the education of librarians. This study revealed that with each amount of increase in the degree of formal education completed by respondents, there was, almost without exception, a corresponding decrease in the approval of repressive measures on the right to read and the freedom of inquiry. Such was found to be true in cases where the increase was with only two or three additional hours of college credit. In view of this finding, continuing education in the form of courses taken for credit may be an important, perhaps even essential, method for promoting among librarians an active commitment to the preservation of the freedom to read for everyone. Less formal methods of education, such as on-the-job or in-service training, workshops, and institutes, might also have similar effects on librarians' attitudes toward censorship; however, this study did not identify or isolate these as variables. Informal education could have been an intervening variable and might account for the fact that a few of the librarians with limited formal education expressed quite liberal views. In any event, the implications are quite clear: the more education, the less repression.

Fifty-one per cent of the respondents were over 45 years of age, and as the ages of respondents increased from the 19-21 bracket to the over-45 bracket, attitudes became more favorable toward censorship practices and authoritarian beliefs. As there was a statistically significant relationship between ages and attitudes and as growing older appeared to have an adverse effect on liberal attitudes, the continuing education of professional librarians could also prove to be a necessary condition for the reduction of that effect on librarians' attitudes toward the freedom of access to books and information.

Because the librarians employed in more urbanized areas of all five states were more anti-censorship than those working in small communities and towns, an assumption seems justifiable that similar attitudes could be found among librarians in other states and regions. The degree to which the population characteristics of other states and areas correspond to those included in the present study, as well as the extent to which characteristics of librarians in other states and areas also correspond with those in this opinion research, should govern generalizations based on the findings outlined here. The degree to which a state or region is urbanized appears to be a significant variable in predicting pro- or anti-censorship attitudes among librarians. Librarians working in areas of the nation such as the south Atlantic, the west north-central, and the east south-central, all of which are relatively rural, might be expected, consequently, to look more favorably on the practice of censorship than would librarians in highly urbanized areas. This assumption remains, however, in need of an empirical test: mobility of librarians would have to be considered.

The 1970s appear to be a period of ferment and change, with an increasing polarization of society on numerous social and political issues. It is imperative that public librarians continually renew and reevaluate their attitudes and actions in respect to the maintenance of library collections, which provide information for all groups of library users and which present views on all sides of all issues. Continuing education, supported by liberal policies for leaves or sabbaticals for that purpose, appears to be one method of assuring that librarians will maintain professional perspectives relevant to and commensurate with the responsibilities inherent in the positions which they occupy in the communication networks of the United States.

All respondents in this study were selected from a population of librarians employed in public library job classifications which, according to professional standards, require educational qualifications consisting of a four-year college degree plus professional library training consisting of a Master's degree in library science or its equivalent; however, many of those selected as respondents from these job classifications did not meet the educational qualifications commensurate with the positions they held. There appear, therefore, to be implications with respect to library manpower. Insofar as attitudes toward censorship are concerned, unqualified librarians without appropriate educational and professional backgrounds were shown to be more likely to favor the restriction of intellectual freedom, and these attitudes are in opposition to standards of library service adopted by the profession as a whole. The "Library Education and Manpower" statement, which was adopted by the Council of the American Library Association on June 19, 1970, and which is concerned primarily with the categorizing of library personnel according to positions and the educational requirements and responsibilities of these positions, may become an effective means for reducing the amount of pro-censorship feeling in the library profession. The manpower statement stipulates that the title "librarian" should carry with it the connotation of "professional" and should be reserved only for those who are qualified by means of education to perform professional duties.

## Recommendations for Additional Research

This study raises some questions concerning librarians and intellectual freedom that can be answered only on the basis of rigorous research. Answers are needed for the following queries:

1. *Role of the Public Library Trustee.* Boards of trustees of public libraries are responsible for the selection and appointment of head librarians and are, as well, responsible for setting policies under which public librarians operate. To what extent do these boards support the application of intellectual freedom policies to book-selection practices and to library services? Are trustees willing to defend actions of librarians who actively support the principles of the freedom to read in public libraries?

2. *Attitudes of Community Leaders.* What are the attitudes of community leaders toward the freedom to read and access to information? Librarians with restrictive attitudes frequently justify a need for censorship by referring to the general climate of opinion within their communities. A statement such as "This sort of thing just won't go over in the community," in reference to some book or material on a sexual topic, or a political one, or even to a volume of modern poetry, is frequently used to justify the exclusion of books and other materials. Opinion research should be conducted among city council members, mayors,

city managers, superintendents of schools, and other community social and political leaders to obtain a measure of their attitudes toward censorship and the freedom to read. Such a study would lead to a better understanding, perhaps, of the attitudes of librarians.

3. *Attitudes of Library Users and Non-users.* What are the attitudes of library users (who may or may not be community leaders) toward freedom of access to books and information, and what do non-users of libraries also feel about censorship and intellectual freedom? How many and what kinds of users care whether they—or other users with differing viewpoints—have access to varying kinds of materials? Do the attitudes of some users contribute to the restrictive practices of librarians, who, because of a fear of complaints from readers, refrain from adding controversial material to their collections?

4. *The Struggle Between Ideologies.* What effects will the current struggle between the ideologies of permissiveness and law and order have on the development of public library collections and the attitudes and behavior of librarians toward censorship? Over a period of years, do changes in selection practices show any relationship to the nature or extent of public controversy?

5. *Role of State Libraries and Library Associations.* How much effort do state libraries, library extension agencies, and library associations exert to promote intellectual freedom in the various states? Do active intellectual freedom committees exist at state and regional levels? How effective are the programs of these groups? Do librarians believe that they will receive the full support of state and regional library associations, as well as that of the state library extension agency, when they defend the user's right to read, or do they feel that they will be essentially alone in resisting censorship?

6. *Role of the American Library Association.* How effective is the American Library Association, the strongest organization of librarians in the United States, in defending intellectual freedom and librarians who resist censorship pressures? Will the Freedom to Read Foundation, which was approved by the American Library Association's Executive Board in November, 1969, serve as an effective deterrent to censorship pressures? Will it prove to be a potent mechanism for the support and defense of librarians who are faced with censorship problems and find their positions in jeopardy as a result of their public defense of intellectual freedom principles?

7. *System Affiliation.* Do librarians in small libraries which are parts of library systems have attitudes toward intellectual freedom which differ from those of librarians in completely independent small libraries? What efforts are being made by librarians within systems to promote the freedom of access to materials for users in member libraries? Do centralized book-selection practices in consolidated systems promote the building of objective and balanced collections in small member libraries? What attempts are being made in consolidated systems to liberalize any narrow attitudes and restrictive practices which librarians in smaller library units may have?

### In Conclusion

If the assumption is accepted that librarianship is a recognized profession, then the supposition must also be accepted that codes of behavior and statements of policy developed by the profession's associations should govern the conduct and practices of members. Consequently, documents such as the *Library Bill of Rights* and the *Freedom to Read* statement, both of which were designed to protect the rights of library users to easy access to books and information, should contribute to the development among librarians of more professional attitudes. Librarians who wish to maintain high standards of library service and professional behavior will not only profess agreement with the contents of these documents, as all librarians in this opinion research basically did; they will also activate the principles which they profess and apply them to their practices—which some of the respondents apparently do not do, if their attitudes are reflections of their actions.

If one culls the statistical data of this study in order to determine whether Midwestern public librarians are predominantly restrictive or permissive in relation to the freedom of inquiry and the freedom to read, the picture which evolves is indeed ambivalent. While these librarians express very strong agreement with "freedom to read" concepts contained in the *Library Bill of Rights* and the *Freedom to Read* statement, the greatest majority of them were much more cautious; they did not strongly oppose restrictiveness. It is evident that Midwestern public librarians did not hesitate to express agreement with clichés of intellectual freedom but that many of them apparently did not feel strongly enough about them as professionals to assert these principles in the face of real or anticipated censorship pressures.

# PART III

# BIBLIOGRAPHY OF CENSORSHIP
# 1950–1971

# INTRODUCTION

This bibliography was compiled in order to provide in one source a listing of current publications about contemporary censorship problems. Publications in subject areas closely related to censorship—such as freedom of inquiry, the freedom of information, and issues of obscenity and pornography in various communication media—are also included. The compiler's purpose in preparing this bibliography was not to provide a comprehensive or definitive bibliography of censorship; every effort was made, on the contrary, to be critical and selective.

While an attempt was undertaken to list publications of scholarly value published between 1950 and 1971, a few not-so-scholarly works were included for one or more of the following reasons: 1) the special nature of a work, 2) unique treatment of the topic, or 3) contents of potential value as historical documents. Works published during the 1960s and 1970s were given priority of inclusion in deference to political and social developments of the recent decade and the impact which changes of the sixties have had on the availability of information and the censorship of expression. A few earlier works published in the 1950s were also included, either because of their contribution as contemporary statements or for their potential usefulness to librarians as parallel studies to current issues of intellectual freedom.

Monographic and research works, including doctoral dissertations, are listed in Section A of this bibliography, while theses written for Master's degrees in library science are listed in Section B. Articles or parts of larger publications are noted in Section C of the list. Descriptive annotations of varying lengths have been provided for the more than 100 books, research studies, and doctoral dissertations in Section A. No attempt was made, however, to annotate or abstract the Master's degree theses in Section B or the 131 periodical and journal articles listed in Section C; titles of many of the articles included are fairly descriptive of their content. All articles and theses in this compilation were deemed to be of current or future value to librarians, to scholars, and to students who might be concerned about the free exchange of information and ideas and the forces at play which attempt to restrict, either overtly or subtly, the free flow of information.

With the exception of some documents listed for which resumes were reprinted from *Research in Education*,[1] almost all works included in Section A were personally examined by the compiler; indeed, many of them were read in their entirety. As it is the compiler's intention to maintain ongoing interest in publications similar in content to those listed here, users of this bibliography are encouraged to communicate with the author if glaring omissions are recognized here or if publications are encountered in the future which merit attention but which—because of their ephemeral nature or limited distribution—might otherwise escape notice.

# FOOTNOTES

[1] *Research in Education*, a monthly publication of the Educational Resources Information Center (ERIC), Office of Education, U. S. Department of Health, Education, and Welfare, is designed to make possible the early identification and acquisition of reports of interest to the educational community.

## SECTION A
## BOOKS, DISSERTATIONS, STUDIES, REPORTS, AND PAMPHLETS
## AN ANNOTATED LIST

Aherns, Nyla H. *Censorship and the Teacher of English: a Survey of a Selected Sample of Secondary School Teachers of English.* Dissertation written for the Ed.D. degree at Columbia University, 1965. 148p. (University Microfilms, No. 65-14, 958)

Based on the results of survey research among members of the· Secondary Section of the National Council of Teachers of English, the study found that 12.6 per cent of the respondent-teachers had experienced incidents of attempts to censor textbooks and other books used in public secondary school English programs. The study also attempted to identify any common characteristics of teachers who had experienced censorship pressures as well as those who had not. Differences in educational backgrounds, in the use by teachers of literary material, and in the size of schools were found between the two groups. Despite incidents of censorship attempts, the study revealed that "in the majority of cases the book was retained for use as originally planned."

American Library Association. Office for Intellectual Freedom. *Censorship and Intellectual Freedom: an Annual Annotated Comprehensive Bibliography, 1968-69.* Chicago, A.L.A., 1970. 42p.

Compiled by James H. Harvey, assistant director of the Office for Intellectual Freedom of the American Library Association, this bibliography contains citations for current articles, pamphlets, and books on the following topics: principles of intellectual freedom; practice of intellectual freedom; defense and support of the *Library Bill of Rights*; censorship, the law, and obscenity; activities related to intellectual freedom; and intellectual freedom and censorship in fields related to librarianship. Brief descriptive annotations are provided for each entry.

Balmuth, Daniel. *Censorship in Russia, 1848-1855.* Dissertation written for the Ph.D. degree at Cornell University, 1959. 555p. (University Microfilms, No. 59-6127)

This thesis is a study of the regular and extraordinary censorship institutions which existed during the last years of the reign of Nicholas I of Russia.

Blanshard, Paul. *The Right to Read: the Battle Against Censorship.* Boston: Beacon Press, 1955. 339p.

A general introduction to the subject of the freedom to read designed for the average person who might want to know why and how he should defend his right to read. In such chapters as "Textbooks and the Schools" and "Communism and Capitalism," the control and the distribution of reading materials in the United States are examined. The volume is valuable for its analysis of the issues involved in the right to read rather than for its presentation of censorship cases.

Booth, Wayne C. *Censorship and the Values of Fiction.* 1964. 10p. (EDRS Document Ed 014 484)

General statements about the moral value of literature have proven to be unsuccessful in dissuading potential censors. More effective are arguments which convince the person who attempts to censor literature that he is violating his own social, political, or moral standards. However, these also are frequently too general to be convincing. Therefore, the teacher should be prepared with reasonable and articulate defenses of the specific works he plans to teach, based upon anticipated criticism by potential censors. In preparing defenses, teachers should lead potential censors to 1) consider the objectionable elements in the context of the work, 2) reread the book carefully to avoid being misled by first impressions which are modified by sustained reflection, and 3) realize that the real moral center of a work cannot usually be identified with the expressed values of any one character. *Catcher in the Rye* serves as a ready example of the kind of book frequently under attack. If the teacher can briefly explicate the book, emphasizing its moral context and the contribution of Holden's reaction to the prostitute and the words scrawled on the stairwell, the potential censor not only may be dissuaded from pursuing his desires, but also may begin to understand the complexities of literature itself and how the "immoral" book may be, in fact, moral by the censor's own standards.

Boyer, Paul S. *Purity in Print; the Vice-Society Movement and Book Censorship in America.* New York: Scribner, 1968. 362p.

A history of book censorship in the United States, from the rise of the vice societies in the mid-1880s to their decline in the 1930s. Boyer's stated purpose in writing this account of censorship attitudes as they existed 50 years ago is to place modern attitudes toward censorship in perspective. The author believes that we may be headed toward a period of increased censorship; he offers this history of past suppression as a basis for forming new criteria. Information for the book was obtained from newspaper accounts, memoirs, court records, and personal interviews. Includes a bibliography.

Burress, Lee A., Jr. *How Censorship Affects the School.* Wisconsin Council of Teachers of English, 1963. 24p. (Special Bulletin, No. 8; EDRS Document ED 053 110)

Questionnaires were sent to 914 public school administrators and 724 public school teachers in Wisconsin. Of the 1,640 sent, over 600 were returned. A major purpose of the questionnaire was to discover the prevalence of censorship pressures on the public schools of Wisconsin. The returns showed that the pressure of censorship is a prominent part of school life in this state. Censorship is defined as the use of nonprofessional standards for accepting or rejecting a book. Some teachers are discontented with school policy that seems to favor bowing to community standards and tastes. However, the information accumulated by this study does not permit more than certain qualified observations concerning the impact of censorship on the schools. Conditions vary widely in the schools: excellent work is done in many, while severe limitations exist in others.

Burke, Redmond A. *The Control of Reading by the Catholic Church.* Dissertation written for the Ph.D. degree at the University of Chicago, 1948.

This dissertation discusses the role of the Catholic Church in controlling reading material for the layman. The study used authoritative statements by the Catholic Church or regulations concerning the reading of Catholics, the official application of these principles by canonists, and informal discussions. The study points out that the Catholic Church has always had a great respect for books and that it maintains a twofold policy: to stimulate the reading of good books and to discourage the reading of books which might endanger faith or morals, as defined by the Church. The historical background of three views of Church policy regarding censorship is reviewed: 1) *imprimatur* prior to publication; 2) prohibition of books after publication, including methods of examination and evaluation; 3) invocation of penalties against violators. Selected lists of forbidden authors and titles are included.

Busha, Charles H. *The Attitudes of Midwestern Public Librarians toward Intellectual Freedom and Censorship.* Dissertation written for the Ph.D. degree at Indiana University, 1971. 175p. (University Microfilms, No. 71-29, 561)

The purposes of this opinion research among Midwestern public librarians were the determination of 1) extent to which librarians accept intellectual freedom principles of the *Library Bill of Rights* and the *Freedom to Read* statement, 2) the attitudes of librarians toward censorship, 3) the relationship of librarians' censorship attitudes to their attitudes toward selected authoritarian beliefs, and 4) the relationship between librarians' intellectual freedom and censorship attitudes. Data were collected by means of a questionnaire sent to 900 librarians selected at random from a population of 3,253 public librarians in Illinois, Indiana, Michigan, Ohio and Wisconsin. There was a very high degree of agreement among the librarians with statements favoring intellectual freedom; however, a marked disparity existed between the attitudes of some librarians toward intellectual freedom as a concept and their attitudes toward censorship as an activity. Librarians who agreed with authoritarian beliefs also tended, very strongly, to approve of censorship measures. Fourteen per cent of the public librarians were found to be predominantly sympathetic toward censorship. Only 22 per cent of the public librarians were strongly opposed to censorship practices. Findings of the study also suggested that the remaining 64 per cent of Midwestern public librarians were somewhat neutral; they were neither highly in favor of nor opposed to repression of books and information. The older the librarians, the more likely they were to look favorably on censorship measures, and there was more approval of censorship and authoritarian measures among female than among male librarians. The opinion research also revealed that as community size increased, the attitudes of librarians working within them tended to become less tolerant of censorship.

Busha, Charles H. *Authoritarianism and Censorship: Attitudes and Opinions of Students in the Graduate Library School of Indiana University.* Bloomington, Indiana, 1969. 48p. (EDRS Document ED 033 727)

This study bears the subtitle: "A Report of an Exploratory Project Conducted as a Preliminary for a Proposed Nationwide Study of American Public Librarians and Intellectual Freedom." While that proposed study was not conducted on a nationwide basis, this study did serve as a pretest for an opinion survey conducted later among Midwestern public librarians. The pretest measured the attitudes held by a group of future librarians toward intellectual freedom and correlated those findings with certain syndromes of authoritarianism as reported in *The Authoritarian Personality* by T. W. Adorno and others (New York: Harper, 1950). The hypothesis was that graduate library students who expressed approval of restrictive controls on intellectual freedom would also concur with many of the attitudes characteristic of the authoritarian syndrome. If the hypothesis was correct, those students whose opinions scored high on a censorship scale would also score high on the authoritarianism scale (fascism or F scale). The questionnaire distributed to students in December 1968 contained 27 statements about intellectual freedom, book selection, and the role of the librarian, interspersed with the 18 F scale items. The findings of the study supported the hypothesis. Students who agreed with restrictive measures on intellectual freedom also agreed with authoritarian attitudes. The coefficient of correlation between the two attitude scores was .69. The study did not reveal that a large number of students agreed with either censorship measures or with authoritarian attitudes; however, those students who did approve of censorship also approved of authoritarian statements.

Cage, Penelope B. *A Constitutional Dilemma: Censorship of the Obscene.* Dissertation written for the Ph.D. degree at the University of Virginia, 1967. 173p. (University Microfilms, No. 67-17, 594)

Examines the reasons underlying the U. S. Supreme Court's position on censorship in relation to obscenity; analyzes rulings on obscenity cases handed down between 1959 and 1966. The study concludes: "the Supreme Court has become entangled in a dilemma of its own making: by basing the *Roth* decision on the idea that obscene expression is not protected by the First Amendment, the court made it imperative that the term 'obscene' be precisely defined." The dissertation points out the difficulty of defining obscenity and shows how the Court has attempted to establish a new test for that term.

Carmen, Ira H. *Movies, Censorship, and the Law.* Ann Arbor, University of Michigan Press, 1966. 339p.

Dealing primarily with the legal aspects of motion picture censorship, this book covers recent history of restraints against one medium of communication and extends the survey into additional fields such as book publishing. The functions of local censorship boards are also discussed at length in this work.

Chandos, John, ed. *'To Deprave and Corrupt . . .' Original Studies in the Nature and Definition of 'Obscenity.'* London: Souvenir Press, 1962. 207p.

A collection of studies designed to throw light on the concepts of obscenity and censorship, this book contains essays brought together by John Chandos, author, editor, broadcaster, and director of productions of Nonesuch Record Series. Contributors to the volume are: William B. Lockhart, Dean and Professor of Law, and Robert C. McClure, Professor of Law at the University of Minnesota Law School; the Rt. Hon. Lord Birkett, P. C., former Lord Justice of Appeal; Norman St. John-Steves, Academic lawyer and journalist; Ernest Van Den Haag,

Adjunct Professor of Social Philosophy at the University of New York and lecturer at the New School of Social Research; Claire and W.M.S. Russel, behavioral scientists interested in the evolution of human behavior; Maurice Girodias, publisher and journalist; and Walter Allen, author, literary journalist, broadcaster, and former literary editor of the *New Statesman*. The studies are presented in an attempt to explain "the divergence of standards and inconsistency of judgments displayed whenever ... the concepts of obscenity and censorship have arisen." The contributors were chosen because of their expertise relative to the cause and effect of censorship.

Clor, Harry M. *Obscenity and Public Morality; Censorship in a Liberal Society.* Chicago: University of Chicago Press, 1969. 315p.

Clor's central theme is that there are certain minimal moral requirements for the performance of social and political duties and that public morality is something real. The purpose of the study undertaken in the book is threefold: 1) to analyze and evaluate the arguments, evidence, and assumptions employed in the controversy over obscenity; 2) to explore the difficulties encountered by the law when it seeks to define public morality in a constitutional democracy and in a society characterized by pluralism and rapid change; and 3) to contribute to the development of a philosophy of censorship and a test of obscenity which will do justice to the public interests in morality, in free expression, and in literature. Chapters one and two examine the contemporary legal situation and the legal developments which have contributed to it. Chapter three evaluates the libertarian approaches to the First Amendment of the U. S. Constitution and the doctrines from which they derive. The other chapters deal with the rationale for a certain kind of legal control. A selection of notes is included as well as a selected bibliography.

Comstock, Anthony. *Traps for the Young.* Reprint edition, edited by Robert Bremner. Cambridge: The Belknap Press of Harvard University Press, 1967. 262p.

Published originally in 1883 by Funk & Wagnalls, this is a photo-offset edition of the original book. Only advertisements and old illustrations have been eliminated; new illustrations and an excellent introduction by the editor, Robert Bremner, have been added. In the introduction, the rise of Comstockery is traced from its beginnings in 1872 until its decline in 1915, when the portly crusader against indecent literature died. In 1872 Comstock obtained the arrest of six employees of stationery stores for selling "obscene" books and pictures, and by the end of his infamous career he had caused more than 3,600 men, women, and children to be arrested on similar charges. The editor's introduction relates some of Comstock's efforts to rid the country of "infidels," "free lusters," and "abortionist's pimps"; traces his efforts to insure that only "good" literature with "pure thoughts" was made available; and discusses the crusader's activities as Secretary and Chief Special Agent of the New York Society for the Suppression of Vice and as Post Office Inspector. Following the editor's introduction, *Traps for the Young* is presented in its entirety, including an introduction by James Monroe Buckley, Methodist minister and vice-president of the New York Society for the Suppression of Vice. In a series of 14 chapters Comstock tells the reader how to avoid household traps, gambling traps, half-dime novels, death traps by mail, quack traps, free-love traps, advertising traps, artistic and classical traps, infidel traps, and liberal traps. While Comstock's advice to the young might be outrageously hilarious to many today, once our laughter has ceased we are struck by the realization that there are among us an all too uncomfortable number of people who still agree with Comstock and who would employ the same trickery and arbitrary power which he employed to restrict and repress books and ideas. Because of Comstock's role in the history of American censorship and repression, his book is important as a historical document. It also serves as an example of generally accepted attitudes and restrictive measures in the United States during the latter nineteenth and early twentieth centuries.

Conferences on Intellectual Freedom, Washington, D. C., 1965. Proceedings. *Freedom of Inquiry, Supporting the Library Bill of Rights.* Chicago: American Library Association, 1965. 70p.

This publication contains 16 papers presented at the Conference on Intellectual Freedom held in Washington in January 1965. The papers deal with censorship and recommend what librarians, teachers, members of the clergy, lawyers and private citizens can do to make libraries free from the pressures of censorship. The appendix includes a copy of the *Library Bill of Rights* and recommendations of the Conference's discussion group in regard to instituting a program of legal assistance to support the *Library Bill of Rights* and to giving practical assistance to librarians.

Craig, Alec. *Suppressed Books; a History of the Conception of Literary Obscenity.* Cleveland: The World Publishing Company. 1963. 285p.

First published in England in 1937 with the title *The Banned Books of England and Other Countries*, this book represents a pioneer work in the field of literary censorship, and it reveals the "absurdity of man's fears with respect to sexual titillation in print or picture." Censorship battles in England in the nineteenth century are discussed at length, and parallels in the United States are made in a chapter entitled "Censorship in America." Morris L. Ernst, who wrote the foreword, suggests that "this volume . . . can be an effective instrument to tidy up the law of censorship" and that "it might even educate us to a more adult approach to the mystery of life." A selected bibliography of publications and articles relative to the concept of literary obscenity is included; it is particularly valuable for works published during the first half of the twentieth century.

Daniels, Walter M., ed. *The Censorship of Books.* New York: H. W. Wilson Co., 1954. 202p.

Articles and essays containing various opinions on book censorship are reprinted from journals and periodicals in this work. Most of the contributions included center around the theme that legal censorship does more harm than good and that extra-legal censorship by individuals or by pressure groups is a dangerous type of restriction in a democratic society.

DeGrazia, Edward. *Censorship Landmarks.* New York: Bowker, 1969. 675p.

Many court case studies of censorship from 1600 to 1968 are included. The book illustrates the slow progress that has been made from conditions of widespread censorship in the United States to something approaching freedom in respect to the dissemination and use of books, magazines, and motion pictures. Stage presentations and oral expressions having to do with sexual topics are also discussed in relation to suppression.

Donelson, Kenneth L. *Some Responsibilities of the English Teacher Facing Censorship.* Tempe, Arizona: Arizona English Teachers Association, 1969. 10p. (EDRS Document ED 043 603)

The "inevitable and ubiquitous nature of censorship" forces teachers of literature to accept seven responsibilities: 1) to know literature of all types and all periods extremely well and to know what constitutes literary merit and adolescent appeal in any work; 2) to understand the implications of arguments for and against censorship; 3) to build an English department capable of fighting censorship both through discussion of works likely to be attacked and through implementation of a formal policy for handling any attempted censorship; 4) to prepare a rationale and defense for any work to be taught in any class by any teacher; 5) to communicate to the public and to students what is going on in English class and why it is going on; 6) to woo actively community support before censorship strikes; and 7) to recognize that the censor may sometimes have a legitimate complaint and to recognize that not all English teachers are defensible, either for what they teach or for how they teach it.

Downie, Currie S. *Barriers to the Flow of Technical Information: Limitation Statements—Legal Basis.* Arlington, Va.: Office of Aerospace Research (Air Force), 1969. 16p. (EDRS Document ED 032 910)

The new "Freedom of Information Act" and the more important reasons for limitations on the flow of information are discussed. The legal basis for these limitations can be found in the almost 100 statutory provisions which prohibit, exempt, or otherwise protect certain types of information from disclosure. The Export Control Acts of the Department of Commerce and the Mutual Security Act of the Department of State are among the most difficult to administer. Some of the basic reasons and requirements for Department of Defense distribution statements are reviewed. Finally, statistics are presented to show approximately what proportion of the federal reports fall in the various categories of limitations, and the contributions of the Air Force laboratories to the federal technical report literature.

Downs, Robert B., ed. *The First Freedom; Liberty and Justice in the World of Books and Reading.* Chicago: American Library Association, 1960. 469p.

A collection of more than 80 essays and articles by American and British writers on the topic of censorship of the printed word, excluding freedom of the press. Editor Downs, former dean of library administration at the University of Illinois and an active promoter of intellectual freedom in libraries, admits that the book leans heavily toward the liberal view. He states, however, that it was not the purpose of the anthology to present both pro- and anti-censorship arguments. Essays are grouped under twelve broad headings, including "We Have

Been Here Before: A Historical Retrospect," "The Court Looks at Books," "Who or What Is Obscene?" "Political Subversion and Censorship," and "The Schools Under Attack." One chapter is devoted to the stand which librarians have taken on censorship. Texts of several important intellectual freedom documents endorsed by the American Library Association are also provided, including the "Library Bill of Rights," the "Freedom to Read" statement, and the "Overseas Libraries Statement." Dwight D. Eisenhower's letter on intellectual freedom, written to Dr. Downs when he was president of the American Library Association, is also in the chapter, as well as essays by Downs himself ("The Book Burners Cannot Win"), Leon Carnovsky ("The Obligations and Responsibilities of the Librarian Concerning Censorship"), and Archibald MacLeish ("A Tower Which Will Not Yield").

Ernst, Morris L. *Censorship: the Search for the Obscene*. By Morris L. Ernst and Allan U. Schwartz. With an introduction by Philip Scharper. New York: Macmillan, 1964. 288p.

Writing from the point of view that the best censorship is the least censorship, two lawyers have the following objectives in this work: to make laws about censorship more intelligible to the laity and to discuss the law of the obscene, its origins in our culture, the forces that shaped and are still shaping it, and the pivotal opinions rendered by judges. The book is a factual account of censorship; all major judicial decisions from 1821 to early 1963 are discussed. In the final chapter, the law as it existed in 1964 is clearly outlined in relation to what materials were or were not acceptable.

Ernst, Morris L. *To the Pure ... A Study of Obscenity and the Censor*. By Morris L. Ernst and William Seagle. New York: Kraus Reprint Company, 1970. 336p.

A source for information on obscenity and censorship, the book attempts to reveal the absurdity and ineffectiveness of existing censorship laws and to bring about a change of attitude toward obscenity. Appendices include a list of books banned in Boston in 1927 and a list of publications which were prohibited as imports into Canada. This is a reprint of a book originally published in 1928 by The Viking Press.

Estrin, Herman A., ed. *Freedom and Censorship of the College Press*. Edited by Herman A. Estrin and Arthur M. Sanderson. Dubuque, Iowa: W. C. Brown Co., 1966. 310p.

A collection of seminal essays and concepts for the student press, this work explores the complex areas of freedom, censorship, and responsibilities of college newspapers. Appended to the work are several documents pertaining to the student press and its relationship to censorship and freedom, including "Freedom of the College Press," by the American Civil Liberties Union and "Basic Policy Declaration on Freedom and Responsibility of the Student Press," by the U. S. Student Press Association.

Farley, John J. *Book Censorship in the Senior High School Libraries of Nassau County, New York*. Dissertation written for the Ph.D. degree at New York University, 1964. 368p. (University Microfilms, No. 65-969)

The purpose of the study was to determine if voluntary and involuntary censorship was being practiced in libraries of senior high schools. Interviews were conducted with librarians to determine book selection practices and to uncover any incidents of censorship pressures imposed upon libraries. Interviews revealed that voluntary censorship (by the librarian on his own initiative) was more prevalent than involuntary censorship (outside pressures upon the librarian). The greatest majority of the librarians in Nassau County had experienced some kind of outside pressures for the removal of books from library collections, and all of them admitted having performed some voluntary book censorship in order to avoid controversy.

Fiske, Marjorie. *Book Selection and Censorship; a Study of School and Public Libraries in California.* Berkeley and Los Angeles: University of California Press, 1959. 145p.

Based on the results of a rigorous two-year study which took place between 1956 and 1958, this book examines book selection and intramural censorship in selected California school and public libraries. The "Fiske Report," as the book is commonly called, shows with conclusive evidence that some of the librarians who served as respondents in the study were themselves the most active censors of the contents of their libraries. Many librarians had so carefully screened their purchases in the selection process that books likely to have caused complaints from patrons, teachers, or school administrators were not added to collections. The study concluded that librarians were generally following the principle that the best way to avoid censorship controversies or pressures in libraries was to avoid the purchase of controversial books. Nearly two-thirds of the librarians interviewed who were involved in book selection reported instances when a controversy about a book or author resulted in a decision not to purchase a work.

Fowell, Frank. *Censorship in England.* By Frank Fowell and Frank Palmer. New York: Lennox Hill Publishing and Distributing Corp., 1970. 390p. (Originally published in London in 1913)

Traces the origin and development of censorship in England from 1347 to the twentieth century. The book contains many quotations, documents, and illustrations. Numerous footnotes explain text material with reference to the appendices. Appendices include a list of plays licensed and refused, acts for regulating theatres, and speeches and letters of importance.

Frank, John P. *Obscenity, the Law, and the English Teacher.* By John P. Frank and Robert F. Hogan. Champaign, Ill.: National Council of Teachers of English, 1966. 61p.

The first part of this work relates an experiment performed by Frank, who submitted a number of "questionable" materials to a panel of experts in literature and psychology. An analysis of the responses of the experts is made, and there is a discussion of the relevance of judgments. The author also discusses the consequences of using a panel of experts in determining the obscenity content of a particular work. The second part of the book presents various objections to the theories behind the panel method used by Frank; however, the joint author, Hogan, ultimately supports the panel-of-experts' approach as a saving, not condemning, device for books. He also discusses the function of the literature teacher "in the creation of a healthy population."

Full Freedom of Expression, Symposium. *Wilson Library Bulletin*, Vol. 39, No. 8, April 1965. pp. 639-72.

Aside from its regular features, the entire issue of the April 1965 edition of the *Wilson Library Bulletin* was devoted to the topic "Full Freedom of Expression." The symposium consisted of eight articles contributed by noteworthy individuals (mainly in the library and publishing fields) who were directly involved in the fight for freedom of expression. These contributors state that censorship is not new, but at the same time that libraries are increasingly becoming targets for attack. They further state that librarians cannot afford to maintain a neutral position and, as professionals, they must maintain a firm commitment to the freedom to read.

Gardiner, Harold C. *Catholic Viewpoint on Censorship.* Rev. ed. Garden City, N. Y.: Image Books, 1961. 200p. (The Catholic Viewpoint)

This book attempts to contribute to the cause of rational and temperate debate on the controversy between anti- and pro-censorship factions; it also serves as an apology for the Catholic viewpoint. According to the author, if the Legion of Decency and the National Office for Decent Literature ever became defunct, as seems the goal of the anti-censorship bodies, then the American cultural scene would be the poorer for it. In his support of these pro-censorship organizations, the author points out that art has always flourished when it has had to meet the challenge of protest against some of its vagaries, and that law should be the final arbiter on censorship issues.

Gerber, Albert B. *Sex, Pornography, and Justice.* New York: Lyle Stuart, Inc., 1965. 349p.

Using the word "obscenity" only as a legal term, the author investigates legal cases surrounding the "obscenity chaos." The discussion of numerous court decisions in this work provides rather convincing evidence that recent judicial decisions concerning pornographic and obscene materials have only "compounded the confusion."

Gillett, Charles R. *Burned Books; Neglected Chapters in British History and Literature.* Port Washington, N. Y.: Kennikat Press, 1964. 2v.

A rather scholarly, detailed study of condemned books of the fifteenth to the eighteenth centuries in the British Isles; includes a bibliography of condemned books, a chronological list of censorship attacks, and an index. This two-volume work was originally published with the same title by the Columbia University Press in 1932.

Gilmore, Donald H. *Sex, Censorship, and Pornography.* San Diego, Calif.: Greenleaf Classics, 1969. 2v. 511p. (A Greenleaf Classic)

Combines past and present thoughts on controversial subjects. The history of censorship is described rather fully, giving the reader background information on the issues involved. Mr. Gilmore also traces the history of the obscenity law—how it has been interpreted throughout different periods of United States history and its current status.

Ginzburg, Ralph. *An Unhurried View of Erotica.* Introduction by Theodor Reik and preface by George Jean Nathan. New York: Ace Books, Inc., 1958. 128p.

In this provocative and informative volume, Mr. Ginzburg presents the history of erotica in the English-speaking world and discusses the present state of erotic literature in the United States and in England. Dr. Reik, who wrote the introduction, said: "This little book deals with the universal interest the Anglo-Saxons had and have in all aspects of sex in a surprising manner." The book is comprised of seven parts, which have the following titles: "Precursors of English Erotica," "Earliest English Works," "The Two Manias," "London Becomes World Capital," "First American Works," "Reference Works," and "The Erotic Book Market Today." A bibliography of 100 erotic works is also provided; it contains such titles as *The Diary of a Nymphomaniac, The Festival of Love, How to Raise Love. Or the Art of Making Love in More Ways Than One,* and *The Whore's Rhetorick.* This book was also published by Helmsmen Press in a hardcover, slip-cased gift edition.

Gleason, Marian, ed. *Censorship: A Symposium.* Burlington, Vt.: New England Association of Teachers of English, 1969. 47p. (ERIC Document ED 031 495)

These 12 articles on censorship in the schools comprise a collection of "representative opinions expressed by concerned individuals"—professors, teachers, school administrators, clergy, high school students, a publisher and a spokesman for the National Education Association. The essays range in viewpoint from a traditional belief in the prerogative of the censor to select and edit materials to the position that censorship should be abolished. Topics include the effect of censorship in the schools, the kinds of literature that teachers should teach, the role of the censor in selecting educational materials, and the social history of free expression.

Haas, Warren J. *English Book Censorship.* Rochester, N. Y.: University of Rochester Press for the Association of College and Reference Librarians, 1955. 2 microcards. (ACRL Microcard, No. 19)

A study submitted for the degree of Bachelor of Library Science at the University of Wisconsin. Historical in nature, it covers the period of the Early Stuarts, the Interregnum, and the Later Stuarts. It points out how the Tudors, the Stuarts, and certain parliamentary leaders feared that immoderate use of the printed word would lead to surfeits and sickness among the populace. The study provides an indication of the nature of England's early attempts to control the thoughts of people by controlling the press.

Haight, Anne Lyon. *Banned Books; Informal Notes on Some Books Banned for Various Reasons at Various Times and in Various Places.* 3d ed. New York & London: R. R. Bowker Company, 1970. 166p.

A chronological list of books banned from 387 B.C. until the 1960s, this bibliography includes works which were suppressed primarily for religious, political, or moral reasons. Most of the works listed, consequently, were banned on charges of heresy, treason, or obscenity. Included are such works as *The Green Pastures* by Marc Connelly, which was forbidden in England in 1929 "on the ground that the Deity ought not to be represented on the stage," and *Wonder Stories* by Hans Christian Andersen, which was in 1954 stamped in Illinois "For Adult Readers" to make it impossible for children to obtain smut. In addition to the bibliography, this work contains an appendix devoted to essays on trends in censorship and statements relating to the freedom of the press, including Milton's *Areopagitica*, Mill's *On Liberty*, and Eisenhower's "Letter to the American Library Association."

Hall, William E. *An Analysis of Post-World War II Efforts to Expand Press Freedom Internationally.* Dissertation written for the Ph.D. degree at the State University of Iowa, 1954. 435p. (University Microfilms, No. 54-3466)
    The author describes freedom of the press on an international level as it existed in 1954. Data for the study were gathered by questionnaires sent to 72 editors, representing nine nations.

Hamlin, Peter R. *A Case Study of the Fairfax County, Virginia, Censorship Controversy, 1963* (University of Illinois Graduate School of Library Science Occasional Papers, No. 95). Urbana: University of Illinois Graduate School of Library Science, 1968. 22p.
    The Farifax County Library case offers a classic example of a political struggle over differing concepts of library censorship and freedom. This report is about the controversy which spread to the courts and onto the floor of Congress. The Virginia censorship controversy involved a number of issues, including segregation, obscenity, evolution, and communism, and it illustrates the need for an intellectual and sophisticated approach to politics by librarians, as well as the necessity for more research on the library in the political process.

Haney, Robert W. *Comstockery in America; Patterns of Censorship and Control.* Boston: Beacon Press, 1960. 199p.
    Through extensive use of historical and contemporary quotes, the book presents a detailed survey of censorship (Comstockery) from earliest times to the present. Restraints upon the production and distribution of hardcover books, magazines, comics, paperbound books, motion pictures, radio broadcasts, and television by public authorities and by private organizations are dealt with. Included is an extensive bibliography of books and articles about censorship.

Hart, Harold H., ed. *Censorship: For & Against.* New York: Hart Publishing Co., Inc., 1971. 255p.
    According to the editor, "this book is addressed to those who would like to unravel the tangled threads of our laws and our mores." The 12 provocative essays by the following individuals express a variety of viewpoints on the topic of censorship: Hollis Alpert, film critic and contributing editor for *Saturday Review*; Joseph Howard, Executive Secretary of the National Office for Decent

Literature; Judith Crist, film critic for *TV Guide* and the *New York* magazine; Carey McWilliams, editor of *The Nation*; Charles H. Keating, Jr., founder of the Citizens for Decent Literature, Inc., and a member of the Presidential Commission on Obscenity and Pornography; Eugene McCarthy, U. S. Senator from Minnesota; Rebecca West, literary critic and political writer; Ernest van den Haag, practicing psychoanalyst and a professor of philosophy; Arthur Lelyveld, President of the American Jewish Congress; Max Lerner, author, teacher, and journalist; Charles Rembar, New York lawyer and author of *The End of Obscenity*; and Nat Hentoff, staff writer for *The New Yorker*. The essays are significant position papers on the topic of censorship, representing opinions from people who, because of their interests and backgrounds, are eminently qualified to speak on the subject, whether their positions are pro- or anti-censorship.

Hewitt, Cecil R. *Books in the Dock*. London: Deutsch, 1969. 144p.

An examination of the past and present obscenity laws regarding literary censorship in England. The British Obscenity Act of 1959 is interpreted and explained; recountings of court cases illustrate how the existing laws operate and various proposals for reform of the 1959 act are made.

Hohenberg, John. *Free Press/Free People; the Best Cause.* New York: Columbia University Press, 1971. 514p.

Beginning with the dissemination of news in pre-print days, this work is concerned with the development of the idea of a free press and concentrates on individuals who fought for freedom of the press and, through it, the freedom of the individual.

Hollister, Charles A. *School Boards and the U. S. Constitution*; Paper presented at the Annual Session of the National School Boards Association, Miami Beach, Florida, April 1969. (EDRS Document ED 029 387)

As public agencies created by state legislative mandate, school districts and the officers thereof are obligated to abide by several provisions of the United States Constitution. School boards can reduce many of the sources of current student unrest by complying with these provisions. Courts have held that under the Fourteenth Amendment school officials are obligated to provide due process of law and equal protection of the law to their patrons. These provisions strictly prohibit capricious, arbitrary, or unreasonable rule-making and discrimination based on race, color, or economic position. Under the First Amendment the guarantees of freedom of speech and freedom of religion require school officials to recognize the students' rights to speak without prior restraint, subject to penalties for abuse of that right, and requires these officials to maintain a neutral position towards religion. School officials seeking to operate their school system in a lawful, peaceful, and productive manner should be aware that as agents of the state they are subject to constitutional restraints on their authority. Such an awareness should limit the potential for turmoil stemming from decisions affecting the civil liberties of students.

Hove, John. *Meeting Censorship in the School; a Series of Case Studies.* Champaign, Ill.: National Council of Teachers of English, 1967. 57p. (EDRS Document ED 019 268)

Nine case studies illustrative of incidents arising from the objections made by individuals to specific books and poems used in English classrooms and school libraries are reported herein by the National Council of Teachers of English Committee to Report on Case Studies of Censorship. Each study describes anonymously 1) the community's location, size, educational environment, economy, nationality composition, and if relevant, its political or religious temperament; 2) the school's size, inclusive grades, teacher salary schedule, and administrative structure; 3) the school board members' educational backgrounds; 4) the teacher's qualifications, tenure, status, and relationship with colleagues; 5) the complaint and the complainant, including specific charges and method of objecting; and 6) the reaction to the complaint, listing chronologically the procedure followed by the teacher, department, administration, press, and other community members. Both successful and unsuccessful responses to censorship challenges are included. Appended is the book selection procedure used by the English department of the Wappingers Central Junior and Senior High Schools, Wappingers Falls, New York.

Hoyt, Olga. *Censorship in America.* By Olga G. and Edwin P. Hoyt. New York: Seabury Press, 1970. 127p.
    Concerned with cultural censorship, the book examines forces that have tried to supervise American cultural life. Censorship of radio, television, theater, art, and motion pictures is discussed. The book raises the question: who is to be judge of the public morals? According to the author, the great danger of censorship to citizens is the denial of the freedom to read, to see, and to hear.

Hudson, Edward G. *Freedom of Speech and Press in America.* Foreword by William O. Douglas; introduction by Morris L. Ernst. Washington: Public Affairs Press, 1963. 224p.
    Written by a lawyer and librarian at the Supreme Court, this is a scholarly examination of the degree of freedom that the press actually has. The history of legal struggles in defense of freedom of the press is traced in this detailed book, which attempts to place court cases in their historical and philosophical settings.

Hughes, Douglas A., ed. *Perspectives on Pornography.* Edited with an introduction by Douglas A. Hughes. New York: St. Martins, 1970. 223p.
    Fifteen articles by experts such as Harry Levin, Vivian Mercier, Kenneth Tynan, George P. Elliott, Ernest van den Haag, Susan Sontag, and others provide a summary in this work of current views toward pornographic literature. Some of the essays have been published in periodicals such as *Esquire* and *Atlantic Monthly*, and many of them are of historical interest insofar as literary values are concerned.

Hunnings, Neville M. *Film Censors and the Law.* Foreword by Frede Castberg. London: Allen & Unwin Ltd., 1967. 474p.
    Dr. Hunnings has written a thorough comparative law study of the censorship of films. Emphasis is placed on film censorship in England, but restrictive practices in the United States, India, Canada, Australia, Denmark, France, and the Soviet Union are also discussed. While any account of film

censorship will be out of date almost as soon as it is published because of rapid legislative and social changes, the present book provides a rather complete examination of how film censorship works and how it has developed in various countries. The author points out in the preface that "one of the advantages of adopting an historical approach to a subject like censorship is that radical changes in rules do not automatically invalidate what has already been written." In Part I, which is devoted to England, legislation such as The Disorderly House Act, 1751, and the first Cinematography Act, 1909, are discussed. Developments of the system of film censorship employed in England between 1910 and 1924 are also covered, including the creation of the British Board of Film Censors, the State Censorship Board, and the London County Council. Extension and consolidation of control are covered for the period 1925 to 1955. Parts II and III are devoted to censorship in the four federal countries whose restrictive practices are examined and to censorship activities against films in three European countries. In the conclusion, Part IV, the nature of film censorship is examined in detail. A table of film censorship cases, a table of statutes, decrees, and territorial ordinances, and a table of censored films are provided at the end of the book, which also contains an extensive bibliography on film censorship.

Hutchinson, E. R. *Tropic of Cancer on Trial; a Case History of Censorship.* New York: Grove Press, 1968. 300p.

This historical review of Henry Miller's life and books, with an exhaustive analysis of legal action against *Tropic of Cancer* at the state level, is thoroughly documented. Based on a dissertation, the work includes background material and related incidents of censorship. Also included are an appendix listing major court cases which deal with obscenity and a selected bibliography.

Hyde, Hartford M. *A History of Pornography.* With an introduction by Morris L. Ernst. London: Heineman, 1964. 246p.

The relationship between erotic literature and the law during a 300-year period is discussed in this historical, often witty, book. A large number of pornographic works are discussed, but the book deals primarily with classical and Anglo-American pornography.

James, Max H. *Propaganda or Education? Censorship and School Journalism.* Tempe: Arizona English Teacher Association, 1970. 5p. (EDRS Document ED 045 675)

A survey of 95 Arizona high schools and their problems with school newspaper censorship indicates that whether limitations are imposed before or after publication, the essential conflict is one between viewing the student newspaper as an opportunity for education, or seeing the paper as a public relations agent for the school. Some suggestions for teachers and students in promoting responsible school journalism are 1) clarify the publisher-editor relationship; 2) print a balanced selection of opinion; 3) do "enterprise" reporting on serious campus issues—drugs, the draft, racial problems, the relevancy of educational requirements; and 4) employ good reporting techniques.

Jeffries, John A. *Legal Censorship of Obscene Publications: Search for a Censoring Standard.* Dissertation written for the Ph.D. degree at Indiana University, 1968. 200p. (University Microfilms, No. 69-7690)

This dissertation examines the question of whether the threatened danger which is imposed by allegedly obscene publications is sufficient to warrant use of police and judicial power to suppress it. The conclusion is that there are apparently no justifications for the "vague and sometimes abusive" governmental policies toward obscenity censorship. The investigator submits that none of the alleged evils of obscenity is significant enough to justify the legal censoring standard.

Jennison, Peter S. *Freedom to Read.* New York: Public Affairs Committee, Inc., 1963. 20p. (Public Affairs Pamphlet, No. 344)
   This pamphlet is divided into various subheadings: "Roots Deep in History," "Search for Simple Answers," "Libraries and the Censor," etc. Under each subheading, an attempt is made to provide arguments for and against censorship. Specific examples are cited in support of both positions. A short bibliography entitled "What to Read" appears at the end of the publication.

Kamarch, Edward L., ed. "Censorship and the Arts"; an issue of *Arts in Society* (Vol. 4, No. 2, Summer 1967).
   Published by the University of Wisconsin Extension, *Arts in Society* "is dedicated to the augmenting of the arts in society and to the advancement of education in the arts." The greater part of this issue is devoted to the topic of censorship, a term which the editor calls a "very vivid word to most segments of our culture—the novelist, poets, television writers, art gallery directors, concert managers, and librarians." This work is comprised of a number of articles and many comments by representatives from each of these groups. Psychiatrists and psychologists discuss the effects of pornography on man, the question of whether censorship should fall within the province of the law, and factors contributing to the increasing frankness of subject and expression in the arts. Creative writers discuss the effects of censorship on their works. Television writers tell how censorship operates in the television industry and discuss the obligation of television to present avant-garde or "shocking" creative works. Art gallery directors and concert managers discuss official and unofficial censorship and the freedom to present controversial programs or exhibits. Librarians discuss the censorship climate during the 1953-63 decade and the role of the library in relation to the cultural tastes of the community. In his preface, the editor states: "Librarians are, in fact, in the very thick of today's censorship wars, for they have the considerable problem of mediating between sharply differing levels of sophistication." Librarians who contributed to the issue are: Gordon H. Bebeau, Director of the Appleton (Wis.) Public Library; Edwin Castagna, Director of the Enoch Pratt Free Library (Baltimore); Helen Dirtadian, Director of Libraries for the State of Alaska; Ervin J. Gaines, Director of the Minneapolis Public Library; William F. Hayes, Director of the Boise (Idaho) Public Library; Farris J. Martin, Director of the Montgomery (Ala.) Public Library; Margaret Monroe, University of Wisconsin Library School; Everett T. Moore, University of California; Felix Pollak, University of Wisconsin; and Doris L. Shreve, Missouri State Library.

Kerr, Walter. *Criticism and Censorship.* Co-sponsored by the National Catholic Educational Association and Trinity College, Washington, D. C. Milwaukee: Bruce Publishing Co., 1954. 86p. (The Gabriel Richard Lecture, No. 5)

This work deals with the ever-present problem of criticism versus censorship. The author, a drama critic, tries to comment objectively on the difference between the two concepts as related to the arts in general in the different media of communication. Special attention is given to the Catholic point of view, to which the author objects.

Kilpatrick, James J. *The Smut Peddlers.* 1st ed. Garden City, N. Y.: Doubleday, 1960. 323p.

In this thoroughly researched study of obscenity and censorship in the United States, the author reports on mail-order obscenity, censorship of books and motion pictures, and the state of public law and private action in regard to censorship. He presents arguments both for and against censorship. Legalistic attempts to deal with these issues are also discussed through reviews of various cases and court decisions.

Klausler, Alfred P. *Censorship, Obscenity, and Sex.* St. Louis: Concordia Publishing House, 1967. 104p. (The Christian Encounters)

Alfred Klausler, a journalist and an ordained Lutheran minister, deals with the problems of censorship, personal freedom, and the church's relationship to issues of restraint versus the right to read. Although brief, the book provides a view from the pulpit of the problems surrounding controversies over obscenity.

Knudson, Rozanne R. *Censorship in English Programs of California Junior Colleges.* Dissertation written for the Ph.D. degree at Stanford University, 1967. 250p. (University Microfilms, No. 68-6444)

This is a report of a study undertaken to determine if California junior colleges had encountered attempts at extralegal censorship of books included in reading lists for English programs and to discover if English teachers were exercising self-censorship. The study found that 13 per cent of the teachers had received objections about works they included in reading lists. Fifty-two per cent of the teachers had refrained from using certain books because of anticipated objections. The study concludes: "a need is seen for alerting prospective teachers of English to the possibilities of censorship incidents and for preparing them to deal with such extralegal censorship."

Konvitz, Milton R. *Expanding Liberties; Freedom's Gains in Postwar America.* New York: Viking Press, 1966. 429p.

Covers such topics as religious freedom, freedom of association, academic freedom, and the judicial handling of problems of obscenity and pornography. The author, a constitutional lawyer, analyzes problems of civil liberties within the framework of constitutional law in the United States. He attacks the "social utility" theory of the U. S. Supreme Court, which was advocated as a guide for determining whether a book might be obscene. The book is detailed and scholarly in its examination of advances which have been made since World War II.

Kronhausen, Eberhard, and Phyllis Kronhausen. *Pornography and the Law; the Psychology of Erotic Realism and Pornography.* 2d ed., completely revised and enlarged. New York: Ballantine Books, 1964. 416p.

This study of books at which charges of obscenity have been imposed in the courts is, according to Theodor Reik, "a valuable defense of erotically realistic writings." The authors have in both study and in private practice specialized in family therapy and group guidance. They presented their research findings on family milieu therapy with severely disturbed parents at the 2d International Congress of Psychiatry, Zurich, 1957. The present work attempts to differentiate between erotic realism and obscenity, and it clearly demonstrates that "obscenity" is the only crime without a clear definition. It is divided into several major sections, including those devoted to the psychology of erotic realism, obscene books and the law, and the psychology of pornography. In these sections such topics are discussed as erotic wit and humor, "dirty" words, the Supreme Court definition of "obscenity," the concept of "contemporary community standards," the structure of "obscene" books, supersexed males, nymphomaniac females, homosexuality, and flagellation. A bibliography of 139 specialized works relating to eroticism and pornography is included.

Kuh, Richard H. *Foolish Figleaves? Pornography in and out of Court.* New York: Macmillan, 1967. 368p.

Traces the major American court decisions concerning pornography and endeavors to supply a specifically stated model law for use in all obscenity cases. The author, a one-time assistant district attorney of New York City, has been personally involved in many of the cases cited, and he lends this background to an argument for punishing those who traffic in sex for profit.

Kyle-Keith, Richard. *The High Price of Pornography.* Washington: Public Affairs Press, 1961. 230p.

An attempt to examine the nature and history of pornography and the causes for its increase since the Second World War. The actions of anti-pornography groups in various cities of the United States are discussed at length.

LaConte, Ronald T. *The Relationship Between Book Selection Practices and Certain Controversial Elements of Literature in Bergen County, New Jersey Public Senior High School English Departments.* Dissertation written for the Ph.D. degree at Rutgers—The State University, 1967. 202p. (University Microfilms, No. 67-12, 022)

The purposes of this study were: to describe the book selection practices of certain high school English departments, to investigate the relationship between book selection practices and certain controversial elements of literature, and to present the beliefs and opinions of English department chairmen concerning controversial literature. This study of book selection practices and certain elements of books, which at some time had been attacked as unsuitable for students, involved the English department chairmen of 34 public high schools in Bergen County, New Jersey. Data from questionnaires and interviews were tabulated and statistically analyzed, and the existence of a relationship between controversial elements and selection practices was substantiated. The following were among the conclusions supported by data found to be significant at the .05 level: 1) controversial political and religious views are not likely to cause department chairmen to reject a book, 2) department chairmen involved in prior censorship incidents tend to restrict or reject fewer books than those who had not been involved in incidents, and 3) department chairmen from schools having a written policy for handling objections to books restricted or rejected fewer controversial books than those from schools without a policy.

Levy, Leonard W., ed. *Freedom of the Press from Zenger to Jefferson; Early American Libertarian Theories.* Indianapolis: The Bobbs-Merrill Company, Inc., 1966. 409p.

    With original documents, statements, and other records relating to freedom of press from the Zenger case in 1735 to the Croswell case in 1804, Professor Levy clearly demonstrates, in this sequel to *Legacy of Suppression: Freedom of Speech and Press in Early American History*, that the defense of freedom can be stripped of the mythology surrounding it and can be clearly documented with historical evidence. This anthology is a fundamental and comprehensive work on the freedom of the press in America, comprised of authoritative original materials written by such men as Benjamin Franklin, John Peter Zenger, William Livingston, William Bollan, Richard Henry Lee, Alexander Hamilton, George Hay, James Madison, Thomas Jefferson, and many others. The book is divided into six parts: Part I, the Formative Period: "Cato" and Zenger; Part II, The Revolutionary Period: Patriots and Blackstonians; Part III, The Constitutional Period: Neo-Blackstonians; Part IV, The New Libertarianism; Part V, The Special Case of Thomas Jefferson; and Part VI, Epilogue: Zenger Revivivus. The sources included throw considerable light on the history of libertarian theory in the United States.

Levy, Leonard W. *Legacy of Suppression: Freedom of Speech and Press in Early American History.* Cambridge, Mass.: Belknap Press of Harvard University Press, 1960. 353p.

    Free speech and liberty of the press are the primary topics of this scholarly history of civil liberties and the development of freedom in the United States. Professor Levy attempts to reveal that, contrary to popular belief, there was in the early period of our nation's history a "legacy of suppression."

Lockhart, William B. *Censorship of Obscenity: the Developing Constitutional Standards.* By William B. Lockhart and Robert C. McClure, 1960. 119p. (EDRS Document ED 025 497)

    To demonstrate that substantial protection has been given to published material dealing with sex, an analysis of the constitutional criteria governing recent Supreme Court decisions in the area of obscenity censorship is presented. It is found that the Supreme Court uses "hard core pornography" as the foundation of a "constant" concept of obscenity. A "variable" concept making the validity of censorship dependent upon the particular material's primary audience and the nature of its appeal to that audience is endorsed and explained. Also discussed are 1) the requirement that material be judged as a whole on the basis of its dominant theme, 2) the weight to be given "redeeming social importance," 3) the protection of "immoral" ideas, 4) the requirement of "scienter," 5) the meaning and application of "contemporary community standards," and 6) the need for independent judicial review of obscenity findings.

Loth, David G. *The Erotic in Literature; a Historical Survey of Pornography as Delightful as It Is Indiscreet.* New York: J. Messner, 1961, 256p.

Judging by the title, one might expect this book to contain a wealth of illustrated pornographic material; however, the work is a detailed, historical, and critical analysis of erotic and pornographic literature from ancient Greece to the present time. In chapter one, which is entitled "The Jungle of Censorship," the author sets the stage for his book. "Unfortunately this book will have to chronicle a sad story of unwarranted interference in the natural processes by which the standards of the public are formed and executed. It is a tale of literature emasculated while books on crude sexual aestheticism is encouraged."

McClallan, Grant S., ed. *Censorship in the United States.* New York: H. W. Wilson Co., 1967. 222p. (The Reference Shelf, Vol. 39, No. 3)

A compilation of articles, parts of books, and speeches on the subject of censorship. The question examined is that of the prevalence of censorship today. Supreme Court decisions are discussed, in addition to debates on fair trial versus free press and the withholding of information by government agencies. An extensive bibliography is included.

McConnell, John L.C., ed. *To Deprave and Corrupt; Original Studies in the Nature and Definition of Obscenity.* Edited by John Chandos, pseud. New York: Association Press, 1962. 207p.

Noted contributors from Britain, France, and the United States discuss aspects of censorship from various points of view in this collection of essays on the problems of obscenity and censorship. The points of view taken by each contributor vary: legal, literary, psychological, moral, etc. The book is entertaining as well as informative, and included are biographical sketches of contributors as well as bibliographic footnotes.

McCormick, John, ed. *Versions of Censorship; an Anthology.* Edited by John McCormick and Mairi MacInnes. Garden City, N. Y.: Doubleday and Company, Inc., 1962. 374p. (A Doubleday Anchor Original)

By presenting texts of famous statements by such men as John Milton, Henry Miller, Benedict de Spinoza, Thomas Hobbs, Alexis de Tocqueville, and George Orwell, and by including comments on the texts, the editors of this book have attempted to construct a definition of censorship out of cases, both historical and contemporary. The book is arranged into four main parts: censorship and belief, censorship and fact, censorship and imagination, and self-censorship. The editors "have tried to provide notes toward a chapter in the history of ideas, both to fill out the past and to indicate the complexity, ubiquity, and urgency of censorship in the modern time."

McCoy, Ralph E. *Banned in Boston: The Development of Literary Censorship in Massachusetts.* Dissertation for the Ph.D. degree at the University of Illinois, 1956. 349p. (University Microfilms, No. 56-3020)

Historical study which traces book-banning in Boston from Puritan times to the present and which points out that legal awareness of obscenity did not come to Massachusetts until early in the eighteenth century, at which time it was closely related to blasphemy. The study describes the atmosphere surrounding the creation of the New England Watch and Ward Society in 1878 and its subsequent attempts to enforce a rigid concept of purity in written expression. This work points out that after 1909 Boston booksellers joined the New England Watch and Ward Society in deciding what books might be sold in Boston, and that the joint decisions of these two groups were not challenged until 1926, when H. L. Mencken defiantly sold an issue of the *American Mercury* on Boston Common. Shortly thereafter, intellectual leaders in the state demanded changes in the obscenity laws. The study points out that in 1956 there was a strong civil liberties movement in Boston, supported by lawyers, librarians, booksellers, and publishers, and that the Massachusetts experience with censorship should ultimately provide a basis for accommodation between the ideologies of puritanism and democracy.

McCoy, Ralph E. *Freedom of the Press; an Annotated Bibliography.* With a foreword by Robert B. Downs. Carbondale; Southern Illinois University Press, 1969. 1v. (unpaged)
Approximately 8,000 books, pamphlets, journal articles, films, and other materials dealing with freedom of the press are contained in this bibliography, which was compiled by the director of libraries at Southern Illinois University. The bibliography is an attempt at comprehensiveness; entries are annotated.

McKeon, Richard P., et al. *The Freedom to Read: Perspective and Program.* New York: Published for the National Book Committee by R. R. Bowker Co., 1957. 110p.
The National Book Committee began a preliminary inquiry in 1955 into the theory of censorship and the freedom to read. With a grant from the Fund for the Republic, the Committee established an exploratory commission comprised of three scholars for the purpose of conducting the study. They were: Richard McKeon, University of Chicago professor of philosophy; Robert K. Merton, Columbia University sociology professor; and Walter Gellhorn, Columbia Law School professor. These scholars were asked to outline the problems of censorship, to explore questions related to censorship in the light of philosophical, sociological and legal ramifications, and to "raise its own questions and formulate its own terms." This book is the result of the scholars' investigations and reflections, and it provides insights into problems of censorship and the freedom to read books. A detailed plan for a three-sided program to insure and to promote the freedom to read is included in the book, and the authors discuss the philosophical arguments, political and social arguments, and the legal and moral arguments concerning censorship, freedom, and security. Incidents and mechanisms of censorship are also discussed. The book is a must for every librarian's reading list, since it contains basic background information for an understanding of why there are those in our society who restrict or would restrict the freedom to read by external and internal censorship.

Marcus, Steven. *The Other Victorians; a Study of Sexuality and Pornography in Mid-nineteenth-century England.* New York: Basic Books, 1966. 292p. (Studies in Sex and Society)

175

Using materials in the library and archives of the Institute of Sex Research, Marcus has written an historical and critical survey of English literature of the 1850s. Victorian hypocrisy is stripped bare in this examination of various past attitudes to sex as reflected in literature of the period. The book includes chapters devoted to: views of Dr. William Acton, Victorian sexologist; the research of Henry Spencer Ashbee, compiler of erotic and pornographic bibliographies; the autobiography *My Secret Life*, written anonymously by a Victorian gentleman of means; some nineteenth-century pornographic novels; and the role of pornography during the Victorian period.

Marcuse, Ludwig. *Obscene; the History of an Indignation.* Translated from the German by Karen Gershon. London: MacGibbon & Kee, 1965. 327p.

With the premise that "obscene is not a fact but a serviceable scare" and a belief that the term "obscene" has no right to exist, Marcuse has written an indignant book about "the history of an indignation." Definitions of the concept "obscene" by the Pope, the U. S. Supreme Court, and a German *Candidatus Philosophiae* are offered initially to set the tone of this somewhat bitter examination of how the term has been used and misused. Chapters are entitled: "Jena 1799, One Hundred Years of German Indignation"; "Paris 1857, Emma Bovary and Other Flowers of Evil"; "New York 1873, Anthony Comstock, a Cross Between Barnum and McCarthy"; "Berlin 1920, Sex, Politics and Art—in a Round Dance"; "London 1960, D. H. Lawrence or *purissimus penis*"; "Los Angeles 1962, the Most Obscene Writer in World Literature"; and "Seven Theses to Disarm Indignation."

Marquette University. *Problems of Communication in a Pluralistic Society; Papers Delivered at a Conference on Communication, the Fourth in a Series of Anniversary Celebrations, March 20, 21, 22, and 23, 1956.* Milwaukee: Marquette University Press, 1956. 166p.

The first four papers deal with the difficulties of developing better communication and understanding between people. The three papers which follow are concerned with the people's "Right to Know," and two additional papers deal with the topic of censorship: a philosopher examines moral problems and a jurist examines legal problems germane to the censoring of mass communications media.

Marshall, Max L. *The "Right-to-Read" Controversy.* Columbia, Mo.: Freedom of Information Center, 1969. 14p. (EDRS Document ED 039 225)

The growing amount of activity by pressure groups, as well as professional statements like those of the American Library Association and the American Association of Library Teachers, reflect an increased concern with legal, quasi-legal or extra-legal censorship. The National Organization of Decent Literature, a Catholic Church sponsored censorship group, publishes an evaluation of materials, and while they do not intend their lists for boycott or coercion, they admit that that has occurred. The activities of Citizens for Decent Literature (now the most active and successful of the "decency movement" groups) parallel those of the New Jersey Committee for the Right to Read and the National Council for Freedom to Read. Each of these groups has

1) attempted to influence the public through speakers and newsletters, 2) provided some legal assistance, and 3) surveyed psychiatrists as to the effects of pornography, particularly on the young. Of these two forces, the activities of the "decency movement" have enjoyed broader, more vocal public support. (Examples of court decisions and local news concerning censorship are cited throughout the report.)

Meerloo, Abraham M. *The Rape of the Mind; the Psychology of Thought Control, Menticide, and Brainwashing.* 1st ed. Cleveland: World Publishing Co., 1956. 320p.

Dr. Meerloo, a Dutch-American psychiatrist, covers in this psychological treatise some of the techniques of individual and mass submission, and he attempts to reveal what psychoanalysis can do when it is combined with findings of the behavioral sciences. Although the book was written for the layman, the clinical jargon is at times difficult to follow; however, the reader should keep in mind that psychiatric concepts are not easily simplified. Much of the book is based upon the author's personal experience as chief of the Psychological Department of the Netherlands Army during World War II.

Meltzer, Milton. *Conference on Censorship.* By Milton Meltzer and others. Columbia, Mo.: Freedom of Information Center, 1969. 61p. (EDRS Document ED 038 428)

In this collection of seven speeches from the University of Missouri Conference on Censorship, writers focus on the various aspects of censorship. Speeches are by 1) Milton Meltzer, who lauds those writers who were forced to battle with censors; 2) Enid Olson, who explores the censorship problems faced by teachers and school librarians; 3) Margaret Twyman, who recommends education as the best means of changing the climate in which censors can thrive; 4) Irving Levitas, who interprets the censorship and violence problems as subterfuges for an actual political situation that attempts to preserve the status quo at all costs; 5) Joan Bodger, who asserts that the speaking out of youth has rocked our society and will continue to do so; 6) Morris Ernst, who accuses the networks, TV executives, and controllers of the mass media of keeping the public in ignorance; and 7) Anson Mount, who considers personal freedom as the key to the outlook of the young generation. Also included is the question and answer session of the Conference.

Minor, Dale. *The Information War.* New York: Hawthorne Books, 1970. 212p.

Based on experience gained in the field of press coverage, this is a well written, readable, and somewhat detailed critique of news coverage and censorship. Emphasis is placed on government censorship techniques, the press's interpretation of the news, and the struggle between the forces which constrict or manipulate the information reported to the public.

Missouri Library Association. *Guidelines for Insuring Intellectual Freedom in Missouri's Libraries.* Columbia, Mo., 1969. (EDRS Document ED 049 763)

A statement of policy was developed by the Intellectual Freedom Committee of the Missouri Library Association as a means of carrying out its assigned responsibility "to make available such assistance and direction as deemed necessary and proper to any citizen of Missouri involved in a censorship incident." The Association is directly concerned with the freedom of all members of a democratic society to read what they will in the course of making the social, educational, and political judgments on which that society is based. There is evidence that books and libraries are the chief bastion against the pressures toward conformity which are in large part overwhelming the motion picture, radio and television, and the press. Only in libraries can the interested citizen hope to find all the relevant facts concerning current controversial issues. It is appropriate that librarians should deem their freedom, and that of their libraries, of the utmost importance to the continued existence of democracy.

Moon, Eric, ed. *Book Selection and Censorship in the Sixties.* New York, R. R. Bowker Company, 1969. 421p.

An anthology of 55 articles which appeared during the 1960s in *Library Journal*, this book contains essays written by practicing librarians, library school educators, and non-librarian contributors who are actively involved in or interested in the promotion of intellectual freedom. Articles on book selection in libraries are provided in Part I of the anthology, and they are arranged under the following subtopics: "Theory," "Surveys," "Magazines and News Publications," "Audio-visual Materials," "Children's Books," and "Selection Tools and Reviewing." Part II of the volume deals with book censorship. An article by Ervin J. Gaines, entitled "Intellectual Freedom from *Roth* to the Presidential Commission on Obscenity and Pornography," precedes the 23 articles in Part II, which is divided into sections entitled "Views on Censorship–Outside the Profession," "Library Associations Debate Censorship," "Case Histories," "The Politics of Censorship," and "The Library School's Responsibility."

Murphy, Terence J. *Censorship: Government and Obscenity.* Baltimore: Helicon Press, 1963. 294p.

In this work, which is devoted to examining reactions of the government to obscenity, a Catholic priest attempts to define the term "obscene" and to justify censorship of pornography, a repression which he claims does not violate the Constitutional rights of citizens. Taking a pro-censorship position, the author presents a somewhat biased examination of statutes prohibiting obscene literature and the court decisions connected with them.

National Council of Teachers of English. Committee on the Right to Read. *The Students' Right to Read.* Champaign, Ill.: National Council of Teachers of English, 1962. 21p.

This small pamphlet was designed to call the attention of the general public to the danger of attempting to prevent certain books from being read by students. The literary classics are defended. The message of the pamphlet is carried in "an open letter to the citizens of this country" as well as in an outlined program for anti-censorship action. The pamphlet reflects the belief of the Committee on the Right to Read that freedom to read is as important as freedom of the press and freedom of speech.

National Council of Teachers of English. *The Right to Read: An Open Letter to the Citizens of Our Country from the National Council of Teachers of English*. Champaign, Ill., 1962. 7p. (EDRS Document ED 029 864)

Democracy can exist only in a climate in which teachers are free to teach and students are free to learn, a climate conducive to open inquiry and responsible discussion of any and all questions related to the ethical and cultural welfare of mankind. The right of an individual to read rests on the fundamental democratic assumption that an educated free man possesses powers of discrimination and should determine his own actions. To avoid objections from pressure groups, national or local book committees tend carefully to exclude from textbooks and reading lists those sections and volumes that offend such groups. Consequently, several American writers are inadequately represented in the public secondary schools. Cut off from many of the great ideas and feelings of Western man, a student is unlikely to develop into a free, reasoning person who can make up his own mind, who can understand his culture, and who can live compassionately with his fellowman. To preserve the unity of Western thought and culture, American citizens who care about the improvement of education are urged to join teachers, librarians, administrators, boards of trustees, and professional and scholarly organizations in supporting the students' right to read.

National Council of Teachers of English. *The Students' Right to Read*. Champaign, Ill., 1962. 21p. (EDRS Document ED 033 923)

Individuals and groups are exerting increasing pressures on American schools to restrict student access to important and worthwhile books. The success of these attempts at censorship has resulted in teachers being reprimanded, books being removed from libraries and classrooms, and subsequent attacks being expanded to include areas much larger than the target schools. With this danger of censorship, American citizens must be made aware of their rights to read, based on the fundamental democratic assumption that free men possess powers of discrimination and should determine their own actions. Librarians, teachers of English, and school administrators should prepare to protect the students' right to read by 1) establishing a committee of English teachers who, with the approval of the school administration, can determine book selection policy and screen complaints, and 2) fostering a community climate in which citizens will support the freedom to read.

Nelson, Jack. *The Censors and the Schools*. By Jack Nelson and Gene Roberts, Jr. New York and Toronto: Little, Brown, and Company, 1963. 208p.

This book, written by two former Nieman Fellows at Harvard University, deals with the censorship of textbooks. Case after case of textbook censorship by pressure groups is documented; the authors recommend that scholars, not censors or would-be censors, should make the decision about what goes into textbooks.

Paul, James C.N. *Federal Censorship; Obscenity in the Mail*. By James C.N. Paul and Murray L. Schwartz. New York: Free Press of Glencoe, 1961. 368p.

The research upon which this book is based was conducted through the Institute of Legal Research of the Law School of the University of Pennsylvania with a grant from the Fund for the Republic. The book is an investigation of federal controls on obscene publications and other material flowing through the U. S. mail. It will be of interest to individuals concerned about the censorship role of the federal government.

Peckham, Morse. *Art and Pornography; an Experiment in Explanation.* New York: Harper & Row, 1971. 306p. (Studies in Sex and Society)
   First published in 1969 by Basic Books, Inc., this paperback Icon Edition is part of the Studies in Sex and Society series, which is sponsored by the Institute for Sex Research, Indiana University. A study in the interdependence of art, pornography, and sexual behavior, the book is divided into four parts: "What Is Pornography," "The Art of Pornography," "An Explanation for Pornography," and "Pornography and Culture." In his preface the author states: "In short, my proposal has, I believe, something to displease practically everybody, and to please them, too. My immodest wish is to pass on to my readers the same sense of intellectual contradiction and incoherence I feel in myself, the acceptance of which is, it may be, our only real excuse for hope."

Perrin, Noel. *Dr. Bowdler's Legacy; a History of Expurgated Books in England and America.* 1st ed. New York: Atheneum, 1969. 296p.
   Dr. Bowdler was an English editor of an altered and expurgated version of Shakespeare's works, and his "legacy" is an appropriate title for this volume, which contains many wittily and light-heartedly presented examples of the efforts of individuals and groups to eradicate impurities and obscenities from literary works in English.

Perry, Stuart. *The Indecent Publications Tribunal; a Social Experiment; With Text of the Legislation Since 1900 and Classifications of the Tribunal.* Foreword by Sir Kenneth Greeson. Christchurch: Whitcombe and Tombe, 1965. 169p.
   An objective account of New Zealand's history of censorship of books and experimental operations to deal with censorship by the use of legislation. An extensive bibliography and an index are included. Legislative acts dealing with censorship in New Zealand since 1910 and a classification of the tribunals are included in the appendix.

Phelan, John, ed. *Communications Control; Readings in the Motives and Structures of Censorship.* New York: Sheed and Ward, 1969. 238p.
   A scholarly book with ten previously published essays by outstanding authors; each essay presents an author's views on censorship. The book is divided into three parts, each dealing with a combination of theory, critical analysis, and case study of controls which limit the contents of communications. Footnotes are listed at the end of many of the essays, and a selective bibliography covering subjects discussed in the book is also provided.

Popper, William. *The Censorship of Hebrew Books.* First published in New York in 1899. Reprint edition. New York: Burt Franklin, 1968. 156p. (Burt Franklin Research & Source Works, No. 222 and Judaica Series No. 60)

Using material available in the Hebrew Library of Columbia University, which contains numerous censored and expurgated Hebrew *incunabula* and early works that were at one time or another censored, the author wrote his thesis which has been reprinted as a book. An attempt was made to take a broad, historical view of the censorship of Hebrew books and to include information about all restriction placed upon Hebrew literary activity until the end of the eighteenth century. Restrictions by Spanish authorities between 1232 and 1322 are covered, and information is included about the ineffective measures of the fourteenth and fifteenth centuries, the Reuchlin Movement, the Index Expurgatorius, the Mantuan Commission, and Italian expurgators of the seventeenth and eighteenth centuries.

Putnam, George H. *The Censorship of the Church of Rome and Its Influence Upon the Production and Distribution of Literature.* New York: Benjamin Blom, 1967. 2v.

This book has the subtitle "A Study of the History of the Prohibitory and Expurgatory Indexes, Together with Some Consideration of the Effects of Protestant Censorship and of Censorship by the State." A record of the literary restraints placed by the authority of the Church of Rome, the work was first published in 1906 by G. P. Putnam's Sons; it has been reprinted in these two volumes. Sixteen chapters comprise volume one, which discusses, among other subjects, censorship and the early church, prohibition of books in the Middle Ages, the Roman Inquisition and the congregation of the Index, the Council of Trent and the Index of Pius IV, censorship regulations, Roman indexes and decrees, the Index of Alexander VII, and Erasmus and Luther in the Index. Volume two is comprised of 12 chapters concerned with such topics as theological controversies in France, Germany, England, and the Netherlands between 1600 and 1750; the monastic orders and censorship; Roman indexes between 1758 and 1900; issues between church and state; the book trade as affected by censorship between 1450 and 1800; and a number of other related subjects. Although the book makes no claim to completeness of coverage of Church decrees and regulations, it is a valuable source for historical information about the influence of the Church of Rome's general system of censorship upon the production and dissemination of the printed word.

Radcliffe, Cyril J. *Censors.* Cambridge: Cambridge University Press, 1961. 31p. (The Rede Lecture, 1961)

Delivered by Lord Radcliffe in the University of Cambridge on May 4, 1961, this lecture is an historical and philosophical analysis of "the long debate about freedom of expression which began with the seventeenth century and the puritan revolution." Although the starting point is Milton's *Areopagitica*, Radcliffe arrives at what he modestly calls "random conclusions" of relevance for the modern world: "we badly need to develop a modern philosophy of authority for future use instead of just chanting the old choruses of rebellion. That is true both of this country and of the United States, and the reason, I suspect, is for both the same: the heroes, the men who did and said the heroic things, were men who challenged or overthrew authority." The style of the lecture is rather oratory and heavy, but the contents are pregnant with original and challenging ideas.

Randall, Richard S. *Censorship of the Movies; the Social and Political Control of a Mass Medium*. Madison: University of Wisconsin Press, 1968. 280p.

Legal and extralegal forms of censorship of moving pictures is the topic of this work, written by a University of Nebraska political science professor. The historical development of censorship is dealt with, as well as techniques of repression. This work is somewhat of a repeat of what was already said in Carmen's *Movies, Censorship and the Law* and Schumach's *The Face on the Cutting Room Floor.*

Rembar, Charles. *The End of Obscenity; the Trials of Lady Chatterley, Tropic of Cancer, and Fanny Hill.* New York: Random House, 1968. 528p.

Written by a lawyer who has participated in obscenity trials, this book deals with experiences in court cases concerned with three novels: *Lady Chatterley's Lover, The Tropic of Cancer,* and *Fanny Hill.* Witty and informative discussions of the presentation of court cases and the legal strategy involved are included. The author feels that controversies over obscenity in literary works will eventually disappear from our society and that we will thus have "the end of obscenity."

Roberts, Edwin A., Jr. *The Smut Rakers; a Report in Depth on Obscenity and the Censors.* Silver Spring, Md.: National Observer, 1966. 143p. (The National Observer Newsbook)

The ninth title in the Newsbook Series, this publication reports on obscenity and censorship; it includes discussions about censorship of books and motion pictures as well as the individuals involved in obscenity charges. Also discussed are postal inspections, the Customs Bureau's criteria for obscenity, the F.B.I.'s involvement in censorship cases, and the Ginzburg decision. The book provides different views on the nature of obscenity.

St. John-Stevas, Norman. *Obscenity and the Law.* With an introduction by Sir Alan P. Herbert. London: Secker & Warburg, 1956. 289p.

This book is a study of changing law and attitudes in relation to literature and freedom of expression in literature. Emphasis is on the history of obscenity in England; however, Irish and American censorship experiences are also discussed. As the author states in his preface: "Perhaps the most significant point that has emerged . . . is that the law only intervened to suppress serious literature at the close of the nineteenth century, when the Victorian synthesis was breaking down and when Forster's Education Act had created a vast new reading public." Justifying his concentration on nineteenth century censorship developments, the author states that the availability of materials about obscenity cases during that period and a similarity of problems faced by that era with those of our present time caused him to deal with the period at length. This work is a rather thorough historical examination of the efforts of men who attempted to influence the liberalization of English obscenity laws and, in the words of the author, to "draw a fundamental distinction between works written with a serious purpose and those which have no other aim save the making of money by exploiting and degrading the sexual passions."

Schumach, Murry. *The Face on the Cutting Room Floor; the Story of Movie and Television Censorship.* New York: Morrow, 1964. 305p.

A survey of censorship of motion pictures and television programs, this book considers the effects of scandals and leftwing political activities on censorship and examines the censoring methods used by pressure groups. The rise of the Production Code is discussed, as well as voluntary classification or rating of films, the Hollywood "blacklist" of the McCarthy era, foreign censorship and classification, and the moral and religious aspects of motion pictures.

Sharp, Donald B., ed. *Commentaries on Obscenity.* Metuchen, N. J.: The Scarecrow Press, Inc., 1970. 333p.

Edited by Donald B. Sharp, librarian at Carlow College in Pittsburg, this work is an anthology of articles by legal scholars, including: Harry Kelvin, Jr., William G. Lockhart, Robert B. Cairns, Louis Henkin, Louis B. Schwartz, Henry P. Monaghan, and Richard B. Dyson. According to the editor, the anthology was "gathered to aid the scholar concerned with obscenity law and issues pertinent to freedom of the press." Included are essays dealing with sex censorship, morals and the Constitution, the confusion of Supreme Court decisions on obscenity, freedom of expression, and the definition of obscenity. Recent obscenity cases are also discussed in various articles included in the book, and in the last contribution Charles M. Stern discusses a rationale for the use of expert testimony in obscenity litigation.

Spring, Samuel. *Risks and Rights in Publishing; Television, Radio, Motion Pictures, and the Theater.* 2d ed., rev. New York: W. W. Norton, 1956. 365p.

A well-written work designed for both laymen and lawyers, by a recognized expert in the field of risks and rights in the communication and entertainment industries. The book is devoted to an exploration of what the laws are and what, in the author's view, they ought to be. Cases referred to in the text are grouped in Appendix A with citations. The Copyright Statute of the United States is also provided.

Stein, Fritz. *The Censorship of Books in the United States.* Unpublished thesis written for the Master's degree at Case Western Reserve University, 1955. 98p.

The research upon which this study was based was designed to provide an historical outline of book censorship in the United States. Early censorship cases are discussed as well as pro- and anti-censorship opinions, banned books, obscenity, and censorship as a product of American nationalism.

Swayze, Harold. *Political Control of Literature in the USSR, 1946-1959.* Cambridge: Harvard University Press, 1962. 301p. (Russian Research Center Studies, No. 44)

The Russian Research Center at Harvard University, which sponsored this book, is supported by grants from the Carnegie, Ford, and Rockefeller Foundations. The center carries out inter-disciplinary study of Russian institutions and behavior. This publication is a solid, well-documented, and academic work written by Professor Swayze, who spent nine months at Moscow University. A careful soci-politico-literary analysis of the interrelation between Soviet "belles-lettres" and Soviet bureaucracy is made in the book. As the title indicates, the author takes an historical approach, concentrating mainly on controversial writers and works. He also emphasizes the general trends of official government policy. The non-specialist will find the book replete with an overwhelming amount of details and many unfamiliar Russian names.

Symula, James F. *Censorship of High School Literature: a Study of the Incidents of Censorship Involving J. D. Salinger's "The Catcher in the Rye."* Dissertation written for the Ed.D. degree at The State University of New York at Buffalo, 1969. 162p. (University Microfilms, No. 69-19, 035)

This examination of the omnipresent problem of censorship, especially as it affects public high school literature programs, emphasizes the need for book selection policies and formal procedures for handling a complaint against a book. It may prove useful to school personnel in combatting or preventing censorship by its review of studies in censorship incidents together with the critical literature dealing with *Catcher*. Four major conclusions of the study are that 1) censorship is based on ignorance; 2) in choosing classroom literature, the teacher has tremendous responsibility to the students; 3) English teachers must lead the fight against censorship; and 4) there is a great need for honest reporting of facts surrounding an incident of censorship.

Thomas, Donald. *A Long Time Burning; the History of Literary Censorship in England.* New York: Praeger, 1969. 546p. (Books That Matter)

Comprehensive and detailed account of the evolution of British literary censorship from the fifteenth century to the present, with emphasis on the last two and a half centuries. The major political, religious, social, and moral forces are carefully traced, along with their effects on freedom of the press in England. Examples illustrate the contradictions and inequalities of censorship laws, policies, and practices, with suggested explanations for the double standards. Illustrations, bibliographic references, and a sizeable appendix listing censored items are included.

U. S. Department of the Air Force. *Armed Forces Censorship.* Washington: Government Printing Office, 1957. 80p. illus. (Air Force Mannual 205-9)

One of several in a series about security matters in U. S. military forces, this official manual deals with censorship of personal correspondence in times of national emergency. It includes a history of, the purpose for, the principles of, and the responsibility for military censorship. The types of personal communication to be censored are identified, and a procedure for exceptional handling of these materials is outlined.

U. S. President's Commission on Obscenity and Pornography. *The Report of the Commission on Obscenity and Pornography.* Washington: For sale by the Supt. of Docs., U. S. Government Printing Office, 1970. 646p.

The Presidential Commission on Obscenity and Pornography was appointed

184

in January 1968 by President Lyndon B. Johnson for the purpose of investigating the gravity of the production and dissemination of pornography. Among the main charges given to the Commission were the determination of whether pornographic materials were harmful to the public, especially to minors, and whether more effective methods should be devised to control the transmission of such materials. The Commission's report, one of the most controversial documents of the year, is made up of four parts: an overview of the findings, the recommendations of the Commission, the reports of the panels, and separate statements of Commission members. A preface and four appendices are also provided: Public Law 90-100, October 3, 1967, which is the Congressional act authorizing the creation of the Commission; biographies of Commission members; a list of contractors who participated in the research; and a list of hearings conducted in 1970, including names of witnesses. Recommendations of the Commission include the following proposals relating to legislation: "that federal, state, and local legislation prohibiting the sale, exhibition, or distribution of sexual materials to consenting adults should be repealed," "the adoption by the states of legislation set forth in the Drafts of Proposed Statutes in Section III . . . prohibiting the commercial distribution or display for sale of certain sexual materials to young persons," "the enactment of state and local legislation prohibiting public displays of sexually explicit pictorial materials . . . ," "enactment . . . of legislation authorizing prosecutors to obtain declaratory judgments as to whether particular materials fall within existing legal prohibitions and appropriate injunctive relief," and "recommends against the adoption of any legislation which would limit or abolish the jurisdiction of the Supreme Court of the United States or of other federal judges and courts in obscenity cases." A *New York Times* paperback book edition of the report entitled, *The Report of the Commission on Obscenity and Pornography* (Bantam Books, 1970) was published from materials released by the Commission to the press on September 30, 1970. In his introduction to that edition, Clive Barnes of *The New York Times* stated: "The Commission was requested by Congress to address itself to 'a matter of national concern.' But one of the Commission's most significant, and in some quarters most disputed, findings is that obscenity and pornography are not matters of public concern at all."

Widmer, Kingsley, ed. *Literary Censorship: Principles, Cases, Problems.* Edited by Kingsley Widmer and Eleanor Widmer. San Francisco: Wadsworth Publishing Company, 1961. 182p. (Wadsworth Guides to Literary Study)
    This work presents arguments for and against censorship by famous individuals, ranging from Plato to Henry Miller. It also includes discussions by Robert W. Haney, Harold C. Gardner, D. H. Lawrence, and others about restrictive measures of private and religious groups. In the last section, entitled "The Cultural Context of American Censorship," articles by Margaret Mead, Eric Larrabee, and Ernest van den Haag deal with current attitudes toward sex, violence, and art.

Wiggins, James R. *Freedom of Secrecy.* Revised edition. New York: Oxford University Press, 1964. 289p.
    Written to alert the public to the threats of governmental control of

information, the author attacks the cloak of secrecy in which many government agencies have enclosed themselves. In the preface, the author states: "Legislative, executive, and judicial establishments of local, state and federal governments challenge the rights of citizens to scrutinize their transactions." The ten chapters of this work discuss, among other topics, the rights of the people to know about their legislatures, judicial proceedings, the executive department, the military establishment, and private governmental transactions. The right to print without prior restraint is also discussed, as well as reprisal for publication, the right of access to means of publishing, and the right to distribute. The general thesis of this work is that Americans are confronted with a choice between secrecy and freedom; the author presents convincing and documented arguments to support his cause of the free flow of information from the government to the people.


## SECTION B
## THESES

Arden, Carolina. *Analysis of the Reports by Leading News Media of the Activities of the New York Society for the Suppression of Vice, 1916-1947, Regarding the Suppression of Ten Specific Books.* Thesis written for the M. S. degree at Florida State University, 1961. 117p.

Barnes, Frances K. *Policies and Practices Governing Provision of Controversial Materials in the Public School Libraries in Texas in 1965.* Thesis written for the M.L.S. degree at the University of Texas, 1966. 182p.

Bennett, Edward H. *Investigation of Censorship in the Libraries of Massachusetts.* Thesis written for the M.S. degree at Simmons College, 1953. 43p.

Bloomfield, Joy F. *Investigation of Censorship in the Cuyahoga County (Ohio) Library System.* Thesis written for the M.L.S. degree at Kent State University, 1968. 165p.

Boyd, Maurice R. *Effects of Censorship Attempts by Private Pressure Groups on Public Libraries, 1945-1957.* Thesis written for the M.A. degree at Kent State University, 1958. 69p.

Chu, Doris J. *Censorship of Books in the Ch'ing Dynasty, China.* Thesis written for the M.S. degree at Southern Connecticut State College, 1968. 71p.

Coyne, Fumiko H. *Censorship of Publishing in Japan: 1868-1945.* Thesis written for the M.A. degree at the University of Chicago, 1967. 87p.

Dorman, Phae H. *Content Analysis Study of Articles Dealing With Censoring Activities in the United States, 1950-1957.* Thesis written for the M.S. in L.S. degree at Atlanta University, 1959. 39p.

186

Ficklen, Imogene S. *Three Landmarks in the Anglo-Saxon Struggle for Freedom of Speech.* Thesis written for the M.S. in L.S. degree at the University of North Carolina, 1960. 86p.

Hirsch, Jane K. *Critical Reception of Three Controversial Children's Books.* Thesis written for the M.S. in L.S. degree at Catholic University of America, 1966. 77p.

Hohman, Agnes C. *Analysis of the Literature on the Outstanding Issues and Opinions on Censorship, 1940-1950.* Thesis written for the M.S.L.S. degree at Catholic University of America, 1951. 182p.

Lee, Carolyn T. *Contemporary Catholic Attitudes Toward Censorship for Catholics.* Thesis written for the M.A. in L.S. degree at the University of Minnesota, 1958. 93p.

Line, Bryant W. *Study of Incidents and Trends in the Censorship of Books Affecting Public and School Libraries in the United States, 1954-1964.* Thesis written for the M.S. in L.S. degree at Catholic University of America, 1965. 249p.

Louthan, Shirley. *McCarthy Sub-Committee and the American Overseas Libraries.* Thesis written for the M.S. in L.S. at Western Reserve University, 1958. 59p.

Merey, Pakize E. *Analysis of the Books Removed from the United States Information Service Libraries.* Thesis written for the M.S.L.S. degree at Drexel Institute of Technology, 1954. 53p.

Peele, David A. *Lollipops or Dynamite—Shall We Censor the Comics?* Thesis written for the M.S.L.S. degree at Western Reserve University, 1951. 46p.

Rairigh, William N. *Judicial Opinion Concerning Censorship of Library Materials, 1926-1950.* Thesis written for the M.S.L.S. degree at Drexel Institute of Technology, 1950. 59p.

Riordan, Mary E. *Literary Censorship in Ireland 1929-1960.* Thesis written for the M.A. degree at the University of Chicago, 1964. 165p.

Sawilowsky, Yale S. *Censorship and the Librarian.* Thesis written for the M.L.S. degree at the University of Mississippi, 1964. 60p.

Speirs, Charles H. *Effects of Political Censorship in the United States on Public Libraries and Librarians from 1945 to 1955.* Thesis written for the M.S.L.S. degree at Western Reserve University, 1957. 55p.

Stein, Fritz. *Censoring of Books in the United States.* Thesis written for the M.S.L.S. degree at Western Reserve University, 1955. 98p.

Stella, Stefaniex R. *Subversive Literature and Unofficial Censorship: A Study of Organized Patrioric Groups' Tactics and Philosophy, 1960-62.* Thesis written for the M.S. in L.S. degree at the University of North Carolina, 1965. 67p.

Swogetinsky, Betty A. *Study of Censorial Demands on Texas Libraries, 1952-67.* Thesis written for the M.L.S. degree at the University of Texas, 1967. 202p.

Tamblyn, Eldon W. *Censorship in North Carolina Public Libraries.* Thesis written for the M.S. in L.S. degree at the University of North Carolina, 1964. 154p.

Wenning, Dorothy W. *Books Removed from the United States Information Service Libraries; An Analysis and Appraisal.* Thesis written for the M.A. degree at Florida State University, 1956. 213p.

## SECTION C
## ARTICLES AND PARTS OF LARGER WORKS

Asher, Thomas R. "A Lawyer Looks at Libraries and Censorship: Address, 1970," *Library Journal* 95:3247-9 (October 1, 1970).

Ayrton, Michael. "Talking About Censorship: 1. Obscenity in Committee," *Author* 81:69-70 (Summer, 1970).

Baird, Frank. "Program Regulation on the New Frontier," *Journal of Broadcasting* 11:231-44 (Summer, 1967).

Barthel, Joan, and Tom Prideaux. "Sex, Shock and Sensuality: the Lively Arts, With Accounts," *Life* 66:22-35 (April 4, 1969).

Bates, Alan. "The Sad History of Censorship," *Humanist* 82:268-70 (September, 1967).

Berninghausen, David K. "The History of the ALA Intellectual Freedom Committee," *Wilson Library Bulletin* 27:813-17 (June, 1953).

_____."The Librarian's Commitment to the Library Bill of Rights," *Library Trends* 19:19-38 (July, 1970).

Black, Douglas MacCrae. "Addendum to Civil Liberties: The Publisher's Responsibility," *Antioch Review* 13:527-32 (December, 1953).

Blount, William M. "Let's Put the Smut Merchants Out of Businesss," *Nation's Business* 59:34-36 (September, 1971).

Bolte, Charles G. "Security Through Book Burning," *Annals of the Academy of Political and Social Sciences* 2:87-93 (July, 1955).

Bonniwell, Bernard L. "The Social Control of Pornography and Sexual Behavior," *The Annals of the American Academy of Political and Social Sciences* 397:97-104 (September, 1971).

Boyer, P. S. "Boston Book Censorship in the Twenties," *American Quarterly* 15:3-24 (Spring, 1963).

Boyle, Robert. "Literature and Pornography," *Catholic World* 193:295-302 (August, 1961).

Broderick, Dorothy M. "Censorship Reevaluated," *Library Journal* 96:3816-18 (November 15, 1971).

_____."When the Censor Knocks." *Phi Delta Kappan* 52:462-4 (April, 1971).

Bryer, Jackson R. "Joyce, Ulysses, and the Little Review," *South Atlantic Quarterly* 66:148-64 (Spring, 1967).

Burke, John G., and Paxton H. Bowers. "Institutional Censorship: A Proposal for an Effective Mechanism to Protect the Researcher," *Library Journal* 95:468-9 (February 1, 1970).

Burress, Lee A., Jr. "Censorship and the Public Schools," *ALA Bulletin* 59:491-9 (June, 1965).

Busha, Charles H. "Censorship and the Midwestern Public Librarian," *Newsletter on Intellectual Freedom* 20:103-4 (September, 1971).

_____."Student Attitudes Toward Censorship and Authoritarianism," *Journal of Education for Librarianship* 11:118-136 (Fall, 1970).

Castagna, Edwin. "Censorship, Intellectual Freedom, and Libraries," in *Advances in Librarianship* 2:215-51 (Seminar Press, 1971).

Cipes, Robert M. "Controlling Crime News; Excerpts for the Crime War," *Atlantic* 220:47-53 (August, 1967).

Comyn, Andrew F. "Censorship in Ireland," *Studies* 58:42-50 (Spring, 1969).

"Concerning the Obscene," *Wilson Library Bulletin* 42:894-929 (May, 1968).

Couch, W. T. "The Sainted Book Burners," *Freeman* 5:423-26 (April, 1955).

Cowley, Malcom. "Artists, Conscience, and Censors," *Saturday Review* 45:8-10 (July 7, 1962).

Crawford, Donald W. "Can Disputes Over Censorship Be Resolved?" *Ethics* 78:93-108 (January, 1968).

Doebler, Peter D. "Viewpoint: the Printer and Censorship," *Newsletter on Intellectual Freedom* 20:75-76 (May, 1971).

Donelson, Kenneth L. "A Brief Note on Censorship and Junior High Schools in Arizona, 1966-68," *Arizona English Bulletin* 11:26-30 (April, 1969).

_____."Censorship and the Teaching of English: A Few Problems and Fewer Solutions," *Colorado Language Arts Society* 4:5-15, 18-20 (October, 1968).

_____."Challenging the Censor: Some Responsibilities of the English Department," *English Journal* 58:869-76 (September, 1969).

_____."Court Decisions and Legal Arguments About Censorship and the Nature of Obscenity," *Arizona English Bulletin* 11:45-49 (February, 1969).

Downs, Robert B. "Apologist for Censorship," *Library Journal* 86:2042-4 (June 1, 1961).

Dyson, Allan J. "Ripping Off Young Minds: Textbooks, Propaganda, and Librarians," *Wilson Library Bulletin* 46:260-7 (November, 1971).

Elkins, Frederick. "Censorship and Pressure Groups," *Phylon Quarterly* 21:71-80 (Spring, 1960).

Ellenburg, F. C. "Phantasy and Facts: Censorship and Schools," *The Clearing House* 45:515-19 (May, 1971).

Elliott, G. P. "Against Pornography," *Harper's Magazine* 230:51-60 (March, 1965).

Erskin, Hazel G. "The Polls: Freedom of Speech," *Public Opinion Quarterly* 34:483-96 (Fall, 1970).

Esbensen, Thorwald T. "How Far Have the Book Burners Gone?" *School Executive* 76:69-71 (May, 1957).

Everett, T. Moore. "Threats to Intellectual Freedom," *Library Journal* 96:3563-3567 (November 1, 1971).

Fraser, John. "The Erotic and Censorship," *Oxford Review* 9:21-39.

Freilisher, Lila P. "Story Behind the Book: The Little Red Schoolbook," *Publisher's Weekly* 200:32-33 (December 13, 1971).

Friedman, Leon. "Ginzberg Decision and the Law," *American Scholar* 36:71-91 (Winter, 1966-67).

Frisch, Paul. "Censorship and Freedom of Expression in Scandinavia," *American Scandinavian Review* 56:13-19 (March, 1968).

Fryer, Peter. "Censorship at the British Museum: the 'Private Case' and Other Mysteries," *Encounter* 27:68-77 (Autumn, 1966).

_____. "To Deprave and Corrupt," *Encounter* 28:41-44 (March, 1967).

Gaines, Ervin J. "Library Bill of Rights," *Library Journal* 92:984-85 (March 1, 1967).

Gard, Robert A. "Censorship and Public Understanding," *English Journal* 60:255-59 (February, 1971).

Gerber, Albert B. "The Right to Receive and Possess Pornography; an Attorney Foresees the End of Legal Restrictions," *Wilson Library Bulletin* 44:641-44 (February, 1970).

_____. "A Suggested Solution to the Riddle of Obscenity," *University of Pennsylvania Law Review* 112:834-56 (April, 1964).

Gielgud, Val. "Death of the Censor," *Contemporary Review* 219:10-12 (July, 1971).

Gillmor, Donald M. "The Puzzle of Pornography," *Journalism Quarterly* 42:363-72 (Summer, 1965).

Girodias, Maurice. "The Erotic Society," *Encounter* 26:52-58 (February, 1966).

Goodman, Paul. "Pornography, Art and Censorship," *Commentary* 31:203-12 (March, 1961).

Gotshalk, D. W. "Note on the Future of Censorship," *Journal of Aesthetic Education* 4:97-100 (July, 1970).

Gwyn, Robert J. "Opinion Advertising and the Free Market of Ideas," *Public Opinion Quarterly* 34:246-55 (Summer, 1970).

Haefner, John F. "The Battle of the Books," *NEA Journal* 42:227-8 (April, 1953).

Hale, Robert D. "Censorship: What a Bookseller Can Do About It," *Publisher's Weekly* 200:26-27 (July 26, 1971).

Halliday, E. M. "The Man Who Cleaned Up Shakespeare," *Horizon* 5:68-71 (September, 1962).

Hempel, William J., and Patrick M. Wall. "Extralegal Censorship of Literature," *New York University Law Review* 33:989-1026 (November, 1958).

Holmer, Marjorie. "Mother Speaks Up For Censorship," *Today's Health* 40:50-51 (January, 1962).

Holmes, Mary. "Censorship and Civil Rights: The Line Between Freedom and Restraint," *Social Order* 7:242-49 (June, 1957).

Hopkins, Deian. "Domestic Censorship in the First World War," *Journal of Contemporary History* 5:151-69 (October, 1970).

Hughes, Catharine. "Art and Responsibility," *Catholic World* 209:219-21 (August, 1969).

"Intellectual Freedom and the Jurisdictional Jungle," *Library Journal* 96:925-29 (March 15, 1971).

"Irving Wallace on Censorship: An Author Gives His Views on Censorship—Both the Obvious Kind and the Subtle Sort That Some Librarians Practice," interview *Censorship Today* 2:4-20 (October/November, 1969).

Jacobson, D. "An End to Pornography?" *Commentary* 42:76-82 (November, 1966).

Jacoby, Susan. "Russian Book Publishing: Inexorably Wedded to Censorship," *Publisher's Weekly* 200:169-71 (September 27, 1971).

Jarrett, James L. "On Pornography," *Journal of Aesthetic Education* 4:61-67 (July, 1970).

Jenks, George M. "Censorship or Privacy: the U. S. Mails," *RQ* (ALA Reference Services Division) 10:205-7 (Spring, 1971).

Jones, Penny. "Important Moral Issues: the Censorship of Books, Radio, and Television," *Expository Times* 75:333-7 (August, 1966).

Kaelin, E. F. "The Pornographic and the Obscene in Legal and Aesthetic Contexts," *The Journal of Aesthetic Education* 4:69-84 (July, 1970).

Kempton, Murray. "Eros Denied—Yet Again," *Spectator* April 8, 1966, pp. 428-29.

Kermode, Frank. "Obscenities—the Question of Limiting What Can Be Read or Staged," *Listener* 82:98-99 (July 24, 1969).

Kessler, Jascha. "The Censorship of Art and the Art of Censorship," *Literary Review* 12:409-31 (Summer, 1969).

Kohler, Mary. "The Rights of Children—An Unexplored Constituency," *Social Policy* 1:36-43 (March/April, 1971).

Kristol, Irving. "Pornography, Obscenity and the Case for Censorship," *Newsletter on Intellectual Freedom* 20:113-14, 131-33 (September, November, 1971).

Kvapil, Charline R., and Louise S. Schellenberg. "The Right to Read," *Arizona English Bulletin* 11:1-4 (February, 1969).

LaConte, Ronald T. "Who Are the Real Censors? Selection of English Classes," *The Education Digest* 36:44-46 (October, 1970).

Lacy, Dan. "Should the Book Publishing Industry Set Up a Self-Policing Program?" *American Scholar* 29:407 (Summer, 1960).

Lambert, J. W. "The Folly of Censorship," *Encounter* 29:60-62 (July, 1967).

Larrabee, Eric. "Cultural Context of Sex Censorship," *Law and Contemporary Problems* 20:672-88 (Fall, 1955).

Leary, William M., Jr. "Books, Soldiers and Censorship During the Second World War," *American Quarterly* 20:237-45 (Summer, 1968).

"Librarians Take Care," *Economist* 191:1023-24 (June 13, 1959).

Lockhart, William B., and Robert C. McClure. "Censorship of Obscenity: The Developing Constitutional Standards," *Minnesota Law Review* 45:5-121 (November, 1960).

Lunn, Betty. "From Whitest Africa—A Dark Tale of Censorship," [South Africa] *Library Journal* 95:131-33 (January 15, 1970).

Lynch, James J. "The Right to Read—And Not To Read: Censorship in a Permissive America," *Modern Age* 9:18-33 (Winter, 1964-65).

Lyons, Louis M. "What's Fit to Print?" *New Republic* 144:17-19 (June, 1961).

McShean, Gordon. "From Roswell to Richmond . . . to Your Town," *Library Journal* 95:627-31 (February 15, 1970).

Marcus, Steven. "Pornotopia," *Encounter* 27:9-18 (August, 1966).

Medvedev, Zhores. "How Censorship Works in Russia," *Human Events* 31:14-16 (October 23, 1971).

Mendlow, Sylvia, and Irving Morris. "Library Media Committee: Statement, May 5, 1971," *American Libraries* 2:789-90 (September, 1971).

Molz, Kathleen. "Public Custody of the High Pornography," *American Scholar* 36:93-103 (Winter, 1966-67).

Moore, Everett T. "Threats to Intellectual Freedom; Address June, 1971," *Library Journal* 96:3563-67 (November 1, 1971).

Mortimer, John. "Talking About Censorship: 2. After the Chamberlain," *Author* 81:71-73 (Summer, 1970).

Naylor, A. P. "Intellectual Freedom and the Public Library," *Phi Delta Kappan* 52:459-61 (April, 1971).

Oboler, Eli M. "Congress as Censor," *Library Trends* 19:64-73 (July, 1970).

_____. "Everything You Always Wanted to Know About Censorship (But Were Afraid to Ask) Explained," *American Libraries* 2:194-98 (February, 1971).

_____. "The Politics of Pornography," *Library Journal* 95:4225-28 (December 15, 1970).

_____. "Viewpoint: The Case Against 'Liberal' Censorship," *Newsletter on Intellectual Freedom* 21:30 (January, 1972).

O'Malley, William J. "How To Teach 'Dirty' Books in High School," *Educators Guide to Media and Methods* 4:6-11 (November, 1967).

O'Neill, Frank. "Censorship: In the South the Means of Resisting Are Weak," *South Today* 2:4-6 (January/February, 1971).

Osing, Gordon T. "Pornography: Our Concern Also," *Missouri English Bulletin* 27:20-26 (January, 1970).

Piel, Gerard. "Science, Censorship and the Public Interest," *Public Relations Journal* 13:12-13 (July, 1957).

Pilpel, Harriet F. "Evolution of a Sensible Doctrine of Censorship," *Publisher's Weekly* 180:29-30 (September 25, 1961).

Pooley, Beverly. "Librarians and Intellectual Freedom," *Microcosm* June, 1970, p. 1.

Ramsey, Glenn Virgil, and Mary Varley. "Censorship and the Kinsey Report," *Journal of Social Psychology* 33:279-88 (May, 1951).

Rettig, Salomon. "A Note on Censorship and the Changing Ethic of Sex," *Ethics* 78:151-55 (January, 1968).

Richardson, John A. "Dirty Pictures and Campus Comity," *The Journal of Aesthetic Education* 4:85-96 (July, 1970).

Rolph, C. H. "A Backward Glance at the Age of Obscenity," *Encounter* 32:19-28 (June, 1969).

Russell, Bertrand. "Virtue and the Censor," *Encounter* 3:8-11 (July, 1954).

"School Boards, Schoolbooks and the Freedom to Learn," *Yale Law Journal* 59:928-54 (April, 1950).

Segal, Alan. "Censorship, Social Control and Socialization," *The British Journal of Sociology* 21:63-74 (March, 1970).

Serviss, Trevor K. "Freedom to Learn–Censorship in Learning Materials," *Social Education* 17:65-70 (February, 1953).

Shapiro, Sanford. "Big Brother Is Watching Your Kids," *ALA Bulletin* 62:1089-92 (October, 1968).

Sherman, Stuart C. "Defending the Freedom to Read," *Library Journal* 87:479-83 (February 1, 1962).

Shuman, R. Baird. "Making the World Safe for What?" *The Education Digest* 34:36-38 (December, 1968).

Singer, Richard G. "Censorship of Prisoners' Mail and the Constitution," *American Bar Association Journal* 56:1051-55 (November, 1970).

Spangler, Eve. "Surveyor Finds Connecticut Libraries Avoid Controversial Books," *Connecticut Libraries* 13:6-8 (Autumn, 1971).

Spaulding, William E. "Can Textbooks be Subversive?" *Educational Record* 34:297-304 (October, 1953).

Strick, Philip. "Talking About Censorship: 3. Cinema Freedoms," *Author* 81:74-77 (Summer, 1970).

Strout, Donald E. "Intellectual Freedom Landmarks: 1955-60," *Library Journal* 86:2035-42, 2575-79 (July, August, 1961).

Stuart, I. R. "Personality Dynamics and Objectionable Art: Attitudes, Opinions and Experimental Evidence," *The Journal of Aesthetic Education* 4:101-116 (July, 1970).

Symula, James F. "Censorship and Teacher Responsibility," *English Journal* 60:128-31 (January, 1971).

von den Steinen, Karl. "The Harmless Papers: Granville, Gladstone, and the Censorship of the Madagascar Blue Book of 1884," *Victorian Studies* 14:165-76 (December, 1970).

Wassom, Earl. "Education and the Censorship Dilemma," *Kentucky Library Association Bulletin* 35:11-16 (July, 1971).

Wilkins, Barrat. "Censorship and Modernity," *The South Carolina Librarian* 15:15-17,39 (Spring, 1971).

Williams, Pat. "Enemies of the Imagination," *Twentieth Century* 172:79-88 (Spring, 1963).

Wirt, Frederick M. "To See or Not to See: The Case Against Censorship," *Film Quarterly* 13:26-31 (Fall, 1958/Summer, 1960).

Wolff, Geoffrey. "Pornography and Social Value," *New Leader* 51:14-15 (August 5, 1968).

Young, W. Winston. "Censorship: the Need for a Positive Program to Prevent It (Book Selection as Public Relations)." *The Growing Edges of Secondary English: Essays by the Experienced Teacher Fellows at the University of Illinois 1966-67*, edited by Charles Suhor and others. Champaign, Illinois: National Council of Teachers of English, 1968. pp. 201-217.

# APPENDIX I

# LETTERS AND THE
# SURVEY INSTRUMENT*

*Total response for each fixed-alternative choice in the questionnaire is provided to the nearest whole per cent.

# Opinion Survey Of
# Midwestern Public Librarians

Charles H. Busha
Graduate Library School
Indiana University

Bloomington, Indiana 47401
Telephone 812 339-5203

Dear Librarian:

As a doctoral candidate in the Graduate Library School of Indiana University, I am conducting opinion research among Midwestern public librarians. The survey is an attempt to determine how librarians feel about a number of library issues and socially important topics, and it is an important part of my dissertation.

You have been chosen in a random sample of librarians from your state to serve as a respondent in this opinion research, and I sincerely hope that you will participate. You have probably thought about and discussed many of the issues in which I am interested; your opinions about them will be of considerable value. Please complete the enclosed simple questionnaire, which requests opinions only and does not ask for the recall of facts. Only a few minutes of your time will be required.

Items included in this survey cover a number of issues, and your frank opinion about <u>each</u> is the best answer. Strictly speaking, there are no right or wrong answers. You can be sure that, whatever your persuasion may be on a certain issue, a number of librarians will agree with you, while others will disagree. Since your personal opinions are needed, please do not consult with your associates as you complete the questionnaire.

All replies are strictly confidential. Your name is not required on the questionnaire, and references to individuals or to specific libraries will not be made in written reports of this research. The code number on each form is for tabulating purposes only.

Please record your replies and return the questionnaire in the provided, self-addressed, and stamped envelope within the next ten days.

Thank you very much for your help on this study. I look forward to receiving your completed questionnaire.

Sincerely yours,

Charles H. Busha

Enclosures

199

# Opinion Survey Of
# Midwestern Public Librarians

Charles H. Busha
Graduate Library School
Indiana University

Bloomington, Indiana 47401
Telephone 812 339-5203

Dear Librarian:

Several weeks ago you were asked to participate in the Opinion Survey of Midwestern Public Librarians, and a questionnaire was mailed to you. As yet, there is no record of your response.

You are one of a select group of public librarians in your state who was asked to serve as a respondent in this research, and your reply is needed in order to obtain representative data concerning the opinions of all Midwestern public librarians about a number of important issues.

Could you please complete the questionnaire and drop it in the mail in the postage-paid envelope which was provided? It will take only a few minutes of your time.

If you no longer have a copy of the questionnaire, or if you did not receive one in the first place, I will be glad to mail one to you. Please check the appropriate line on the enclosed postcard and drop it in the mail.

Thank you very much for your assistance and for returning the enclosed postcard.

Sincerely yours,

Charles H. Busha

Enclosure

# Opinion Survey Of
# Midwestern Public Librarians

Charles H. Busha
Graduate Library School
Indiana University

Bloomington, Indiana 47401
Telephone 812 339-5203

---

Dear Librarian:

Last summer you were asked to take part in the Opinion Survey of Midwestern Public Librarians; however, the questionnaire which was mailed to you has not been returned. Perhaps you were away on vacation or very busy when the questionnaire arrived. In any event, since the response from your state remains somewhat inadequate at the present time, I hope that you will reconsider participating in the opinion research.

The success or failure of my research as a doctoral candidate at Indiana University depends upon the representativeness of the data which I collect in the opinion research. That is why I am making a final, special plea to you to complete the questionnaire.

In the interest of meaningful research in library science and in helping me to obtain valid data about the opinions of public librarians in your state concerning socially significant issues, won't you please devote just a few minutes of your time to completing the enclosed questionnaire? I will be very grateful to you for your cooperation and for returning the questionnaire in the enclosed postage-paid envelope.

Thank you very much.

Sincerely yours,

Charles H. Busha

Enclosures

No. _____

# OPINION SURVEY OF

# MIDWESTERN PUBLIC LIBRARIANS

## ✪ QUESTIONNAIRE ✪

NAME: _____

SEX: _____     _____
        (male)          (female)

ARE YOU MARRIED?  _____     _____
                          (yes)          (no)

WHAT IS YOUR AGE? (Please check appropriate category.)

Do not write
in above spaces.

| 19-21 | 22-24 | 25-27 | 28-30 | 31-33 |
|-------|-------|-------|-------|-------|

| 34-36 | 37-39 | 40-42 | 43-45 | over 45 |
|-------|-------|-------|-------|---------|

ARE YOU A HIGH SCHOOL GRADUATE?  _____     _____
                                            (yes)          (no)

ARE YOU A JUNIOR COLLEGE GRADUATE?  _____     _____
                                              (yes)          (no)

ARE YOU A GRADUATE OF A FOUR-YEAR COLLEGE?  _____     _____
                                                        (yes)          (no)

IF YOU DO NOT HAVE A COLLEGE DEGREE BUT HAVE ATTENDED
COLLEGE, HOW MANY CREDIT HOURS HAVE YOU EARNED? _____

# ✪ CONFIDENTIAL ✪

**DIRECTIONS FOR COMPLETING SECTIONS I AND II:** Please read all statements carefully and decide for each whether you strongly agree, agree, are undecided, disagree, or strongly disagree. Place a check mark in one of the five squares following each statement corresponding to the response which best expresses your personal opinion. Please be sure to answer every question.

## SECTION I

| | Strongly agree | Agree | Undecided | Disagree | Strongly disagree |
|---|---|---|---|---|---|
| 1. The librarian's moral and aesthetic values must be considered as the chief standard for determining what books should be included in the library's collection . . . . . . | 1 | 9 | 5 | 51 | 34 |
| 2. There is a place in public libraries for periodicals which contain "left wing" articles such as *Ramparts, Evergreen Review, Liberation,* and *Avant Garde* . . . . . . . . | 18 | 59 | 14 | 6 | 2 |
| 3. *Portnoy's Complaint,* a novel by Phillip Roth which describes acts of exhibitionism, voyeurism, auto-eroticism, and oral coitus, does not belong on the open shelves of any public library . . . . . . . . . | 7 | 22 | 10 | 44 | 18 |
| 4. There is a definite need in our society for efforts of civic-minded and religious groups which are working to keep our libraries free of filth . . . . . . . . . . . . . . . . . . . . | 7 | 19 | 13 | 33 | 27 |
| 5. Librarians should be especially watchful to see that books containing unorthodox views are kept from their collections . . . . | 1 | 5 | 4 | 50 | 40 |
| 6. A public library is no place for either right or left wing extremist political literature . . | 2 | 7 | 6 | 53 | 32 |
| 7. Public libraries should not exclude materials because of the race or nationality or the social, political, or religious views of the author. . . . . . . . . . . . . . . . . . . . . . . | 48 | 48 | 0 | 2 | 2 |

| | Strongly agree | Agree | Undecided | Disagree | Strongly disagree |
|---|---|---|---|---|---|
| 8. Since librarians are in a position to recognize dangerous ideas in books and other printed materials, they should carefully control their circulation to the general public . . . . . . . . . . . . . . . . . . . . . . . . | 2 | 9 | 8 | 43 | 37 |
| 9. Librarians should avoid purchasing works of fiction dealing with social, psychological, and sexual problems and concentrate more on building collections of non-offensive literary masterpeices . . . . . . . . . . . | 1 | 6 | 3 | 51 | 38 |
| 10. Materials should not be proscribed or removed from libraries because of partisan or doctrinal disapproval . . . . . . . . . . . . . . | 37 | 53 | 4 | 4 | 3 |
| 11. Your library has received a gift copy of a book about the latest annual Soviet Communist Party Congress from the Russian Embassy. The book was published in the U.S.S.R. and is in English. The library does not have the information contained in the volume, but you feel that there will probably be a need for it. You would not hesitate to accept the book . . . . . . . . . | 22 | 64 | 10 | 3 | 1 |
| 12. No matter how much librarians talk about intellectual freedom, there are just some controversial books in public libraries that should be kept off the open shelves and in restricted rooms or cabinets . . . . . . . . . | 4 | 32 | 15 | 32 | 17 |
| 13. Libraries should provide books and other materials presenting all points of view concerning the problems and issues of our times . . . . . . . . . . . . . . . . . . . . . . . | 54 | 45 | 1 | 0 | 0 |
| 14. A censorship controversy over a single book or magazine is not worth the adverse public relations which it could cause for the library . . . . . . . . . . . . . . . . . . . . . | 3 | 22 | 22 | 40 | 13 |

| | Strongly agree | Agree | Undecided | Disagree | Strongly disagree |
|---|---|---|---|---|---|
| 15. Public libraries should not purchase "right wing" publications such as the *Blue Book of the John Birch Society* .......... | 1 | 8 | 12 | 58 | 21 |
| 16. Censorship should be challenged by libraries in the maintenance of their responsibility to provide public information and enlightenment ................... | 31 | 58 | 6 | 3 | 1 |
| 17. *The 120 Days of Sodom*, a book by French libertine novelist the Marquis de Sade which contains numerous episodes of sexual perversion combined with cruelty, does not belong on the open shelves of any public library ................... | 7 | 29 | 28 | 30 | 6 |
| 18. Libraries should cooperate with all persons and groups concerned with resisting abridgment of free expression and free access to ideas........................ | 17 | 51 | 17 | 12 | 2 |
| 19. Publishers and librarians do not need to endorse every idea or presentation contained in the books they make available .. | 40 | 59 | 1 | 0 | 0 |
| 20. As an institution of education for democratic living, the library should welcome the use of its meeting rooms for socially useful and cultural activities and discussions of current public questions ....... | 37 | 60 | 2 | 1 | 0 |
| 21. If a patron or group in the community complains about a book in a library's collection because of an objectionable sexual theme or because of frank terminology, the librarian should attempt to absolve himself by claiming that sexual themes and four-letter words are included in most present-day novels ..................... | 1 | 19 | 17 | 56 | 8 |

| | Strongly agree | Agree | Undecided | Disagree | Strongly disagree |
|---|---|---|---|---|---|
| 22. It would conflict with the public interest for librarians to establish their own political, moral, or aesthetic views as the sole standards for determining what books should be published or circulated ...... | 41 | 55 | 2 | 2 | 1 |
| 23. It is in the public interest for publishers and librarians to make available the widest diversity of views and expressions, including those which are unorthodox or unpopular with the majority .......... | 32 | 61 | 5 | 2 | 0 |
| 24. The rights of an individual to the use of a public library should not be denied because of age, race, religion, national origins or social or political views ............. | 64 | 35 | 0 | 0 | 0 |
| 25. The circulation of books about marijuana and hallucinating drugs should be carefully controlled by public libraries ........ | 2 | 8 | 7 | 54 | 30 |
| 26. Books which may offend standards of taste should be starred as a guide to those library patrons who wish to avoid these types of works ........................ | 2 | 19 | 16 | 46 | 16 |
| 27. It is the responsibility of publishers and librarians, as guardians of the people's freedom to read, to contest encroachments upon that freedom by indidivuals or groups seeking to impose their own standards or tastes upon the community at large ..... | 30 | 58 | 6 | 4 | 0 |
| 28. Public library meeting rooms or auditoriums should be available equally to all groups in the community regardless of the beliefs and affiliations of their members, provided that the meetings be open to the public ........................ | 21 | 56 | 13 | 10 | 0 |

- 6 -

| | Strongly agree | Agree | Undecided | Disagree | Strongly disagree |
|---|---|---|---|---|---|
| 29. There is no place in our society for extra-legal efforts to coerce the taste of others, to confine adults to the reading matter deemed suitable for adolescents, or inhibit the efforts of writers to achieve artistic expression . . . . . . . . . . . . . . . . . . . . . . | 32 | 58 | 8 | 3 | 0 |
| 30. It is not in the public interest to force a reader to accept with a book the prejudgment of a label characterizing the book or author as subversive or dangerous . . . . . . | 21 | 66 | 9 | 3 | 0 |
| 31. If your library has ordered a controversial book, the reviews of which indicate that it is of literary merit but for which court action is now pending against another library in your state you should cancel the order . . . . . . . . . . . . . . . . . . . . . . . . | 0 | 7 | 25 | 56 | 12 |
| 32. It is the responsibility of publishers and librarians to give full meaning to the freedom to read by providing books that enrich the quality of thought and expression . . . . . . . . . . . . . . . . . . . . . . . . . . . . | 42 | 54 | 3 | 1 | 0 |
| 33. By providing books that enrich the quality of thought and expression, publishers and librarians can demonstrate that the answer to a bad book is a good one and that the answer to a bad idea is a good one . . . . . . | 31 | 51 | 14 | 4 | 0 |
| 34. Library users who want to read erotic novels like *Return to Peyton Place, The Carpetbaggers, God's Little Acre, Candy,* and *Fanny Hill* should not expect to find them in the public library but should buy their own . . . . . . . . . . . . . . . . . . . . . | 10 | 51 | 17 | 18 | 4 |

| | Strongly agree | Agree | Undecided | Disagree | Strongly disagree |
|---|---|---|---|---|---|
| 35. Publishers and librarians have a profound responsibility to give validity to the freedom to read by making it possible for the readers to choose freely from a variety of offerings . . . . . . . . . . . . . . . . . . . . . . | 38 | 60 | 1 | 0 | 0 |
| 36. The suppression of ideas is fatal to a democratic society . . . . . . . . . . . . . . . . | 48 | 46 | 3 | 2 | 0 |

## SECTION II

| | Strongly agree | Agree | Undecided | Disagree | Strongly disagree |
|---|---|---|---|---|---|
| 1. What a child reads should be more the responsibility of parents than booksellers and librarians . . . . . . . . . . . . . . . . . . | 23 | 52 | 6 | 17 | 3 |
| 2. There is a direct causal relationship between reading pornography and juvenile delinquency . . . . . . . . . . . . . . . . . . . . | 2 | 13 | 28 | 39 | 19 |
| 3. Present laws dealing with obscenity in books and other printed matter are too permissive . . . . . . . . . . . . . . . . . . . . | 4 | 21 | 26 | 38 | 10 |
| 4. When it comes to selecting reading materials, most people have little critical judgment: they will usually select the bad rather than the good and the inferior rather than the superior . . . . . . . . . . . . . . . . | 2 | 10 | 15 | 64 | 9 |

**DIRECTIONS FOR COMPLETING SECTION III**: This section differs from previous parts of the questionnaire because it does not have an "undecided" response alternative. Please read each statement carefully and record your opinion according to your first reaction. It is not necessary to spend very much time on any one item. *Please be sure to answer every question.*

- 8 -

## SECTION III

| | Strongly agree | Agree | Disagree | Strongly disagree |
|---|---|---|---|---|
| 1. Obedience and respect for authority are the most important virtues children should learn | 7 | 32 | 53 | 8 |
| 2. Young people sometimes get rebellious ideas, but as they grow up they ought to get over them and settle down | 2 | 42 | 51 | 5 |
| 3. If people would talk less and work more, everybody would be better off | 4 | 40 | 49 | 7 |
| 4. Familiarity breeds contempt | 2 | 20 | 71 | 8 |
| 5. Science has its place, but there are many important things that can never possibly be understood by the human mind | 6 | 48 | 42 | 5 |
| 6. Some people are born with the urge to jump from high places | 1 | 35 | 57 | 7 |
| 7. Most people don't realize how much our lives are controlled by plots hatched in secret places | 1 | 27 | 57 | 15 |
| 8. Human nature being what it is, there will always be war and conflict | 4 | 60 | 31 | 5 |
| 9. The businessman and the manufacturer are much more important to society than the artist and the professor | 0 | 8 | 68 | 24 |
| 10. The wild sex life of the old Greeks and Romans was tame compared to some of the goings-on in this country, even in places where people might least expect it | 1 | 24 | 66 | 9 |
| 11. Some day it will probably be shown that astrology can explain a lot of things | 0 | 23 | 61 | 15 |
| 12. People can be divided into two distinct classes: the weak and the strong | 1 | 14 | 71 | 15 |

209

|  | Strongly agree | Agree | Disagree | Strongly disagree |
|---|---|---|---|---|
| 13. Sex crimes, such as rape and attacks on children, deserve more than mere punishment; such criminals ought to be publicly whipped, or worse . . . . . . . . . . . . . . . | 4 | 17 | 60 | 19 |
| 14. When a person has a problem or worry, it is best for him to not think about it, but to keep busy with more cheerful things . . . . | 2 | 25 | 64 | 9 |
| 15. Homosexuals are hardly better than criminals and ought to be severely punished . . . | 1 | 3 | 71 | 25 |
| 16. Nowadays when so many different kinds of people move around and mix together so much, a person has to protect himself especially carefully against catching an infection or disease from them . . . . . . . . | 1 | 18 | 63 | 18 |
| 17. Wars and social troubles may someday be ended by an earthquake or flood that will destroy the whole world . . . . . . . . . . . | 0 | 16 | 66 | 17 |
| 18. Nowadays more and more people are prying into matters that should remain personal and private . . . . . . . . . . . . . . | 12 | 50 | 33 | 5 |

OPINION SURVEY OF
MIDWESTERN PUBLIC LIBRARIANS
P.O. Box 985
Bloomington, Indiana 47401

# APPENDIX II

# INTELLECTUAL FREEDOM STATEMENTS ADOPTED BY THE AMERICAN LIBRARY ASSOCIATION*

*Reprinted by permission of the Office for Intellectual Freedom of the American Library Association.

# A.
# WHAT TO DO BEFORE THE CENSOR COMES–AND AFTER

## How Librarians Can Resist Censorship

Libraries of all sizes and types continue to be targets of pressure groups and individuals who wish to use the library as an instrument of their own tastes and views. The problem differs somewhat between the public library, with a responsibility to present as wide a spectrum of materials as its budget can afford, and the school or academic library, whose collection is designed to support the educational objectives of the institution. Both, however, involve the freedom of the library to meet its professional responsibilities to the whole community.

To combat censorship efforts from groups and individuals, every library should take certain measures to clarify policies and establish community relations. While these steps should be taken regardless of any attack or prospect of attack, they will provide a firm and clearly defined position if selection policies *are* challenged. As normal operating procedure, each library should:

1. *Maintain a definite materials selection policy.* It should be in written form and approved by the board of trustees, the school board or other administrative authority. It should apply to all library materials equally.

2. *Maintain a clearly defined method for handling complaints.* Basic requirements should be that the complaint be filed in writing and the complainant be properly identified before his request is considered. Action should be deferred until full consideration by appropriate administrative authority. (Upon request, the Office for Intellectual Freedom will provide a sample comment form adapted from one recommended by the National Council of Teachers of English.)

3. *Maintain lines of communication with civic, religious, educational and political bodies in the community.* Participation in local civic organizations and in community affairs is desirable. Because the library and the school are key centers of the community, the librarian should be known publicly as a community leader.

4. *Maintain a vigorous public relations program on behalf of intellectual freedom.* Newspapers, radio and television should be informed of policies governing materials selection and use, and of any special activities pertaining to intellectual freedom.

Adherence to the practices listed above will not preclude confrontations with pressure groups or individuals but may provide a base from which to counter efforts to place restraints on the library. If a confrontation does occur, librarians should remember the following:

1. Remain calm. Don't confuse noise with substance. Require the deliberate handling of the complaint under previously established rules. Treat the group or

individual who complains with dignity, courtesy and good humor. Given the facts, most citizens will support the responsible exercise of professional freedom by teachers and librarians and will insist on protecting their own freedom to read.

2. Take immediate steps to assure that the full facts surrounding a complaint are known to the administration. The school librarian should go through the principal to the superintendent and the school board; the public librarian, to the board of trustees or to the appropriate community administration official; the college or university librarian, to the president and through him to the board of trustees. Present full, written information giving the nature of the complaint and identifying the source.

3. Seek the support of the local press when appropriate. The freedom to read and freedom of the press go hand in hand.

4. Inform local civic organizations of the facts and enlist their support when appropriate. Meet negative pressure with positive pressure.

5. In most cases, defend the *principle* of the freedom to read and the professional responsibility of teachers and librarians. Only rarely is it necessary to defend the individual item. Laws governing obscenity, subversive material and other questionable matter are subject to interpretation by courts. Responsibility for removal of any library materials from public access rests with this established process.

6. Inform the ALA Office for Intellectual Freedom and other appropriate national and state organizations concerned with intellectual freedom of the nature of the problem. Even though censorship must be fought at the local level, there is value in the support and assistance of agencies outside the area which have no personal involvement. They can often cite parallel cases and suggest methods of meeting an attack.

The principles and procedures discussed above apply to all kinds of censorship attacks and are supported by such groups as the National Education Association, the American Civil Liberties Union, and the National Council of Teachers of English, as well as the American Library Association. While the practices provide positive means for preparing for and meeting pressure group complaints, they serve the more general purpose of supporting the *Library Bill of Rights*, particularly Article III, which states that: "Censorship should be challenged by libraries in the maintenance of their responsibility to provide public information and enlightenment." Adherence to this principle is especially necessary when under pressure.

(Adopted February 1, 1962; revised January 28, 1972 by the ALA Council.)

# B.
## LIBRARY BILL OF RIGHTS

The Council of the American Library Association reaffirms its belief in the following basic policies which should govern the services of all libraries.

I. As a responsibility of library service, books and other library materials should be chosen for values of interest, information and enlightenment of all people of the community. In no case should library materials be excluded because of the race or nationality or the social, political, or religious views of the authors.

II. Libraries should provide books and other materials presenting all points of view concerning the problems and issues of our times; no library materials should be proscribed or removed from libraries because of partisan or doctrinal disapproval.

III. Censorship should be challenged by libraries in the maintenance of their responsibility to provide public information and enlightenment.

IV. Libraries should cooperate with all persons and groups concerned with resisting abridgment of free expression and free access to ideas.

V. The rights of an individual to the use of a library should not be denied or abridged because of his age, race, religion, national origins or social or political views.

VI. As an institution of education for democratic living, the library should welcome the use of its meeting rooms for socially useful and cultural activities and discussion of current public questions. Such meeting places should be available on equal terms to all groups in the community regardless of the beliefs and affiliations of their members, provided that the meeting be open to the public.

(Adopted June 18, 1948; amended February 2, 1961, and June 27, 1967, by the ALA Council.)

# C.
## SCHOOL LIBRARY BILL OF RIGHTS

The American Association of School Librarians reaffirms its belief in the Library Bill of Rights of the American Library Association. Media personnel are concerned with generating understanding of American freedoms through the development of informed and responsible citizens. To this end the American Association of School Librarians asserts that the responsibility of the school library media center is:

To provide a comprehensive collection of instructional materials selected in compliance with basic written selection principles, and to provide maximum accessibility to these materials.

To provide materials that will support the curriculum, taking into consideration the individual's needs, and the varied interests, abilities, socio-economic backgrounds, and maturity levels of the students served.

To provide materials for teachers and students that will encourage growth in knowledge, and that will develop literary, cultural and aesthetic appreciation, and ethical standards.

To provide materials which reflect the ideas and beliefs of religious, social, political, historical and ethnic groups and their contribution to the American and world heritage and culture, thereby enabling students to develop an intellectual integrity in forming judgments.

To provide a written statement, approved by the local Boards of Education, of the procedures for meeting the challenge of censorship of materials in school library media centers.

To provide qualified professional personnel to serve teachers and students.

(Approved by American Association of School Librarians Board of Directors, Atlantic City, 1969.)

# D.
## STATEMENT ON LABELING

### An Interpretation of the Library Bill of Rights

Because labeling violates the spirit of the *Library Bill of Rights*, the American Library Association opposes the technique of labeling as a means of predisposing readers against library materials for the following reasons:

1. Labeling[1] is an attempt to prejudice the reader, and as such it is a censor's tool.

2. Although some find it easy and even proper, according to their ethics, to establish criteria for judging publications as objectionable, injustice and ignorance rather than justice and enlightenment result from such practices, and the American Library Association must oppose the establishment of such criteria.

3. Libraries do not advocate the ideas found in their collections. The presence of a magazine or book in a library does not indicate an endorsement of its contents by the library.

4. No one person should take the responsibility of labeling publications. No sizable group of persons would be likely to agree either on the types of material which should be labeled or the sources of information which should be regarded with suspicion. As a practical consideration, a librarian who labels a book or magazine might be sued for libel.

5. If materials are labeled to pacify one group, there is no excuse for refusing to label any item in the library's collection. Because authoritarians tend to suppress ideas and attempt to coerce individuals to conform to a specific ideology, the American Library Association opposes such efforts which aim at closing any path to knowledge.

(Adopted July 13, 1951; amended June 25, 1971, by the ALA Council.)

## FOOTNOTES

[1] "Labeling," as it is referred to in the *Statement on Labeling*, is the practice of describing or designating certain library materials, by affixing a prejudicial label to them or segregating them by a prejudicial system, so as to predispose readers against the materials.

# E.
# RESOLUTION ON CHALLENGED MATERIALS

## An Interpretation of the Library Bill of Rights

WHEREAS, The *Library Bill of Rights* states that no library materials should be proscribed or removed because of partisan or doctrinal disapproval, and

WHEREAS, Constitutionally protected expression is often separated from unprotected expression only by a dim and uncertain line, and

WHEREAS, Any attempt, be it legal or extra-legal, to regulate or suppress material must be closely scrutinized to the end that protected expression is not abridged in the process, and

WHEREAS, The Constitution requires a procedure designed to focus searchingly on the question before speech can be suppressed, and

WHEREAS, The dissemination of a particular work which is alleged to be unprotected should be completely undisturbed until an independent determination has been made by a judicial officer, including an adversary hearing,

THEREFORE, THE PREMISES CONSIDERED, BE IT RESOLVED, That the American Library Association declares as a matter of firm principle that no challenged library material should be removed from any library under any legal or extra-legal pressure, save after an independent determination by a judicial officer in a court of competent jurisdiction and only after an adversary hearing, in accordance with well-established principles of law.

(Adopted June 25, 1971, by the ALA Council.)

# F.
# WHAT THE AMERICAN LIBRARY ASSOCIATION
# CAN DO FOR YOU TO HELP COMBAT CENSORSHIP

The American Library Association maintains a total program for the promotion and defense of intellectual freedom, composed of the Intellectual Freedom Committee, the Office for Intellectual Freedom, the Freedom to Read Foundation, and the *Program of Action for Mediation, Arbitration, and Inquiry.* Each of these performs a unique role in the overall challenge of censorship.

*Intellectual Freedom Committee.* Established by the ALA Council in 1940 as the Committee on Intellectual Freedom to Safeguard the Rights of Library Users to Freedom of Inquiry, the present Intellectual Freedom Committee is the oldest of the Association's units involved in combating censorship and promoting intellectual freedom. As amended at the 1971 Midwinter Meeting, its statement of responsibility is: "To recommend such steps as may be necessary to safeguard the rights of library users, libraries, and librarians, in accordance with the First Amendment to the *United States Constitution* and the *Library Bill of Rights* as adopted by the ALA Council; and to work closely with the Office for Intellectual Freedom and with other units and officers of the Association in matters touching intellectual freedom and censorship."

Recommending policies concerning intellectual freedom to Council, therefore, is the Intellectual Freedom Committee's main responsibility. Its area of concern is limited to a degree: "steps . . . necessary to safeguard the rights of library users, libraries, and librarians, in accordance with the First Amendment . . . and the *Library Bill of Rights* . . ." The second sentence of the statement of responsibility makes explicit the close association among the Committee, the Office for Intellectual Freedom, and other ALA units such as the ALTA Intellectual Freedom Committee.

The Committee's underlying concern is always educational in nature. The most effective "safeguards" for the rights of library users are an informed electorate and a library profession aware of repressive activities and how to combat them.

*The Office for Intellectual Freedom.* The goal of the Office for Intellectual Freedom, established in December 1967, is to educate librarians to the importance of the concept of intellectual freedom. Toward this end, the Office serves as the administrative arm of the Intellectual Freedom Committee and bears the responsibility for implementing ALA policies on intellectual freedom.

Educating librarians to the importance of intellectual freedom principles requires teaching an understanding of the concept as it relates to the individual, the institution, and the functioning of our society. Hopefully, with understanding comes the ability to teach others. To aid this understanding, the Office maintains a complete program of educational and informational publications, projects, and services. The three major publications of the Office are the bi-monthly *Newsletter on Intellectual Freedom*, the monthly column in *American Libraries*, and the monthly *OIF Memorandum*.

The Office also distributes documents, articles, and ALA policies concerning intellectual freedom, among which are the *Library Bill of Rights*, the Association's basic policy statement on intellectual freedom; the *Freedom to Read Statement*; and the *School Library Bill of Rights*. As special circumstances require, materials distributed by the Office are augmented. During nationwide controversies concerning individual titles, press clippings, editorials, and public statements detailing the ways various libraries around the country handled requests to remove specific materials are compiled and sent out to others with problems. The special packets are publicized through the *OIF Memorandum*, the *Newsletter on Intellectual Freedom*, special mailings, and word of mouth. Inquiries and requests for these materials come to the Office from every part of the country.

One of the most often used and least heard about functions of the Office is its provision of advice and consultation to librarians in the throes of potential or actual censorship problems. Rarely does a day go by without a letter or phone call requesting advice about a specific book which has drawn the censorial attention of an individual or group in the community. In these cases, every effort is made to provide information or give any other assistance. Sometimes this takes the form of a written position statement, defending the principles of intellectual freedom in materials selection. Other times it requires names of persons available to offer testimony before library boards. In extreme cases, it demands visiting the community to view the problem first-hand and provide moral and professional support for the librarian and board. The alternative chosen is always the prerogative of the individual requesting assistance.

*Freedom to Read Foundation.* Through their respective responsibilities and cooperative activities, the Intellectual Freedom Committee and the Office for Intellectual Freedom comprise two-thirds of the American Library Association's educational program in support and defense of intellectual freedom. The other part of the program is the Freedom to Read Foundation, established outside the structure of ALA but closely affiliated through its board of trustees and executive director, who also serves as the director of the Office for Intellectual Freedom. The Foundation was incorporated in November 1969, as ALA's response to the increased interest of its members in having machinery to support and defend librarians whose jobs are jeopardized because they challenge violations of intellectual freedom. Another primary objective of the Foundation is to provide a means through which librarians and others can set legal precedents for the freedom to read.

Educating to the importance of, and the necessity for, a commitment to the principles of intellectual freedom requires, also, an assurance that such a commitment will not result in legal prosecution, financial loss, or personal damage. It is the responsibility of the Freedom to Read Foundation to provide that assurance through financial assistance, legal assistance, and judicial challenge of restrictive legislation, thereby helping to establish a favorable climate for intellectual freedom.

Through the provision of financial and legal assistance, the Foundation attempts to negate the necessity for librarians to make the difficult choice between practical expediency and principle in materials selection.

Fighting repressive legislation before it is utilized is another area in which the Foundation attempts to benefit the profession. Librarians can cite many state penal codes prohibiting distribution of so-called "harmful matter." Generally, however, these codes give only the vaguest definition of what constitutes "harmful matter." Such statutes are significantly dangerous to individuals and institutions, for some permit, and even encourage, prosecution of noncommercial interests which have neither the incentive nor the resources to defend the propriety of individual publications. To render librarians vulnerable to criminal prosecution for purchasing and disseminating works which have not previously been held illegal through adversary hearings is to require every librarian to reject the primary philosophical basis of his role in society. Under such an obligation, he either knowingly becomes a censor or unknowingly breaks a law. The choice is inimical to the concept of intellectual freedom and a derogation of the professional responsibilities of librarians. Thus, the Foundation will challenge the constitutionality of those laws which can inhibit librarians from including in their collections and disseminating to the public every work which has not previously been ruled illegal. Through such projects, the Foundation will lay the basis for a favorable climate for the functioning of intellectual freedom in libraries.

Still another aspect of the Foundation is the LeRoy C. Merritt Humanitarian Fund. It was established by the Foundation's Board of Trustees in recognition of the need for support at the moment an individual finds his position in jeopardy or is fired in the cause of intellectual freedom. This special fund allows for an immediate response prior to the development of all pertinent facts in a particular case. Although the fund is separate from other monies in the Foundation, its purpose is integrally related to the larger program of the Foundation.

While grants of assistance from the Foundation can only be made in cases where substantiating facts are available from the Office for Intellectual Freedom, the Intellectual Freedom Committee, or other sources, and in those cases where there is definitely an intellectual freedom issue at stake, monies from the LeRoy C. Merritt Humanitarian Fund can be made available under less rigid circumstances. Depending on the situation, grants can be made prior to establishment of claims that intellectual freedom is involved.

*The Program of Action for Mediation, Arbitration and Inquiry.* In June 1971, the ALA Council approved the *Program of Action for Mediation, Arbitration and Inquiry*, establishing a means for ALA to gather facts regarding violations of ALA policies concerning status, tenure, due process, employment practices, ethical considerations, and certainly, the principles of intellectual freedom.

Thus, on the one hand, the Intellectual Freedom Committee recommends policies for ALA in the area of intellectual freedom; these policies are made known and implemented through the Office for Intellectual Freedom. When violations of these policies are alleged, the problem falls under the *Program of Action* . . . and is referred to the Staff Committee on Mediation, Arbitration and Inquiry, so that facts can be gathered in an objective manner. The Staff

Committee's procedures are dictated by the *Program of Action for Mediation, Arbitration and Inquiry*, as follows:

## I. ESTABLISHMENT OF COMMITTEE

In order to carry out the intent and purposes of this policy as hereinafter set forth, a Committee, composed of senior staff members of the units of the Association with policy assignments in the areas hereinafter delineated, along with one staff member-at-large, is hereby established. The Committee shall be composed of five members, as follows:

Executive Secretary, Association of College and Research Libraries

Executive Secretary, Library Administration Division

Director, Office for Intellectual Freedom

One staff member-at-large, chosen at the discretion of the Executive Director of ALA

Executive Director of ALA, Chairman

Nothing herein shall preclude the Committee, or its chairman, from drawing into the Committee, on a temporary basis, from time to time, and as may be necessary or desirable, senior staff members of other units of the Association when those other units may have interests involved or can supply needed expertise.

## II. NAME OF THE COMMITTEE

The Committee shall be known as the Staff Committee on Mediation, Arbitration and Inquiry (hereinafter referred to as the Committee).

## III. SCOPE OF RESPONSIBILITY

The Committee is hereby assigned responsibility for mediation, arbitration, and inquiry, relating to tenure, status, fair employment practices, due process, ethical practices, and the principles of intellectual freedom as set forth in policies adopted by the Council of the American Library Association.

The Committee shall have full authority to interpret all pertinent ALA approved policies in implementing this *Program of Action for Mediation, Arbitration and Inquiry* and conducting activities to meet its Committee responsibilities.

Nothing in this *Program of Action for Mediation, Arbitration and Inquiry* nor in the authority assigned to the Committee shall be understood, implied or interpreted as granting or vesting in the Committee any policy-making function for any unit of the American Library Association. Nothing in this limitation, however, shall preclude the Committee from referring to any appropriate unit the need for ALA policy.

## IV. COMPLAINTS

A. All complaints of alleged violations received at ALA Headquarters, regardless of the unit or individual receiving such, shall be forthwith transmitted to the Committee. No complaint of any alleged violation shall be considered unless it is made by a party directly involved in the alleged violation.

1. When a complaint is received, whether oral or written, the Committee shall supply a standard form, to be called Request for Action. The

form is to be completed and signed, and returned to the Committee by the complainant.

    2. Until a completed and signed Request for Action is received by the Committee, no formal action* will be taken.

    3. That a completed and signed form is necessary for formal action in no way precludes the Committee from taking informal action, such as, but in no way limited to, telephoning the complainant to offer reassurance or to gather additional information, helping the complainant find a position if he is unemployed, advising the complainant, whether by a member of the Committee, or by another person or persons the Committee so designates. Such visits, however, will be undertaken only on the approval of the chairman of the Committee, or his designate. "Informal" action may include such emergency action as the Committee agrees is necessary and appropriate.

    B. After receiving a completed and signed form, it shall be the responsibility of the Committee to determine whether the matter is one which comes under its jurisdiction.

    C. If the Committee determines that it has jurisdiction, it shall then determine the most appropriate course of action. Prior to undertaking the action deemed appropriate, however, the Committee shall ascertain that no adequate remedy is available from any alternative source.

    1. Among, but not limited to, the possible courses of action are formal mediation and/or arbitration, an inquiry or referral of the matter to a more appropriate agency or organization.

    2. If at any time after filing the Request for Action, the case involves a law suit, the Committee may determine to file, and may file, an *amicus curiae* brief, or take other appropriate action. The filing of an *amicus curiae* brief, however, should be limited to cases involving issues of primary importance to the American Library Association which have not yet been determined by the courts.

    D. Except as provided in Section V, A., complaints may be withdrawn by the complainant, upon written notification to the Committee, or its chairman, at any time prior to the institution of formal action but not thereafter.

    E. The Committee may decline to proceed further with a complaint at any point in the proceedings when, in the judgment of the Committee, further action is unfeasible. In any instance when the Committee declines to proceed, a report of the reasons shall be made by the chairman to the ALA Executive Board.

## V. INQUIRIES

    A. When the Committee determines that a just and equitable resolution of the problem cannot be reached through arbitration and/or mediation, and that the matter warrants a formal inquiry, the Committee shall so notify the complainant. In such notification, the complainant shall be apprised of the seriousness of such an undertaking, and shall further be informed that he has ten days to withdraw his Request for Action. If, at the end of the ten-day period, the complainant has not withdrawn his Request for Action, a fact-finding

---

*Formal action means mediation, arbitration, filing of a brief, or inquiry.

subcommittee shall be appointed. (This paragraph is to be interpreted as meaning that the Committee may decide to attempt to arbitrate and mediate the problem, or it may determine that arbitration and mediation are not appropriate and/or would be to no avail and may proceed directly to an inquiry. However, no formal inquiry shall be made into cases which are in the process of local hearings, except in extraordinary circumstances, and no formal inquiry will be made into cases which are in litigation.)

B. The Committee shall appoint a fact-finding subcommittee whose duty it shall be to gather all of the facts involved in the matter, by interviewing the parties concerned, and through other appropriate means.

1. The fact-finding subcommittee shall be composed, generally, of three persons, including one member of Headquarters staff. Two persons, with the appropriate background of knowledge and experience in regard to the specific situation, shall be drawn from the ALA membership. In all cases, review by peers shall be provided, so that academic librarians conduct inquiries concerning academic librarians and libraries; public librarians conduct inquiries concerning school librarians and libraries; and so forth.

2. All interviews by fact-finding subcommittees shall be conducted in the following manner:

a. All interviews shall be recorded and transcribed.

b. Immediately after the completion of all interviews, the subcommittee will prepare a detailed outline to be used by staff in writing the report.

c. Transcripts shall be made by the Committee for use by staff in writing the report.

d. Transcripts, after review, when necessary, by ALA Legal Counsel and deletion of any actionable material, shall be forwarded to interviewees with certificates of endorsement, for signature and certification. The certificate of endorsement shall read as follows:

### CERTIFICATE

I certify that the above and foregoing is a transcript of the interview given by me to the Fact-Finding Subcommittee composed of

_____(NAME)_____, _____(NAME)_____, and _____(NAME)_____, in

the matter of _____(NAME)_____, on the day of

_____     _____     _____

_____

SIGNATURE

e. Certified transcripts shall be used as background to write the report, after which the transcripts shall be placed in a confidential file designated by the Committee. This file will be accessible only to members of the Committee on Mediation, Arbitration and Inquiry, to such persons as the Committee may authorize, and to persons who may require the transcripts for reference in any further hearing(s) by the ALA Executive Board.

3. Following the completion of a fact-finding investigation a written

report of the findings shall be prepared. Such reports of fact-finding subcommittees shall be sent to the ALA Executive Director, who shall direct copies to the ALA Legal Counsel and to the Committee for further action.

4. It shall be the responsibility of the Committee to recommend appropriate action, based on the facts gathered in the investigation and reported in written form, to the ALA Executive Board. (Members of the fact-finding subcommittees shall not vote on actions.)

a. Reports of fact-finding investigations shall be considered highly confidential and shall not be made public, except as authorized by the ALA Executive Board.

b. Reports of fact-finding investigations, including revisions and recommendations for further action, as determined by the Committee shall be reviewed by ALA Legal Counsel prior to submission to the Executive Board.

c. Upon acceptance and approval of reports of fact-finding investigations by the Executive Board, the full report, a summary thereof, or a statement shall be published in *American Libraries* if so determined by the Executive Board.

## VI. SANCTIONS

Sanctions may be defined as the appropriate penalty or penalties incurred for violations of one or more of the ALA approved policies to which this *Program of Action* relates.

A. Publication of a report that includes a statement of censure, indicating the strong disapproval of ALA because of a violation of one or more of the policies to which this *Program of Action* relates.

B. Suspension or expulsion from membership in ALA.

C. Listing of parties under censure in *American Libraries* as a warning to persons considering employment in an institution under censure that its practices and policies are in conflict with ALA policies concerning tenure, status, fair employment practices, due process, ethical practices, and/or the principles of intellectual freedom. On the same page with such listings of censured libraries shall appear the following statement:

"The fact that the name of an institution appears on the censured list of administrations does not establish a boycott of a library, nor does it visit censure on the staff. There is no obligation for ALA members to refrain from accepting appointment in censured libraries. The ALA advises only that librarians, before accepting appointments, seek information on present conditions from the Staff Committee on Mediation, Arbitration and Inquiry at Headquarters."

## VII. APPLICATION OF SANCTIONS

Sanctions can only be applied upon the completion of a full fact-finding inquiry, leading to a formal report on the basis of which the Committee recommends the imposition of appropriate sanctions. No sanction shall be imposed except with the approval of the ALA Executive Board.

## VIII. HEARINGS

Should the Committee recommend and the Executive Board approve the application of sanctions, the principals shall be notified that a hearing may be held to allow a final opportunity for appeals. Copies of the *full report* shall be forwarded to the principal(s) at this time.

## IX. REMOVAL OF SANCTIONS

Sanctions may be withdrawn when the conditions causing their original imposition are corrected, and when there is reason to believe that ALA principles concerning tenure, status, fair employment practices, due process, ethical practices and/or the principles of intellectual freedom will be observed in the future. To effect the removal of sanctions:

A. Each year the Committee shall query sanctioned institutions to determine if conditions warrant removal of sanctions; and/or

B. The sanctioned administration shall request review of the case, furnishing pertinent information as to why the sanctions should be removed;

C. The Committee votes to recommend to the ALA Executive Board that sanctions be removed or retained.

## X. ALTERNATIVE ACTIONS

In addition to the possible sanctions, other recommendations for action can include, but are not limited to, the following:

A. Distribute summaries of the final report to the library and educational press, to national newspapers, and to other appropriate media, with a statement that copies of the full report are available from the Committee.

B. Assist, as appropriate, in finding suitable temporary or permanent employment for individuals who have lost their positions.

(The ALA Executive Board, at its meeting on April 28, 1971, adopted the following item, which became effective when Council adopted the *Program of Action for Mediation, Arbitration and Inquiry.*)

## XI. COMMITTEE ON POLICY AND IMPLEMENTATION

A. In order to assure Council and the membership of full implementation of the *Program of Action for Mediation, Arbitration and Inquiry*, a Committee on Policy and Implementation is hereby established by the ALA Executive Board. The Committee on Policy and Implementation shall be composed of five members as follows:

President of the Association of College and Research Libraries, or his representative;

President of the Library Administration Division, or his representative;

Chairman of the Intellectual Freedom Committee, or his representative;

One member-at-large, appointed by the President of ALA;

President of ALA, Chairman

B. Function of Committee on Policy and Implementation. The Committee on Policy and Implementation is authorized and charged with ascertaining that the intent of the *Program of Action for Mediation, Arbitration and Inquiry* is fulfilled and implemented, and that the Staff Committee on Mediation, Arbitration and Inquiry is working within the scope of the *Program of Action for Mediation, Arbitration and Inquiry* and is expediting with reasonable speed the just resolution of the complaints received.

(Adopted by ALA Council June 25, 1971.)

# G.
# THE FREEDOM TO READ STATEMENT*

The Freedom to read is essential to our democracy. It is under attack. Private groups and public authorities in various parts of the country are working to remove books from sale, to censor textbooks, to label "controversial" books, to distribute lists of "objectionable" books or authors, and to purge libraries. These actions apparently rise from a view that our national tradition of free expression is no longer valid; that censorship and suppression are needed to avoid the subversion of politics and the corruption of morals. We, as citizens devoted to the use of books and as librarians and publishers responsible for disseminating them, wish to assert the public interest in the preservation of the freedom to read.

We are deeply concerned about these attempts at suppression. Most such attempts rest on a denial of the fundamental premise of democracy: that the ordinary citizen, by exercising his critical judgment, will accept the good and reject the bad. The censors, public and private, assume that they should determine what is good and what is bad for their fellow citizens.

We trust Americans to recognize propaganda, and to reject obscenity. We do not believe they need the help of censors to assist them in this task. We do not believe they are prepared to sacrifice their heritage of a free press in order to be "protected" against what others think may be bad for them. We believe they still favor free enterprise in ideas and expression.

We are aware, of course, that books are not alone in being subjected to efforts at suppression. We are aware that these efforts are related to a larger pattern of pressures being brought against education, the press, films, radio and television. The problem is not only one of actual censorship. The shadow of fear cast by these pressures leads, we suspect, to an even larger voluntary curtailment of expression by those who seek to avoid controversy.

Such pressure toward conformity is perhaps natural to a time of uneasy change and pervading fear. Especially when so many of our apprehensions are directed against an ideology, the expression of a dissident idea becomes a thing

---

*The *Freedom to Read* statement, sometimes referred to as the "Westchester Statement," was prepared by a committee of librarians, publishers, and others concerned about the threats to the free communication of ideas after a meeting held in Rye, New York, May 2-3, 1953. The *Freedom to Read* statement was endorsed officially by the Council of American Library Association on June 25, 1953. It has also been officially approved by the American Book Publishers Council, the American Booksellers Association, the Defense Commission of the National Education Association, and other national organizations.

feared in itself, and we tend to move against it as against a hostile deed, with suppression.

And yet, suppression is never more dangerous than in such a time of social tension. Freedom has given the United States the elasticity to endure strain. Freedom keeps open the path of novel and creative solutions, and enables change to come by choice. Every silencing of a heresy, every enforcement of an orthodoxy, diminishes the toughness and resilience of our society and leaves it the less able to deal with stress.

Now as always in our history, books are among our greatest instruments of freedom. They are almost the only means for making generally available ideas or manners of expression that can initially command only a small audience. They are the natural medium for the new idea and the untried voice, from which come the original contributions to social growth. They are essential to the extended discussion which serious thought requires, and to the accumulation of knowledge and ideas into organized collections.

We believe that free communication is essential to the preservation of a free society and a creative culture. We believe that these pressures towards conformity present the danger of limiting the range and variety of inquiry and expression on which our democracy and our culture depend. We believe that every American community must jealously guard the freedom to publish and to circulate, in order to preserve its own freedom to read. We believe that publishers and librarians have a profound responsibility to give validity to that freedom to read by making it possible for the reader to choose freely from a variety of offerings.

The freedom to read is guaranteed by the Constitution. Those with faith in free men will stand firm on these constitutional guarantees of essential rights and will exercise the responsibilities that accompany these rights.

1. *It is in the public interest for publishers and librarians to make available the widest diversity of views and expressions, including those which are unorthodox or unpopular with the majority.*

Creative thought is by definition new, and what is new is different. The bearer of every new thought is a rebel until his idea is refined and tested. Totalitarian systems attempt to maintain themselves in power by the ruthless suppression of any concept which challenges the established orthodoxy. The power of a democratic system to adapt to change is vastly strengthened by the freedom of its citizens to choose widely from among conflicting opinions offered freely to them. To stifle every non-conformist idea at birth would mark the end of the democratic process. Furthermore, only through the constant activity of weighing and selecting can the democratic mind attain the strength demanded by times like these. We need to know not only what we believe but why we believe it.

2. *Publishers and librarians do not need to endorse every idea or presentation contained in the books they make available. It would conflict with the public interest for them to establish their own political, moral or aesthetic views as the sole standard for determining what books should be published or circulated.*

Publishers and librarians serve the educational process by helping to make available knowledge and ideas required for the growth of the mind and the increase of learning. They do not foster education by imposing as mentors the patterns of their own thought. The people should have the freedom to read and consider a broader range of ideas than those that may be held by any single librarian or publisher or government or church. It is wrong that what one man can read should be confined to what another thinks proper.

3. *It is contrary to the public interest for publishers or librarians to determine the acceptability of a book solely on the basis of the personal history or political affiliations of the author.*

A book should be judged as a book. No art or literature can flourish if it is to be measured by the political views or private lives of its creators. No society of free men can flourish which draws up lists of writers to whom it will not listen, whatever they may have to say.

4. *The present laws dealing with obscenity should be vigorously enforced. Beyond that, there is no place in our society for extra-legal efforts to coerce the taste of others, to confine adults to reading matter deemed suitable for adolescents, or to inhibit the efforts of writers to achieve artistic expression.*

To some, much of modern literature is shocking. But is not much of life itself shocking? We cut off literature at the source if we prevent serious artists from dealing with the stuff of life. Parents and teachers have a responsibility to prepare the young to meet the diversity of experience in life to which they will be exposed, as they have a responsibility to help them learn to think critically for themselves. These are affirmative responsibilities, not discharged simply by preventing them from reading works for which they are not yet prepared. In these matters taste differs, and taste cannot be legislated; nor can machinery be devised which will suit the demands of one group without limiting the freedom of others. We deplore the catering to the immature, the retarded, or the maladjusted taste. But those concerned with freedom have the responsibility of seeing to it that each individual book or publication, whatever its contents, price, or method of distribution, is dealt with in accordance with due process of law.

5. *It is not in the public interest to force a reader to accept with any book the prejudgment of a label characterizing the book or author as subversive or dangerous.*

The idea of labeling supposes the existence of individuals or groups with the wisdom to determine by authority what is good or bad for the citizen. It supposes that each individual must be directed in making up his mind about the ideas he examines. But Americans do not need others to do their thinking for them.

6. *It is the responsibility of publishers and librarians, as guardians of the people's freedom to read, to contest encroachments upon that freedom by individuals or groups seeking to impose their own standards or tastes upon the community at large.*

It is inevitable in the give and take of the democratic process that the political, the moral, or the aesthetic concepts of an individual or group will occasionally collide with those of another individual or group. In a free society each individual is free to determine for himself what he wishes to read, and each group is free to determine what it will recommend to its freely associated members. But no group has the right to take the law into its own hands, and to impose its own concepts of politics or morality upon other members of a democratic society. Freedom is no freedom if it is accorded only to the accepted and the inoffensive.

7. *It is the responsibility of publishers and librarians to give full meaning to the freedom to read by providing books that enrich the quality of thought and expression. By the exercise of this affirmative responsibility, bookmen can demonstrate that the answer to a bad book is a good one, the answer to a bad idea is a good one.*

The freedom to read is of little consequence when expended on the trivial; it is frustrated when the reader cannot obtain matter fit for his purpose. What is needed is not only the absence of restraint, but the positive provision of opportunity for the people to read the best that can be thought and said. Books are the major channel by which the intellectual inheritance is handed down, and the principal means of its testing and growth. The defense of their freedom and integrity, and the enlargement of their service to society, requires of all bookmen the utmost of their faculties, and deserves of all citizens the fullest of their support.

We state these propositions neither lightly nor as easy generalizations. We here stake out a lofty claim for the value of books. We do so because we believe that they are good, possessed of enormous variety and usefulness, worthy of cherishing and keeping free. We realize that the application of these propositions may mean the dissemination of ideas and manners of expression that are repugnant to many persons. We do not state these propositions in the comfortable belief that what people read is unimportant. We believe rather that what people read is deeply important; that ideas can be dangerous; but that the suppression of ideas is fatal to a democratic society. Freedom itself is a dangerous way of life, but it is ours.

# INDEX

Abraham, Henry J., 84
Academic freedom, 32
Adams, Charles J., 98
Adler, Mortimer, 78
Age, influence of, 130-2
Agnew, Spiro T., 24-5, 60
Alien and Sedition Acts, 27
Allentown Farm Camp, Pa., 40
American Book Publishers Council, 24
American Civil Liberties Union, 26, 55, 68, 71
American establishment, 50
American Geological Institute, 33
American Indians, 68
American Legion, 54
American Library Association, 27, 66, 67, 73, 80, 85, 88, 140, 149, 150
*American Library Directory*, 98
American Opinion Bookstores, 56
Americanism, 63
Amish, 68
*An Analysis of Post-World War II Efforts to Expand Press Freedom Internationally*, 166
Anti-censorship librarians, 143
Anti-intellectualism, 32
Arbuthnot, May Hill, 78
*Aeropagitica*, 64
*Armed Forces Censorship*, 184
*Art and Pornography*, 180
Asher, Thomas R., 71
*Aspects of Liberty*, 34
Atlanta, Ga., 27
Attitude scales, 102-4
Attitude scales, reliability of, 114, 141

Attitudes, classification of, 111-12
*The Authoritarian Personality*, 93-4
Authoritarianism, 94

Baldwin, James, 53
*The Banned Books of England*, 64, 160
*Banned in Boston*, 174-5
Berninghausen, David K., 59, 69, 107
Bill of Rights, 44, 64, 66, 67, 68
*Birchism Was My Business*, 57
*Black Panther*, 59
Blanshard, Paul, 84, 155
*The Blue Book of the John Birch Society*, 56, 68
*The Bolshevik Revolution*, 54
Bonner, Paul Hyde, 36
Book publication in 1970, 76
*Book Selection and Censorship*, 163
*Book Selection and Censorship in the Sixties*, 79, 178
Books, controversial, 80
*Books in the Dock*, 167
Boyer, Paul S., 63, 156
*Building Library Collections*, 78, 86
*Bulletin of the John Birch Society*, 58
Burger, Warren E., 46
Burke, Redmond A., 156
*Burned Books*, 164
Busha, Charles H., 157
Butler, Pierce, 78

Cage, Penelope B., 158
Caldecott award, 52

California, 88-90
*The Californian*, 59
Camden, S.C., 52
*Candy*, 116
Capital punishment, 46
Carmen, Ira H., 158
*The Carpetbaggers*, 88, 116
Carswell, G. Harrold, 45
Carter, Mary, 78, 86
Cary, Joyce, 36
Castagna, Edwin, 79, 86
*Catcher in the Rye*, 52, 53
*Catholic Viewpoint on Censorship*, 164
*Censors*, 181
*The Censors and the Schools*, 179
*Censorship and the Arts*, 170
*Censorship and the Teacher of English*, 155
*Censorship: A Symposium*, 165
Censorship, causes of, 28-9
Censorship, definition of, 83, 84
*Censorship: For and Against*, 166
*Censorship: Government and Obscenity*, 178
*Censorship in America*, 168
*Censorship in England*, 163
*Censorship in English Programs of California Junior Colleges*, 171
*Censorship in Russia, 1848-1855*, 155
*Censorship in the United States*, 174
Censorship, intramural, 87-8
*Censorship Landmarks*, 160-1
*Censorship, Obscenity, and Sex*, 171
*The Censorship of Books*, 160
*The Censorship of Books in the United States*, 183
*The Censorship of Hebrew Books*, 180
*Censorship of High School Literature*, 184
*Censorship of Obscenity*, 173
*Censorship of the Church of Rome*, 181
*Censorship of the Movies*, 182
*Censorship: The Search for the Obscene*, 162
*Census of the Population of the United States*, 98

Center for Policy Research, 30
Chandos, John, 158
Chicago, Ill., 52, 145
Chicanos, 68
*Children and Books*, 78
*Cincinnati Enquirer*, 55
Cincinnati, Ohio, 54-5
Citizens for Decent Literature, 60
*A Citizen's Guide to Legal Rights*, 66
Cleaver, Eldridge, 52
Clifton, N.J., 51
Clor, Harry M., 159
Coefficient of correlation, 146
Coldwater, Mich., 50
Collins, Mrs. Hilda, 58
*Columbia Law Review*, 30
*Commentaries on Obscenity*, 49, 183
*Commission on Obscenity and Pornography*, 41-2
*Communications Control*, 180
Community leaders, 149
Community, size of, 127-30
Comstock Act of 1873, 27
Comstock, Anthony, 27, 159
*Comstockery in America*, 88, 166
*Conference on Censorship*, 177
Conference on Intellectual Freedom, 70
Conformity, 36
Conservatism, 34-5
*A Constitutional Dilemma*, 158
Constitutional Heritage Club, 54
*The Control of Reading by the Catholic Church*, 156-7
Controversial materials, 87
Conway, N.H., 53
Coplan, Kate, 79
Corbin, John, 78
Craig, Alec, 64, 160
Creamer, J. Shane, 66
Crime rates, 29
Crist, Judith, 63, 167
*Criticism and Censorship*, 170
Cronbach alpha coefficients, 141
Cuyahoga County, Ohio, 52

Daniels, Walter M., 160
Decatur, Ind., 53
Declaration of Independence, 68
DeGrazia, Edward, 160
DeKalb County, Ga., 27
Denmark, 42
Denver Public Library, 51
de Sade, Marquis, 116
Des Moines Public Library, 69
*The Dictionary of American Slang*, 58
Dixon, W. J., 123
*Do It!*, 51
Dorsen, Norman, 28
Doubleday & Co., 33
Douglas, William O., 45-7
*Down These Main Streets*, 59
Downs, Robert B., 85, 161
*Dr. Bowdler's Legacy*, 180
Duncan, D. B., 123

*Earth in Upheaval*, 32
Earth, rotation of, 33
East north-central states, 95
Eaton, Nancy, 81
Educational-attainment levels, 101
*The End of Obscenity*, 182
*English Book Censorship*, 165
Enoch Pratt Free Library, 85
Ernst, Morris L., 162
*Eros*, 40, 43-4
*The Erotic in Literature*, 174
Espionage Act (1917), 27
Estrin, Herman A., 162
Etzioni, Amitai, 30
*Evergreen Review*, 51
Exodus of Jews, 33
*Expanding Liberties*, 171
Extremist groups, 54-60

*The Face on the Cutting Room Floor*, 183
*Fanny Hill*, 116
Faulkner, William, 36
*Federal Censorship; Obscenity in the Mail*, 179

Fennimore, Wis., 100
Fielding, Henry, 80
*Film Censors and the Law*, 168
*The First Freedom*, 161
Fisher, John, 36
Fiske, Marjorie, 80, 88-90, 93-4, 163
Fixed-alternative responses, 106
Food and Drug Administration, 26
*Foolish Figleaves?*, 172
Ford, Gerald C., 45
Fort Wayne-Allen County (Ind.) Public Library, 53
Fowell, John P., 163
Fox, John, 84
Freeport, Ill., 52
*Free Libraries and Unclean Books*, 80
*Free Press/Free People*, 167
*Freedom and Censorship of the College Press*, 162
*Freedom of the Press*, 175
Freedom of speech, 68
*Freedom of Speech and Press in America*, 168
*Freedom to Read*, 170
*Freedom to Read: Perspective and Program*, 175
Freedom to Read Foundation, 72-3
*Freedom to Read* statement, 70, 78, 93, 104, 105, 118, 139, 144, 147
Fund for the Republic, 89

Gaines, Erwin, 59
Garceau, Oliver, 87
Gardiner, Harold C., 164
Gay Liberation Front, 68
Gerber, Albert B., 164
Gillett, Charles R., 164
Gilmore, Donald H., 164
Ginzburg, Ralph, 40-4, 165
Gleason, Marian, 165
*The Goddam White Man*, 88
*God's Little Acre*, 116
Goldhor, Herbert, 87
Goldwater, Barry, 27

Hachten, William, 44
Hall, William E., 166
Haney, Robert W., 88, 166
Harvard University Observatory, 33
Haas, Warren J., 165
Hart, Harold H., 166
Haynesworth, Clement F., Jr., 45
Hemingway, Ernest, 36
Hewitt, Cecil R., 167
*The High Price of Pornography*, 172
*The History of Jonathan Wild the Great*, 80
*A History of Pornography*, 169
Hohenberg, John, 167
Homosexuality, 31, 49, 77
*Homosexuality in America*, 52
*The Honored Society*, 52
*Hotline*, 58
*Housewife's Handbook on Selective Promiscuity*, 40-1
Hoyt, Olga, 168
Hubbard, James M., 79
Hudson, Edward G., 168
Hughes, Douglas A., 168
*Human Sexual Inadequacy*, 52
Hunnings, Neville M., 168
Hutchins, Margaret, 79
Hutchinson, E. R., 169
Hyde, Hartford M., 169
Hypotheses, list of, 94-5
Hypotheses, testing of, 132

*The Indecent Publications Tribunal*, 180
Indiana, 95
Indiana University, 32
Indiana University Graduate Library School, 105
Indiana University Research Computing Center, 110
*The Information War*, 177
Inge, William, 53
Institute of Sex Research, 32
Intellectual Freedom Committee, 70
Intellectual freedom, definition of, 84
*Introduction to Reference Work*, 79

Iowa, 105

Johoda, Marie, 90
Javits, Jacob K., 60
Jeffries, John A., 169
Jennison, Peter S., 170
Jewish Community Relations Council, Cincinnati, 55
Job classifications, 96
John Birch Society, 54, 56-9
Johnson, Lyndon B., 41
Jones, Howard Mumford, 67
Jones, Leroi, 54

Kamarch, Edward L., 170
Katz, Bill, 80
Katz, Daniel, 90
Kershaw County, S.C., 52
Kerr, Walter, 170
Kilpatrick, James J., 171
Kinsey, Alfred, 32
Klausler, Alfred P., 171
Knudson, Rozanne R., 171
Koestler, Arthur, 36
Konvitz, Milton R., 171
Kraeling, Carl, 33
Kronhausen, Eberhard, 171
Kuh, Richard, 44, 172
Kyle-Keith, Richard, 172

LaConte, Ronald T., 172
Lacy, Dan, 24
*Lady Chatterly's Lover*, 88
Lake, Albert C., 87
LaPorte (Ind.) Public Library, 98
Lambert, J. W., 72
Lasswell, Harold D., 83
*Legacy of Suppression*, 34, 173
*Legal Censorship of Obscene Publications*, 169
Leigh, Robert, 86
Letter, cover, 105
Levy, Leonard W., 34, 173
*Liaison*, 40
*Library Bill of Rights*, 38, 67, 69, 73,

236

*Library Bill of Rights* (cont'd.) 88, 93, 94, 104, 105, 118, 139, 144, 147
Library directors, 138
Library Education and Manpower, 149
*Library Journal*, 76
*The Library Reaches Out*, 79, 87
Library trustees, 149
Likert-type scales, 102
*Literary Censorship*, 185
Literature, realistic movement of, 31
Lockhart, William B., 29, 173
*Lolita*, 88
*A Long Time Burning*, 184
Lorain, Ohio, 100
Los Angeles, Calif., 60
Loth, David G., 174
Lubalin, Herb, 40

McCarthy, Joseph, 27
McCarthyism, 63, 70, 84
McClallan, Grant S., 174
McClure, Robert C., 29
McConnell, John L.C., 174
McCormick, John, 174
McCoy, Ralph E., 174-5
McKenney, Mary, 77
Macmillan Co., 33
*The Mafia and Politics*, 52
*Magna Carta*, 66
Maloff, Saul, 56
Manistique, Mich., 52
Marcus, Steven, 175
Marcuse, Ludwig, 176
Marquette University, 176
Mason City (Iowa) Public Library, 78
Meerloo, Abraham M., 177
Meltzer, Milton, 177
Memphis Public Library, 51
Michigan, 95
Middle-class, beliefs of, 31
Midwesterners, characteristics of, 96
Milton, John, 64
Milwaukee, Wis., 27
*Minimum Standards for Public Library Systems*, 85

Minor, Dale, 177
Minnesota, 105
Missouri, 105
Mitchell, John N., 67
Moon, Eric, 79, 178
Moore, Everett, 60
Montgomery, Ala., 51
*Movies, Censorship, and the Law*, 158
Multiple range test, 123
Murphy, Terence J., 178

Nabokov, Vladimir, 53
National Advisory Commission on Libraries, 24
National Book Committee, 88
National Committee for Impeachment of the President, 25
National Council of Teachers of English, 178-9
National Office for Decent Literature, 35-6
Nelson, Jack, 179
*New Left Notes*, 59
New morality, 31
*The New Underground Theater*, 53
New York Printing Pressman's Union No. 2, 25
New York Society for the Suppression of Vice, 27
*The New York Times*, 25, 42, 72
*Newsletter on Intellectual Freedom*, 50-2, 85, 107
Nixon, Richard M., 24-5
*None Dare Call It Treason*, 56
*The North American Midwest*, 96
North Little Rock, Ark., 52
North Miami, Fla., 51

*Obscene; the History of an Indignation*, 176
*Obscenity and the Law*, 182
*Obscenity and Public Morality*, 159
*Obscenity, the Law and the English Teacher*, 163
Office of Censorship, 28

O'Hara, John, 36, 53
Ohio, 95
*120 Days of Sodom*, 116
Opinion Survey of Midwestern Public
    Librarians, 93-107
Ostle, Bernard, 123
*The Other Victorians*, 175


Pandering, 40, 43, 46
Paul, James C.N., 179
Payne-Gasposchkin, Cecilia, 33
Peckham, Morse, 180
*Pensée*, 33
Pentagon Papers, 72
Perkins, F. B., 79
Perrin, Noel, 180
Perry, Stuart, 180
*Perspectives on Pornography*, 168
Phelan, John, 180
Philadelphia, Pa., 51
*Political Control of Literature in
    the USSR*, 183
Popper, William, 180
Population-size categories, 98-100
*Portnoy's Complaint*, 51
Pornography, 41-2, 49, 65, 80
*Pornography and the Law*, 171
Powell, Lewis F., Jr., 45-6
Pressure groups, 70
Princeton University, 33, 60
Printing, invention of, 35
*Problems of Communication in a
    Pluralistic Society*, 176
Pro-censorship librarians, 141-2
Prostitution, 49
Protestant Church, 35
Protestant ethic, 35
Public libraries, standards of, 85
Public Library Assn., 85
*The Public Library in the United
    States*, 86
Public Library of Cincinnati and
    Hamilton County, 54
Puerto Ricans, 68
Puritan ethic, 34-6
Puritans, 34
*Purity in Print*, 63, 156

Putnam, George H., 181


Qualitative variables, 100
Quantitative Guide to Public Library
    Operations, 98
Quantitative variables, 101
Questionnaire, construction of,
    101-4
Questionnaire pre-testing, 104-5
Questionnaire, response to, 107
Questionnaire, scoring of, 110-13
Questionnaires, return of, 109-10


Radcliffe, Cyril J., 181
Radicals, 31
Rafferty, Max, 58
*Ramparts*, 51, 54
Randall, Richard S., 182
*Rape of the Mind*, 177
*Red Star over China*, 54
Rehnquist, William H., 46
Reid, Charles, 80
Religion, effects of, 34-5
Rembar, Charles, 30, 182
*Research Methods in Social Rela-
    tions*, 107
Reseda, Calif., 51
Resolution on Challenged Materials,
    72
*Return to Peyton Place*, 116
*Revolution for the Hell of It*, 51
*The Right to Read*, 84, 155
*Risks and Rights in Publishing*, 183
Roberts, Edwin A., Jr., 182
Roche, John P., 34
Rogers, Donald F., 25
*Rolling Stone*, 59
Roman Catholic Church, 35
Roosevelt, Franklin D., 45


St. John-Stevas, Norman, 182
Salem witch hunts, 34
Salinas, Calif., 59
Sample, characteristics of, 109-10
Sample, stratification of, 98-100
Sampling procedures, 98-100

San Francisco Public Library, 80
Schomp, Gerald, 57
School libraries, 52-3
Schumach, Murry, 183
Science, censorship of, 32-4
Scores, classification of, 98-100
*The Secret Rulers*, 52
Selltiz, Claire, 107
*The Sensuous Woman*, 51, 52
*Sex, Censorship, and Pornography*, 164
Sex, influences of attitudes of, 132
*Sex, Pornography, and Justice*, 164
Sexual behavior, research in, 32
Sexually-explicit materials, 30
Shapley, Harlow, 33
Sharp, Donald, 49, 183
Shawnee Mission, Kans., 53
Shera, Jesse, 79
Situation ethics, 35
Smith Act (1940), 27
Smith, Hannis, 59
Smith, Ray, 78
Smoot-Hawley Tariff Bill, 27
*The Smut Peddlers*, 171
*The Smut Rakers*, 182
Society for Psychological Study of Social Issues, 90
*Soul on Ice*, 52
South Atlantic states, 148
Spaulding, Forest, 69
Spokane, Wash., 52
Spring, Samuel, 183
Standard deviations, 111, 114, 115
State libraries, 150
State library associations, 150
*Statistics in Research*, 123
Stein, Fritz, 183
Stewart, John Q., 33
Stewart, Potter, 46
Stone, Elizabeth W., 87
Stormer, John, 56
Student Academic Forum, 33
Students, attitudes of, 104-5
Styron, William, 53
*Suppressed Books*, 160
Swayze, Harold, 183
Sweden, 42

*Sylvester and the Magic Pebble*, 52-3
Symula, James F., 184
Systems, library, 150

Thomas, Piri, 59
Thurmond, Strom, 27
*Times Literary Supplement*, 72
*To Deprave and Corrupt*, 158
*To the Pure*, 162
Toledo, Ohio, 53
Toledo Police Patrolmen's Assn., 53
*Traps for the Young*, 159
*Tropic of Cancer*, 88
*Tropic of Cancer on Trial*, 169
Tulare County (Calif.) Public Library, 58
Tulsa, Okla, 51

U.S. Congress, 24-28
U.S. Congress, Subcommittee on Constitutional Rights, 26
U.S. Constitution, 25, 28, 43-4, 66-8, 81
U.S. Department of the Air Force, 184
U.S. Federal Bureau of Investigation, 26
U.S. Internal Revenue Service, 26-7
U.S. Justice Department, 26
U.S. President's Commission on Obscenity and Pornography, 41, 184
U.S. Social Security Adm., 26
U.S. State Department, Passport Div., 26
U.S. Supreme Court, 43-9, 72, 81
*U.S. v. Ginzburg*, 40-50
*An Unhurried View of Erotica*, 165
University of California School of Librarianship, 89

Vagabonds, 31
*Vallachi Papers*, 52
Variables, 100-1
Variance, 123-4

Velikovsky, Immanuel, 32-4
*Versions of Censorship*, 174
Vietnam War, 24, 72


Waldor, Milton A., 57
Wallace, George, 54
Warren, Earl, 56
Warwick, R.I., 50
Welch, Robert, 56-7
West north-central states, 148
Wheeler, Joseph, 87
White, Byron R., 46
Widmer, Kingsley, 185

Wiggins, James R., 185
Williamsville, N.Y., 52
Wiretapping, 45
Wisconsin, 95
Women's City Club, Cincinnati, 55
Women's Liberation, 68
*Woodstock Nation*, 51
*Worlds in Collision*, 32-4


Yale University, 25
Youth, 37


Zola, Emile, 36